STUDY GUIDE

STUDY GUIDE

Stephanie Stolarz-Fantino
University of California, San Diego

to accompany

Lightfoot, Cole, and Cole

The Development of Children

Sixth Edition

WORTH PUBLISHERS

Study Guide
by Stephanie Stolarz-Fantino
to accompany
Lightfoot, Cole, and Cole: **The Development of Children**, Sixth Edition

ISBN-13: 978-1-4292-1783-5
ISBN-10: 1-4292-1783-9

First Printing, 2009

Worth Publishers
41 Madison Avenue
New York, NY 10010
www.worthpublishers.com

Contents

To the Student

This Study Guide was designed for use with *The Development of Children*, Sixth Edition, by Cynthia Lightfoot, Michael Cole, and Sheila R. Cole. It is intended to help you understand and remember the ideas and facts presented in the textbook. The guide has 15 chapters corresponding to the 15 chapters of the textbook; each chapter has the following sections:

- The introduction will orient you to the ideas presented. You may want to read it before reading the text chapter.
- The **Learning Objectives** are questions to keep in mind while studying each chapter.
- The detailed **Chapter Summary** can be read before the textbook chapter, as preparation, or afterward, as a review; it will also be useful when studying for quizzes and exams. Reading the outline cannot, however, substitute for reading the text; while it contains the basic ideas, it leaves out many important examples and illustrations that will help you understand and remember these ideas.
- The **Key Terms** listed at the end of each textbook chapter are reproduced. The matching exercise will give you the opportunity to test your understanding by identifying examples that illustrate key terms.
- **Multiple-Choice Practice Questions** cover material that is especially likely to appear on exams.
- **Short-Answer Practice Questions** are intended to make you think about important topics introduced in the chapter. Sometimes you will need to utilize ideas presented in different sections of the chapter to answer these questions.
- **Putting It All Together** appears in some, but not all, chapters of the guide. It contains exercises that require you to combine material from the chapter you are currently studying with information from previous chapters to help you gain a better overall view of development.
- **Sources of More Information** supplement the additional readings listed at the end of each text chapter.
- An **Answer Key** in each chapter lists the correct answers for the key terms matching exercise, the multiple-choice questions, and, where appropriate, for the putting it all together section.

It is hoped that by using this Study Guide, you will find your study of child development to be interesting and enjoyable.

1

The Study of Human Development

For centuries, people have wondered about how individual humans become what they are, and about how the events of their lives help or hinder their development.

Today, developmentalists from a variety of academic disciplines bring the techniques of scientific research to bear on these questions. Using interviews, observations, and experiments, they gather information on human development and interpret it within various theoretical frameworks.

This research is not of interest solely to researchers and theoreticians. It helps all of us to make informed decisions in diverse areas: for example, in public policy, by asking what kinds of programs for children should receive public support; in education, by asking under what conditions children learn best; and in child rearing, by asking what practices are most likely to help children grow up happy and well-adjusted.

Developmental science does not yet have answers to all our questions. But each year developmental research adds something to our understanding of human nature and to our appreciation of the development of individual children.

Learning Objectives

Keep these questions in mind while studying Chapter 1.

1. How did developmental science become an area of scientific study?
2. What are the four central issues that inform research in the area of human development?
3. What are the major theoretical perspectives into which we can organize most work in developmental science ("grand theories") and which theorists are associated with each? What modern approaches characterize recent research into development?

4. All scientific research must conform to certain standards in order for the results to be accepted by other scientists. What are the criteria by which scientific research is judged, and how can we tell if they have been met?
5. Which methods of data collection are commonly used by developmental scientists? What are the advantages and disadvantages of each?
6. What types of research designs are used for understanding how behavior changes over time? What are the strengths and weaknesses of each?
7. What are the broad frameworks into which we can organize most work in developmental science, and how does each perspective explain developmental change?
8. How do researchers protect the rights and privacy of children who participate in developmental studies?

Chapter Summary

Victor, the "Wild Boy of Aveyron," remains something of a mystery two centuries after his discovery. Was he, as believed by many authorities of his time, abandoned by his parents because of innate mental deficiency? Or, as his benefactor Jean-Marc Itard believed, was his development stunted by years of isolation in the forest?

I. DEVELOPMENTAL SCIENCE

In Itard's time, philosophers, social reformers, and scientists were already expressing interest in children and their development. Eventually, this interest grew into **developmental science**—the study of physical, cognitive, social, and emotional changes that children undergo from conception onward.

Once established as a discipline, the study of development was pursued mainly by psychologists. In recent years, however, developmental science has become more interdisciplinary and also more international, reflecting the importance of cultural contexts in development. Developmentalists have always worked to understand the basic biological and cultural underpinnings of development and also to devise ways of safeguarding children's health and well-being. Today, technological advances in data collection and analysis allow developmentalists to seek answers to increasingly complex and wide-ranging questions.

A. Periods of Development

Developmentalists, and people in most cultures, organize the time between conception and the start of adulthood into five broad periods: the prenatal period, infancy, early childhood, middle childhood, and adolescence.

B. Domains of Development

Domains are major areas of development: social, emotional, cognitive (intellectual), and physical. Development in each domain is influenced by and, in turn, influences development occurring in the others.

C. Contexts of Development

The contexts in which development takes place—whether at the physical, family, community, cultural, or institutional level—present children with both resources and risks that affect the course of their development.

II. CHILDREN, SOCIETY, AND SCIENCE

Over time changes in beliefs about children have set the stage for the emergence of developmental science.

A. Historical Beliefs about Children and Childhood

Societies' beliefs about children's nature and their development affect adults' expectations and shape their caregiving practices. Historians can follow changes in these beliefs over the last few centuries by examining objects and written information; less information is available about how adults viewed children in medieval times. There is evidence that during medieval times childhood was not viewed as a unique period of life. Children were considered to be much like adults; as a consequence, they were not provided with special toys or clothes. From the 1600s to the early 1900s, Puritan ideas about children were widely influential, and mothers were urged to adopt childrearing practices that encouraged obedience and limited arousal, so as to help children overcome their sinful natures. At the same time, during the late 1700s and early 1800s, the Industrial Revolution caused changes in families, resulting in a shift toward viewing childhood as a unique period of development. By the late 1800s, children and childhood were receiving the attention of parents, educators, and scientists.

B. The Emergence of Developmental Science

The Industrial Revolution in Western Europe and the United States brought large numbers of children into factories. There they worked long hours in unhealthy conditions, causing concern in the social and scientific communities.

Charles Darwin's *Origin of Species* also focused interest on children, as their development was thought to provide clues to the stages of human evolution. William Preyer, a nineteenth-century embryologist, wrote the first textbook on child development and developed a set of rules for observing children's behavior (described in Table 1.1 of the textbook). Many early developmentalists believed that adult abilities were already fully formed in children, simply waiting to emerge. James Mark Baldwin reversed this notion, proposing that children's abilities progress through a series of specific stages on the way to their adult forms.

Other early developmentalists turned to practical applications of knowledge. For example, Alfred Binet developed methods of testing that could help identify schoolchildren who would benefit from special instruction.

C. The New Field of Developmental Science

By the early twentieth century, the study of development was recognized as a field of scientific inquiry in universities, and government agencies and philanthropic organizations began to support developmental research. The same scientific and practical questions that influenced earlier research continue to motivate developmental science today.

III. THE CENTRAL ISSUES OF DEVELOPMENTAL SCIENCE

Developmentalists share an interest in four fundamental questions:

1. What are the contributions of heredity and the environment to development? This is a question about *the sources of development*.
2. To what extent does the course of development change, through accident or through intervention? This is a question about *plasticity*.
3. Is development a gradual process of change or do periodic sudden, rapid changes result in new forms of thought and behavior? This is a question about *continuity* and *discontinuity*.
4. How do *individual differences* develop, making each human being unique?

A. Questions about the Sources of Development

The question about the roles of genes and environment in development is often thought of as a debate about the relative importance of **nature** (an individual's inherited biological predispositions) and **nurture** (the influences of the social and cultural environments on the individual). This debate is illustrated by the argument over Victor, the Wild Boy of Aveyron. What were the causes of his disabilities of speech and social interaction? Modern developmentalists continue to debate the roles of nature and nurture, but they recognize that development cannot be adequately explained by either factor in isolation.

B. Questions about Plasticity

Are there times during development when behavior is especially open to influence by the environment—that is, when it displays **plasticity**? In some nonhuman species, **critical periods** are times during which particular events must occur in order for development to proceed normally. An example is the period after hatching during which chicks or ducklings become attached to their mothers. In humans, true critical periods seem to occur only during prenatal development. Therefore, when observing human development, researchers look for **sensitive periods**—times when environmental influences are likely to be most pronounced. An example would be the period in childhood during which children typically acquire language.

C. Questions about Continuity/Discontinuity

Some developmentalists emphasize quantitative change in development—a gradual process such as may be seen in the increase in a child's vocabulary. Others emphasize the appearance of more abrupt, qualitative changes at particular points of development—for example, at the boundary between infancy and early childhood. These qualitatively new patterns are called **developmental stages.** According to John Flavell, the transition from one stage to another is marked by (1) qualitative changes; (2) simultaneous changes in many, if not all, domains of a child's development; (3) rapid change from one state to the next; and (4) a coherent pattern of changes across developmental domains. Observations of discontinuities in children's behavior support the existence of stages; however, there is also evidence to support the view that young children and adults experience the world quite similarly. Of particular difficulty for stage theories are observations that, at a given time, children often exhibit behaviors associated with more than one developmental stage.

D. Questions about Individual Differences

The question about individual differences is really two questions: (1) What makes people different from one another (really, another form of the question about sources of development)? and (2) Do people's characteristics remain stable over their lifetimes—for example, can you predict their behavior as adults from their traits in infancy? Apparently, the stability of characteristics over time depends, to some degree, on how they are measured. If different testing measures are used at different ages—as they often must be—characteristics may appear unstable over time. Stability of characteristics is also influenced by the stability of a person's environment; if the environment changes, personal characteristics may change as well.

IV. THEORIES OF DEVELOPMENT

The information psychologists obtain about children's behavior is only meaningful in the context of a **theory**—a collection of ideas or principles that can be used to guide the collection and interpretation of data.

A. Theory in Developmental Science

At present, no single theoretical perspective exists that unifies knowledge about development. However, there are several important theoretical perspectives that differ in a number of ways: (1) the domains of development under investigation; (2) the research methods used; and (3) the central issues addressed.

B. Grand Theories

Four theoretical perspectives—psychodynamic, social learning, constructivist, and sociocultural—are sweeping ("grand") in scope; they have laid the foundations for the modern theories that have followed.

- **Psychodynamic theories** have shown that developmental processes can be illuminated by examining the life experiences of individual people.

  Sigmund Freud constructed a theory of psychological development that emphasized the ways in which children satisfy their basic biological drives. At each psychosexual stage of development, children experience conflicts between their desires and the expectations of society. Freud also contributed the idea that the personality is made up of three structures—the id, the ego, and the superego—and the method of treatment for psychological disorders known as *psychoanalysis*.

Erik Erikson, another psychodynamic theorist, emphasized social and cultural factors as the major force behind development. He believed that children and adults pass through a series of psychosocial stages, each of which is associated with a task related to the quest for identity. Each task—or "crisis"—can be resolved positively or negatively, and each must be resolved in order to move on to the next stage. Development does not end with physical maturity but continues throughout life.

- **Social learning theories** emphasize the idea that learning occurs through the association of behaviors with their consequences. An early social learning theorist—John B. Watson—believed that development mainly resulted from learning (nurture) alone. B. F. Skinner contributed the theory of *operant conditioning,* which explains how behaviors are strengthened when they are followed by reinforcement and weakened when followed by punishment. Albert Bandura contributed the concept of *modeling,* through which children learn by observing and imitating others, and the idea of *self-efficacy,* which refers to people's beliefs about their ability to deal effectively with the environment. Social learning theory has given rise to the treatment known as *behavior modification,* which—among other things—helps to eliminate problem behaviors by breaking the associations between the behaviors and the consequences that maintain them.

- Jean Piaget based his **constructivist theory** on the idea that children actively construct their knowledge about the world on the basis of their experiences. Piaget believed that children progress through a series of stages of cognitive development, described in Table 1.3 of the textbook. He further believed that variations in the environment can speed up or slow down this process, but that all children go through the same stages in the same sequence.

  In Piaget's view, the basic unit of cognitive functioning is the *schema*—a mental structure that provides a model for understanding the world. Schemas are strengthened and transformed through two processes of *adaptation: assimilation* (the process by which experiences are incorporated into existing schemas) and *accommodation* (the process by which schemas are modified so that they can be applied to both old and new experiences). So, for example, infants may assimilate breast, bottle, pacifier, and fingers to the inborn sucking schema. Because different techniques are necessary for sucking on these different objects, the infant must accommodate the sucking schema to each. **Equilibration** is a balancing of the back-and-forth of assimilation and accommodation, bringing children to a new stage of development.

- Lev Vygotsky's **sociocultural theory** emphasizes the role of culture as a force in development. In this view, nature and nurture exert their influence on development by interacting indirectly, through culture. Vygotsky contributed the idea of the **zone of proximal development**—the gap between what children can accomplish on their own and what they can accomplish when interacting with others who are more competent. Ideally, in helping children to learn, adults provide assistance to them that goes just beyond, and builds on, their current abilities.

The grand theories are compared in Table 1.4 of the textbook.

C. Modern Theories

Although the grand theories continue to be important influences, modern theories have also generated insights into thinking about development.

- **Evolutionary theories** attempt to explain how human physical and behavioral characteristics contribute to the survival of our species and to understand how our evolutionary history influences each person's development. Recently, as described in the box "High-Tech Research on Brain Development and Disorders," technological advances allow biological processes to be measured more directly; this has led to increased interest in biologically based theories.

    The evolutionary approach is important in **ethology,** which is the study of behavior of species in their natural environments, as discussed in the box "In the Field: Probing the Mysteries of Learning." Using naturalistic observation, ethologists investigate the ways in which the characteristics of young organisms, and the adults who care for them, are adaptive—that is, how they increase the likelihood of the young surviving to have offspring of their own.

- **Information-processing theories** explain cognitive development in terms of the workings of a computer; they are concerned with how children come to process, store, organize, retrieve, and manipulate information, in increasingly efficient ways. The "hardware" of intellectual functioning includes structural components, such as brain structures and neural features, where data are stored and retrieved. The "software" is the set of strategies and methods that people use to help them process and remember information (for example, rehearsal).

- **Systems theories** view development in terms of complex wholes made up of systems that are organized, interact, and change over time. **Dynamic systems theory** addresses the ways complex systems of behavior develop through the interaction of less complex parts, for example, the way visual and motor behaviors coordinate to become the smooth reaching-and-grasping motion that allows a child to capture a dangling toy. **Ecological systems theory** focuses on the interactions among the environmental contexts in which development takes place. For example, Uri Bronfenbrenner visualized the developing child at the center of a set of nested, interacting systems: the *microsystem,* representing everyday settings; the *mesosystem,* in which everyday settings are linked to one another; the *exosystem,* representing outside settings that indirectly influence children's development; and the *macrosystem,* the culture's dominant beliefs and ideologies that shape what happens in the systems nested within.

- **Critical theories** call attention to cultural biases that may be present in traditional views of development. For example, they may seek to understand how development is affected by such factors as gender, race, ethnicity, and socioeconomic class, or by a society's social categories, institutions, and power relations.

Although no theory provides a full picture of development, each frames a unique aspect of development, allowing researchers to formulate **hypotheses**—explanations that can be tested and found to be true or false. The research methods used to test these hypotheses are described in the next section.

IV. METHODS FOR STUDYING DEVELOPMENT

It is important that the methods researchers use to collect information about development are appropriate for answering the questions they seek to answer.

A. The Goals of Developmental Research

Research in development can be described as belonging to one of several categories, depending on its goals:

- *Basic research* is carried out to advance scientific knowledge of human development; this research often explores major theoretical issues.
- *Applied research* is carried out to answer practical questions to help solve specific problems.
- *Action research,* also known as "mission-oriented" research, is carried out to provide data that can be used to influence decisions about social policy.

B. Criteria for Developmental Research

Researchers judge their findings according to specific scientific criteria:

- Observations should have **objectivity**—that is, they should not be biased by the investigator's preconceived ideas.
- Observations should have **reliablility**—they should be consistent when observed on more than one occasion, and particular observations should be agreed on by independent observers.
- Observations should have **replicability**—that is, when others perform the same study using the same procedures, they should obtain the same results.
- The measures used should have **validity**—the data being collected should actually reflect the underlying process the researcher is studying.

C. Methods of Data Collection

There are a variety of ways in which developmentalists collect data:

- **Naturalistic observation** is a method in which behavior is observed in the context of everyday life. It is an important method in the study of **ethnography,** in which researchers attempt to explain the meaning of children's behaviors in light of their culture's customs, beliefs, and values. Observation can take place in a single context or in many contexts.

  A limitation on the usefulness of naturalistic observation is that behavior may change when people know they are being observed. Also, because it is difficult for observers to record everything, their preconceived ideas may influence what actually is recorded.

Audio or video recordings can help preserve information, though they are time-consuming to analyze.

- In a psychological **experiment,** investigators can study cause-and-effect relationships. They may introduce a change (the *independent variable*) into the experience of a person or group of people; their behavior in response to that change (the *dependent variable*) is compared with that of people who are randomly assigned to not receive the experimental treatment. The group whose experience is changed is called the **experimental group.** Their behavior is compared with that of the **control group,** who are treated as much as possible like the experimental group except for not undergoing the experimental manipulation. An example of the experimental method is the study by Nathalie Charpak and her colleagues, in which they tested the effectiveness of "kangaroo care" in promoting the development of preterm infants.

  An important advantage of using experimental methods is that experiments can isolate causal factors. **Causation** refers to a relationship in which one event (or factor) *depends on* the occurrence of a prior event (or factor). Researchers may also be interested in the **correlation** between these factors and various measures of development. The **correlation coefficient** is a measure of the strength of association between two factors, but does not reveal if Factor A causes Factor B, if Factor B causes Factor A, or if some other factor causes both. The issue of correlation and causation is discussed in the box "Understanding the Causes and Correlations of Children's Behavior and Development."

  A limitation of experiments, according to some researchers, is that they may lack **ecological validity;** that is, children's behavior studied in one environment—the laboratory, in particular—may not be characteristic of their behavior in more natural settings.

- In the **clinical method,** researchers tailor questions to the individual subject. The answers to questions determine the direction the questioning will take. Jean Piaget made effective use of this method in his studies of children's thinking at different ages. The clinical method can reveal a great deal about developmental patterns; however, this method also relies heavily on verbal expression and therefore may underestimate the abilities of young children, because they may understand things well before they are able to express them.

The various methods of data collection are compared in Table 1.5 in the textbook.

D. Research Designs

Before beginning a study, researchers need to develop an overall plan describing how the study is put together—a **research design.** The most commonly used research designs are discussed in this section.

- In a **longitudinal design,** data are collected from the same group of people over an extended period as they grow older. Carrying out a longitudinal study is costly and time-consuming; in addition, the study may suffer *selective dropout*—that is, subjects may drop out during the course of the study, changing the sample from its original composition. Longitudinal designs also may confound age changes in behavior with changes due to other influences relating to the subjects' **cohort**—the group of people born at about the same time who share particular experiences unique to those growing up during that era.

- The **cross-sectional design,** in which different groups of people of different ages are each studied once, is the most commonly used design in developmental research. This type of design is less expensive and time-consuming and requires less commitment from participants. However, it is important, when carrying out a cross-sectional study, to be sure that participants in each age group are comparable in many characteristics besides age, such as sex, ethnicity, education, and socioeconomic status. Also, because of the way a cross-sectional study "slices up" development, it does not allow researchers to see how behavior actually changes over time and they must fill in the gaps through extrapolation and guesswork. As with a longitudinal design, it is possible for cohort-related confounding to occur, so this must be taken into account when interpreting the results.
- Using a **cohort sequential design,** in which a longitudinal study is replicated with several cohorts, helps researchers to separate cohort-related factors from changes due to age.
- To get closer to actually observing developmental processes in action, researchers can use a **microgenetic design,** which focuses on development over the course of a relatively short time interval, sometimes only a few hours or days. This method is generally used with children who are thought to be on the threshold of a significant developmental change.

The advantages and disadvantages of each type of design are discussed in the textbook in Table 1.6.

E. Ethical Standards

Today, research is evaluated for its ethical soundness as much as for its scientific accuracy; many universities and governmental agencies have **institutional review boards (IRBs)** that oversee the ethical soundness of research conducted at their institutions. Most of the ethical guidelines for the treatment of human research participants are based on the *Nuremberg Code,* the first formal international standard for evaluating the ethics of research involving subjects. These guidelines share several main concerns:

- Freedom from harm, both physical and psychological
- Informed consent, including parental consent for research with children
- Confidentiality of the information collected

The Society for Research in Child Development has devised a special set of ethical standards for conducting research with child participants; institutional review boards in the United States use these guidelines in their evaluations.

V. LOOKING AHEAD

The following chapters will trace development across the five major periods of child development, taking a *biocultural approach* that will emphasize the ways in which biological and cultural processes intertwine over the course of childhood.

Key Terms I

Following are important terms introduced in Chapter 1. Match each term with the letter of the example that best illustrates the term.

1. _____ causation

2. _____ clinical method

3. _____ cohort

4. _____ cohort sequential design

5. _____ control group

6. _____ correlation

7. _____ correlation coefficient

8. _____ cross-sectional design

9. _____ ecological validity

10. _____ experiment

11. _____ experimental group

12. _____ hypothesis

13. _____ institutional review boards (IRBs)

14. _____ longitudinal design

15. _____ microgenetic design

16. _____ naturalistic observation

17. _____ objectivity

18. _____ reliability

19. _____ replicability

20. _____ theory

21. _____ validity

a. A broad conceptual framework within which facts can be interpreted is called this.
b. Watching children interact on the playground at recess is a form of this.
c. This describes research designs that are not biased by preconceived ideas.
d. A measure has this characteristic when it reflects what it is purported to. (For example, in order to have this characteristic, a written memory test would need to be given to subjects who could read.)
e. A group of subjects in an experiment who undergo a manipulation of their environment.
f. A psychologist who is comparing a group of 8-year-olds, a group of 10-year-olds, and a group of 12-year-olds on a problem-solving task is conducting this type of study.
g. In order to be useful, this must be capable of being disconfirmed.
h. Subjects in an experiment who do not receive the experimental manipulation, but are otherwise treated the same as those who do are called this.
i. A measure has this if when subjects are tested on more than one occasion, they earn nearly the same scores.
j. An example is "American children beginning kindergarten in 1992."
k. In this way of studying development, questions are tailored to the person being interviewed.
l. An example is the relationship between age and height in children.

m. This is demonstrated when the occurrence of an event depends on some other event that has already occurred.

n. This characterizes a study that yields the same results when carried out by another set of researchers using the same method.

o. Some laboratory experiments are criticized as lacking this characteristic.

p. A researcher studying adolescence follows several groups of children from 10 through 15 years, adding a new group of 10-year-olds to the study every five years.

q. Researchers are doing this when they test the effectiveness of a new way to teach math by teaching one group with the new method and compare the results to those from a group taught by the earlier method.

r. A psychologist who studies one group of children's social relationships from kindergarten through sixth grade is conducting this type of study.

s. This is most often used when children are on the verge of a significant developmental change.

t. This can vary between -1.0 and $+1.0$.

u. This is a group that oversees research to make sure that participants are protected from risk.

Key Terms II

Following are important terms introduced in Chapter 1. Match each term with the letter of the example that best illustrates the term.

1. _____ constructivist theory

2. _____ critical period

3. _____ critical theory

4. _____ developmental science

5. _____ developmental stages

6. _____ dynamic systems theory

7. _____ ecological systems theory

8. _____ equilibration

9. _____ ethnography

10. _____ ethology

11. _____ evolutionary theory

12. _____ information-processing theory

13. _____ nature

14. _____ nurture

15. _____ psychodynamic theory

16. _____ research design

17. _____ sensitive period

18. _____ social learning theory

19. _____ sociocultural theory

20. _____ systems theory

21. _____ zone of proximal development

a. This type of theory may look at particular behaviors (for example, walking) as made up of parts that change in their development, organization, and interaction over time.

b. This may address one or more biases that characterize traditional approaches to development (as, for example, when development is defined in terms of typical male behavior patterns).

c. This balance between existing schemas and environmental experience is a "back and forth" process that brings the child to new levels of development.

d. Distinctive periods of development marked by discontinuity from the periods occurring before and after.

e. Sigmund Freud's theory of development is an example.

f. This is an interdisciplinary field of study with twin goals of studying children's development scientifically and of promoting their health and welfare.

g. This represents the influence of the environment on the individual.

h. This may provide an explanation of how children learn to reach for and grasp objects.

i. This refers to the individual's inborn, biologically based capacities.

j. This takes into account the multiple contexts in which development occurs.

k. An example is when a child's mother puts applesauce on a spoon, then lets the infant guide it to his mouth.

l. This term describes Lev Vygotsky's developmental theory.

m. This explanation of development assumes that children grow in understanding through active interaction with the world.

n. This is a time in an organism's life when certain experiences are necessary if normal development is to occur.

o. Albert Bandura's approach to development is an example.

p. A researcher needs to put this plan together before beginning a project.

q. This involves observing behavior in the settings in which it ordinarily occurs, rather than in the laboratory.

r. Some researchers feel that this occurs, during early childhood, for children's language development.

s. The study of the cultural organization of behavior is called this.

t. This uses the analogy of a computer to help understand how children's thinking develops.

u. This way of looking at development considers children's behavior in light of how it contributes to survival of the human species.

Multiple-Choice Practice Questions

Circle the letter of the word or phrase that correctly completes each statement.

1. Developmentalists work in which of the following settings?
    a. schools and child-care centers
    b. hospitals
    c. universities
    d. All these answers are correct.

2. The physical environments, families, and cultures in which children grow up are called the
    _____ of their development.
    a. domains
    b. contexts
    c. stages
    d. sources

3. Research by historians suggests that during medieval times
    a. children were treated in much the same way as adults.
    b. children were given clothes and toys appropriate to their levels of development.
    c. children were rarely left with anyone but a competent caregiver.
    d. children's ability levels were taken into account by those who provided them with education.

4. The work of Charles Darwin stimulated interest in the study of children's development for
    which of the following reasons?
    a. Economic and social changes led to concern about children's health and welfare.
    b. Scientists thought that children's behavior might shed light on our evolutionary past.
    c. Educators were searching for the causes of learning difficulties.
    d. Darwin's work highlighted the vast differences between the development of humans and
        that of other species.

5. During _____, a particular experience has a greater effect on development than
    it would at another time.
    a. a sensitive period
    b. a developmental stage
    c. phylogeny
    d. plasticity

6. According to John Flavell, reaching a new stage of development is characterized by
    a. quantitative change (for example, the ability to remember more words).
    b. slow, steady improvement (for example, being able to walk more quickly).
    c. simultaneous change in several areas of behavior.
    d. the appearance of new behaviors with no obvious input from the environment.

7. A(n) _____ provides a framework for investigating and interpreting facts.
    a. theory
    b. experiment
    c. observation
    d. cohort

8. Erik Erikson viewed _____ as the main challenge confronting each person.
    a. achieving equilibrium between assimilation and accommodation
    b. conflict between the id and the superego
    c. overcoming restrictions imposed by society
    d. the quest for identity

9. The work of which of the following researchers reflects a social learning approach to the study of development?
   a. Jean Piaget
   b. Sigmund Freud
   c. B. F. Skinner
   d. Lev Vygotsky

10. According to Jean Piaget, children gain knowledge about the world
    a. by constructing it on the basis of experience.
    b. through explicit teaching by adults.
    c. through the activation of genetic programs.
    d. by imitating their parents and peers.

11. Lev Vygotsky's most important contribution to our understanding of children's development is
    a. the study of the evolutionary roots of behavior.
    b. the concept of the zone of proximal development.
    c. the technique of behavior modification.
    d. the analogy of the brain being like a computer.

12. We say that observations have _____ when they are agreed on by independent observers.
    a. validity
    b. plasticity
    c. objectivity
    d. reliability

13. A teacher who keeps track of preschool children's cooperative play during recess is participating in which form of data collection?
    a. clinical interview
    b. experimental
    c. naturalistic observation
    d. ethnographic

14. In the study conducted by Nathalie Charpak, "kangaroo care" of preterm infants was the
    a. control condition.
    b. dependent variable.
    c. clinical method.
    d. experimental treatment.

15. A problem with the experimental method is that experiments
    a. cannot uncover causal influences on behavior.
    b. take place in artificial environments.
    c. are difficult and expensive to carry out.
    d. are harmful to the participants.

16. In general, as children's shoe sizes increase, so do their vocabularies. This is an example of
    a. a positive correlation.
    b. a negative correlation.
    c. a causal relationship.
    d. a zero correlation.

17. In using the clinical method, investigators
    a. ask each subject the same set of questions in the same way.
    b. introduce a change into each subject's experience and measure the effect on behavior.
    c. tailor questions to the individual subject.
    d. restrict their questions to those aimed at uncovering psychological problems.

18. When researchers compare the performance of three groups of children—3-year-olds, 5-year-olds, and 7-year-olds—on a test of picture recognition, they are conducting
    a. a cross-sectional study.
    b. a cohort-sequential study.
    c. a longitudinal study.
    d. a microgenetic study.

19. Compared to other research methods, _____ give the clearest picture of the actual process of development.
    a. experiments
    b. microgenetic designs
    c. naturalistic observations
    d. clinical interviews

20. Guidelines for conducting research require that scientists
    a. submit their research plans to the institution review board of their institution.
    b. get informed consent from research participants (and their parents, in the case of children).
    c. keep personal information about participants confidential.
    d. All these answers are correct.

Short-Answer Practice Questions

Write a brief answer in the space below each question.

1. What might be some reasons why Victor, the Wild Boy of Aveyron, never developed completely normal behavior, despite Itard's educational efforts?

2. How have views of children and childhood changed over the last five centuries? What impact have these changes had on interest in studying human development?

3. Discuss the ways in which changing technology has allowed developmentalists to study a wider range of questions.

4. Compare the advantages and disadvantages of naturalistic observation and experiments for studying children's behavior.

5. Describe how researchers may use a longitudinal design or a cross-sectional design to gather information on the same aspect of development. What are the advantages and disadvantages of each?

6. Why is it necessary to make sure that research studies meet the ethical standards for developmental research?

Sources of More Information

Azar, B. (May 1997). Nature, nurture: not mutually exclusive. *APA Monitor 1,* 28.
In this article, published in the news bulletin of the American Psychological Association, the author shows how genes affect our experience of the environment and how the environment influences the effects of our genes.

Barker, R. G., & Wright, H. F. (1951). *One Boy's Day: A Specimen Record of Behavior.* New York: Harper & Row.

This book, which records in detail a day in the life of a 7-year-old boy, illustrates one method of naturalistic observation.

Cole, M. (1999). Culture in development. In *Developmental Psychology: An Advanced Textbook,* 4th ed., M. H. Bornstein & M. E. Lamb (Eds.). Mahwah, NJ: Lawrence Erlbaum. This chapter presents examples of research on the role of culture in development.

Horvat, J., & Davis, S. (1998). *Doing Psychological Research.* Upper Saddle River, NJ: Prentice-Hall. This discussion of psychological research techniques includes many examples from published studies and effectively explains the logic of research design.

Hubbs-Tait, L., Nation, J. R., Krebs, N. F., & Bellinger, D. C. (2005). Neurotoxicants, micronutrients, and social environments: Individual and combined effects on children's development. *Psychological Science in the Public Interest* 6(3), 57–121. This special journal issue provides an excellent example of developmental research that addresses important practical problems and has implications for public policy decisions.

Jones, N. B. (Ed.) (1972). *Ethological Studies of Child Behaviour.* New York: Cambridge University Press. This book contains many different ethological studies, including examples of child–child and mother–child interaction.

Lerner, R. M. (2001). *Concepts and Theories of Human Development,* 3rd ed. New York: Psychology Press. Many different approaches to development, both historical and contemporary, are covered in this book.

Miller, S. A. (1998). *Developmental Research Methods,* 2nd ed. Upper Saddle River, NJ: Prentice-Hall. This book on research methods is tailored to students of developmental psychology.

Patterson, G. (1976). *Living with Children: New Methods for Parents and Teachers.* Champaign, IL: Research Press. In this book, parents and teachers are shown how to change children's behavior for the better by arranging environmental contingencies to encourage desired behaviors and eliminate undesired ones. This book illustrates the social learning approach to development.

Pelligrini, A. D., Symons, F. J., & Hoch, J. (2004). *Observing Children in Their Natural Worlds: A Methodological Primer,* 2nd ed. Mahwah, NJ: Lawrence Erlbaum. This book gives ideas and instructions for conducting observational studies with children.

Singer, D. G., & Revenson, T. A. (1996). *A Piaget Primer: How a Child Thinks,* rev. ed. New York: Penguin Books.

The authors discuss Piaget's conceptualization of children's thinking and how it can be applied to teaching and parenting.

Smuts, Alice B., & Hagen, J. W. (Eds.). (1985). History and research in child development. *Monographs of the Society for Research in Child Development 50* (4–5, Serial No. 211). This monograph, published to commemorate the 50th anniversary of the Society for Research in Child Development, contains chapters on the history of the family and on scientific developments within the field of child development, set within their social contexts.

Answer Key

Answers to Key Terms I: 1.m, 2.k, 3.j, 4.p, 5.h, 6.l, 7.t, 8.f, 9.o, 10.q, 11.e, 12.g, 13.u, 14.r, 15.s, 16.b, 17.c, 18.i, 19.n, 20.a, 21.d.

Answers to Key Terms II: 1.m, 2.n, 3.b, 4.f, 5.d, 6.h, 7.j, 8.c, 9.s, 10.q, 11.u, 12.t, 13.i, 14.g, 15.e, 16.p, 17.r, 18.o, 19.l, 20.a, 21.k.

Answers to Multiple-Choice Questions: 1.d, 2.b, 3.a, 4.b, 5.a, 6.c, 7.a, 8.d, 9.c, 10.a, 11.b, 12.d, 13.c, 14.d, 15.b, 16.a, 17.c, 18.a, 19.b, 20.d.

2 Biocultural Foundations

In many ways, all human beings seem very much alike. Yet within that basic similarity, the details of appearance and behavior vary a great deal. In fact, people exhibit an amazing diversity of both talents and troubles.

How do genes and the environment combine to create our unique characteristics as human beings? If we were all raised in identical environments, would we behave completely alike? Nearly all developmentalists would say "No." Human development is an interaction between biologically based tendencies and the environmental circumstances in which people live. Nearly all of us are genetically unique, so a hypothetical universal environment would affect each person in a different way. Even genetically identical individuals—monozygotic twins—develop individual interests, abilities, and characters.

Some of the differences among people are shaped systematically by the cultures in which they live. Human beings can adapt to changing conditions through cultural evolution, building on the expertise of countless generations.

Because biological and cultural evolution have occurred together for so long, it is not easy to distinguish their separate influences on development. But by comparing members of the same families and by studying the effects on development of mutations—mistakes in gene replication—and inherited genetic disorders, psychologists can learn more about how biology and culture interact to produce each unique person.

Learning Objectives

Keep these questions in mind while studying Chapter 2.

1. What are some of the ways in which culture organizes our behavior and our relationship to the environment?
2. How does culture accomplish the transmission of adaptive behaviors from one generation to the next?

3. What is the relation between genotype and phenotype? Why do adaptive phenotypic traits become more widespread and less adaptive traits become rarer?
4. How is a person's genetic sex determined?
5. What are the different ways in which alleles—the genetic variants of a gene—can express themselves?
6. How is development affected by genetic mutations and abnormalities?
7. In what ways do researchers use kinship studies to help them estimate the degree to which characteristics are influenced by heredity and environment? What are some of the ways in which individuals act to modify their own environments?
8. What are some examples of the interaction of biology and culture in the process of coevolution?

Chapter Summary

The similarities and differences among people result from both their cultural heritage and their genetic heritage; these influences interact in relation to the particular life experiences of each individual, resulting in distinct developmental patterns.

I. INHERITING CULTURE

Observations of macaque monkeys in Japan have shown that, even among nonhuman primates, culture is rooted in everyday activities such as getting and preparing food, caring for children, and children's play. **Culture,** as defined by most developmentalists, consists of *material and symbolic tools that accumulate through time, are passed on through social processes, and provide resources for the developing child.*

A. The Tools of Culture

The **material tools** of culture include not only physical objects such as hammers and computers but also observable patterns of behavior such as family routines and social practices. The **symbolic tools** are more abstract and are related to knowledge, beliefs, and values—for example, a society's expectation of male and female sex roles. Many tools of culture are both material and symbolic. The term **mediation** refers to the way people's activities are organized through the use of tools. There is debate about the ways in which a culture's material and symbolic tools mediate children's behavior and development; for example, will playing with toy weapons lead children to behave more aggressively?

B. Processes of Cultural Inheritance

How is culture transmitted from one generation to another?

- Social processes involved in cultural inheritance are **social enhancement,** in which children make use of resources that happen to be available to them because of other people's activities; **imitation,** in which children learn from observing and copying the activities of others; and **explicit instruction,** in which children are purposefully taught to use the material and symbolic resources of their culture. Explicit instruction makes use of *symbolic communication* (for example, language, drawing, and music); thus, it is possible to inform children about objects and events that are not present in the environment.

- Symbolic communication also allows the expression of abstract ideas, and the expression of feelings and cultural values. For example, Stephanie Carlson and her colleagues found that children performed better on a self-control task (in which they needed to pick the smaller set of candies in order to get the larger one) when the choices were marked with symbols compared to when the choices were visibly present.

C. The Complexity of Culture

The people of a culture produce individual variations in the material and symbolic cultural tools they use; this process of change through variation is called **cumulative cultural evolution.** Much as cultural variation is necessary to cultural evolution, variation in biological inheritance is essential to biological evolution.

II. BIOLOGICAL INHERITANCE

How is an individual's genetic endowment expressed in physical and psychological traits? How does genetic endowment relate to the process of evolution?

A. Genes and Traits

Heredity is the transmission of biological characteristics from one generation to the next; the units of heredity are **genes,** which contain instructions that guide the formation of physical and psychological traits. An individual's **genotype** represents that person's exact genetic makeup. The individual's **phenotype,** or observable characteristics, develops as a result of the interaction between that person's inherited traits and the environment.

B. EVOLUTION'S PROCESS OF NATURAL SELECTION

According to Charles Darwin, **natural selection** determines which phenotypes survive. Individuals whose phenotypes are successfully adapted to their environments are more likely to survive to reproduce. Variation in phenotypes is necessary for natural selection to occur.

- As humans changed in physical structure related to walking upright (bipedalism), women developed smaller birth canals while infants' brains—and heads—became larger. Thus, women whose babies were born after shorter pregnancies (that is, when the infants were smaller) were more likely to survive and to have babies undamaged by the birth process. Over a period of many thousands of years, natural selection would have favored a shortening of the length of human pregnancies.
- Another development favored by natural selection is the emergence of baby-talk or **infant-directed speech.** Because infants born after a shorter pregnancy were less mature (and less able to cling to their mothers), mothers may have had to put them down in order

to carry out tasks such as food gathering. The soothing, melodic quality of infant-directed speech would have had the effect of quieting and calming babies, and would have been an expression of maternal responsiveness. Responsive mothers would have been more likely to have offspring who survived to have offspring of their own and to pass on their mothers' tendency to use baby-talk.

C. Genetic Inheritance Through Sexual Reproduction

How is an individual's genotype formed? Each person's genes are found on 46 threadlike **chromosomes,** each a single molecule of **DNA (deoxyribonucleic acid)** in the shape of a double helix. There are thousands of genes on each chromosome. The father's sperm and mother's ovum each contain 23 chromosomes, half the number necessary for a new individual to develop. Sperm and ovum fuse to form the **zygote,** a single cell containing 46 chromosomes from which all the child's cells will develop.

• Our bodies contain two types of cells: **germ cells** (sperm and ova) and **somatic** (body) **cells.**

    Somatic cells are created by **mitosis,** a process of duplication and division. This is also the way new cells are created and replaced throughout a person's lifetime. Under ordinary circumstances, the genetic information in the new cells is an exact copy of that in the original.

    Meiosis is the cell-division process by which germ cells are formed. It results in cells with 23 unpaired chromosomes—half the original set from the parent cell. When a sperm cell fertilizes an ovum, the resulting zygote will have 46 chromosomes.

    The mixing of genes from both parents during sexual reproduction makes each human being genetically unique. The exception to this uniqueness is the case of **monozygotic (MZ) twins.** Occasionally, the zygote separates to form two genetically alike individuals: monozygotic twins. Monozygotic twins are called "identical twins"; however, they are not really identical, in appearance or in behavior. **Dizygotic (DZ) twins,** or fraternal twins, result from the fertilization of two ova by two sperm; these twins are no more alike than non-twin siblings.

• The twenty-third pair of chromosomes in normal females are both **X chromosomes;** normal males have one X chromosome and one much smaller **Y chromosome.** Whereas an ovum always contains an X chromosome, a sperm may contain an X or a Y. The twenty-third chromosome determines the genetic sex of the child; however, other characteristics have more complex origins.

D. Laws of Genetic Inheritance

Some characteristics are inherited through a simple type of genetic transmission in which a pair of genes, one from each parent, contributes to a trait. The genes that influence the trait may have alternative forms or **alleles.** People who have inherited the same allele from both parents are **homozygous** for the trait; those who have inherited a different allele from each parent are **heterozygous.** How an allelic form of a trait is expressed in a heterozygous person depends on whether the allele is **dominant** (in which case it will be expressed) or **reces-**

sive (in which case it will not be expressed). **Carriers** of recessive alleles can still pass them to their offspring. A recessive trait is expressed when both parents contribute the same recessive allele; Table 2.2 of the textbook shows some examples of disorders that are transmitted through recessive genes. In some cases, two alleles have **codominance,** in which case a distinctively different outcome will result; the blood type "AB" is an example of this. In other instances, both alleles have some influence and an intermediate outcome will occur; thus, children of one light-skinned parent and one dark-skinned parent may have skin tones that are intermediate between the two.

E. Mutations and Genetic Abnormalities

Changes in the human **gene pool**—the total genetic information possessed by a sexually reproducing population—can occur through **mutation,** an error in gene replication that results in a change in the structure of an individual's DNA. Mutations in somatic cells affect only the person in whom they occur, whereas mutations in the germ cells may result in changed genetic information being passed on to the next generation. Mutations are a natural part of life; they provide a source of variation needed for natural selection to occur. However, the majority of mutations are lethal, resulting in miscarriage early in pregnancy. About 3.5 percent of babies born have some kind of genetic abnormality. Table 2.2 shows common disorders related to genetic abnormalities.

- Phenylketonuria (PKU) is an inherited metabolic disorder that results from a recessive gene; it occurs through normal genetic transmission when both parents pass the recessive allele to their child. Children with PKU have difficulty in metabolizing phenylalanine; the buildup of phenylalanine in the bloodstream causes brain damage, leading to mental retardation. However, by altering the environment of children with this disorder—specifically, by removing from their diets foods high in the amino acid phenylalanine—the effects of the disorder can be greatly reduced. Blood tests given to newborns can detect most cases of PKU, so that dietary intervention may begin immediately. PKU can also be detected prenatally, and a test to identify carriers of the recessive gene for the disorder is also available. GA1, another inherited metabolic disorder, is discussed in the box "In the Field: Doctor of the Plain People." The box titled "Genetic Counseling" discusses options available to those who are carriers of genes for genetically based disorders.
- Down syndrome occurs, not through normal genetic transmission, but through a chromosomal error, usually during the process of meiosis. The affected person has extra genetic material on chromosome 21 or—in most cases—an extra copy of the chromosome (this is called *trisomy 21*). The disorder results in mental retardation as well as a number of distinctive physical characteristics. However, the severity of the disorder varies and supportive intervention can improve the functioning of Down syndrome children. Down syndrome affects about 1 of every 1000 children born in the United States. The older a woman is when she conceives, the greater her chance of producing a child with this disorder.
- Half of all chromosomal abnormalities in newborns involve the X and Y chromosomes—those that determine the baby's sex. The most common sex-linked chromosomal abnormality is Klinefelter's syndrome, in which a boy has an extra X chromosome (XXY). This

disorder occurs in 1 of every 500 to 1000 males born in the United States. The boys develop normally until adolescence, at which point they fail to develop the characteristics of sexual maturity; they may also have speech and language problems, leading to difficulties in school. Testosterone replacement therapy, beginning at age 11 or 12, has beneficial effects on the physical development and sexual functioning of men affected by this disorder; however, they are sterile.

F. The Phenotype: From Genes to Traits

Developmentalists ask whether any given phenotypic trait is determined by an individual's genotype and to what extent it is open to environmental influence.

- The degree to which a phenotype is open to influence by the environment is called **phenotypic plasticity.** Some traits, such as eye color, have little plasticity; others, such as intellectual skills, have greater plasticity. The British geneticist Conrad Waddington imagined the development of a phenotypic trait as the journey of a ball across a landscape; as the ball rolls downhill, it meets "forks in the road" where development can turn one way or the other. The interaction of genes with environment results in changes in the landscape over time, depending on the individual's experiences.
- Some genetically determined traits are not easily influenced by the environment; they are said to be **canalized.** The tendency for children to learn language is a highly canalized process; only severe and prolonged deprivation would prevent it from occurring.

  Phenotypic plasticity allows individuals to adapt to changes in the environment, whereas canalization ensures that important traits are not thrown off track by genetic or environmental changes.

G. Heritability

Because of the complexity of the gene-behavior relationship, we usually speak of human characteristics as being "genetically influenced" rather than "genetically caused."

- **Heritability** is the amount of phenotypic variation in a population that results from genetic variation. Heritability can be estimated by comparing the incidence of a trait among people who have different degrees of genetic relationship to one another. There is no universal heritability for any given trait. Instead, estimates of heritability apply to a particular population at a particular time. A high heritability estimate for a trait—height, for example—does not mean that it cannot be influenced by environmental factors, such as nutrition. Instead, it may mean that the environment in question is quite uniform—as, in the United States, where nearly all children receive nutrition adequate for growth. Thus, nearly all variation in children's height in the U.S. population is due to genetic variability.
- **Kinship studies** allow developmentalists to estimate the genetic and environmental contributions to a phenotypic trait by examining the similarity among relatives who vary in their degree of genetic closeness. A strong correlation between genetic closeness and similarity on the trait implies that the trait is highly heritable; weaker correlations indicate lower heritability.

*In a **family study**, comparisons among members* of the same household show how similar people with varying degrees of genetic relationship are with respect to a specific characteristic. Of course, people who are biologically related also share similar environments; therefore, similarities can be attributed to environmental as well as genetic similarity.

In a **twin study,** monozygotic twins and same-sex dizygotic twins are compared to one another and to other family members for similarity on a trait. Monozygotic twins should resemble one another more than dizygotic twins or other siblings with respect to a heritable trait.

An **adoption study** is another strategy for estimating the contribution of genes and environment to particular traits. Adopted children may be compared with both their adopted relatives, with whom they share an environment, and their biological relatives, to whom they are biologically related.

Studies have shown a pattern of greater similarity with closer genetic relationships for a number of characteristics, including intelligence, some personality traits, and susceptibility to schizophrenia. It is also true that family members are often quite different from one another, despite their close genetic relationship. Table 2.3 in the textbook illustrates the effects of both genetic factors and environmental influences on the personality trait of extroversion.

Researchers studying individual differences have pointed out problems with kinship studies. For example, monozygotic twins may be treated more similarly than dizygotic twins because they look more similar. And, besides having different combinations of genes, individuals in a family experience unique environments, having their own particular teachers, friends, and sibling relationships. A study of identical twins by Spanish researcher Manuel Esteller has found that the twins' phenotypic traits become increasingly different as they grow older, presumably due to the effects of social and environmental factors.

H. Genotypes, Phenotypes, and Human Behavior

Waddington's analogy of a ball rolling through a landscape leaves two important questions unanswered: What role do developing individuals play in the process of their own development? And how do the individual's cultural and social environments form and transform the landscape over the course of a lifetime?

- Developmentalists use the term **niche construction** to refer to the ways individuals actively shape and modify the environments in which they live. For example, a quiet and undemanding infant evokes different responses from adults than one who is fussy and demanding. But because niche construction is a social process that proceeds through interactions with parents, siblings, playmates, and others, it is best thought of as a process of **co-construction** between developing individuals and the important people in their lives.
- Children's physical environments are also important to their development. The term **ecological inheritance** refers to environmental modifications that affect the development of offspring or descendants. Examples of ecological inheritance are *selection of habitat* (for

example, migrating to a new land or relocating from a rural to an urban environment) and *changes to the existing habitat* (for example, building homes and schools or depleting natural resources). Research from the ecological perspective can show how human activity affects the genotype and phenotype of developing individuals.

III. THE COEVOLUTION OF CULTURE AND BIOLOGY

Rudimentary forms of culture were already present during early phases of human evolution. Humans' biological evolution did not end with the appearance of culture. Instead, biology and culture have interacted with each other in a process called **coevolution.** James Mark Baldwin, an early developmentalist mentioned in Chapter 1, proposed that cultural factors influence the likelihood that people with particular traits will survive; this idea is called the **Baldwin effect.** Individuals who have access to knowledge that enhances survival—for example, how to build shelters, prepare food, and heal illness—are more likely to live long enough to reproduce and pass their knowledge on to their children.

A. Lactose Tolerance

The ability to digest fresh milk—known as *lactose tolerance*—is an example of the coevolution of biology and culture. Most adults no longer produce lactase, the enzyme that aids in the digestion of milk. However, a genetic variant exists that allows lactase production to continue after the age of weaning; this variant is widespread in certain cultures where dairy products became an important source of nutrition, for example, among pastoral nomads in the Middle East and Africa. This genetic variant is also common among people of Northern European descent; in their case, the selective advantage comes from their need to be able to absorb calcium in the absence of sufficient Vitamin D-producing sunlight in the northern climate.

B. Sickle-Cell Anemia

Another example of the coevolution of biology and culture is sickle-cell anemia, a serious blood disorder that occurs in people who are homozygous for the recessive sickle-cell trait; they inherit it from both parents. People who are heterozygous for the gene have the sickle-cell trait but do not suffer from severe symptoms of the disease. The sickle-cell trait is found primarily among people of African descent; heterozygous carriers have the advantage of greater resistance to malaria than those without the trait. In West Africa, the area from which the ancestors of most African Americans came, and where malaria is still a serious problem, more than 20 percent of the population carry the sickle-cell trait. There is a great deal of malaria in the region due to the cultural practice of cutting forests, thus enlarging the habitat of malaria-carrying mosquitoes. In contrast, in the United States, malaria is rare. Therefore, the sickle-cell trait no longer provides an advantage and is gradually being eliminated from the gene pool; it is carried by only 8 to 9 percent of Americans of African descent.

IV. RETRACING THE LAETOLI FOOTPRINTS

Our evolutionary forebears had lives and experiences that were different from, and yet quite similar to, our own. Like them, we are affected by biology, physical environment, and culture. In later chapters, we will see how these factors interact in complex ways throughout the course of development.

Key Terms I

Following are important terms introduced in Chapter 2. Match each term with the letter of the example that best illustrates the term.

1. _____ allele

2. _____ Baldwin effect

3. _____ canalized

4. _____ carriers

5. _____ chromosome

6. _____ codominance

7. _____ cumulative cultural evolution

8. _____ DNA (deoxyribonucleic acid)

9. _____ dominant allele

10. _____ genes

11. _____ gene pool

12. _____ genotype

13. _____ heredity

14. _____ heterozygous

15. _____ homozygous

16. _____ infant-directed speech

17. _____ kinship studies

18. _____ natural selection

19. _____ phenotype

20. _____ recessive allele

21. _____ X chromosome

22. _____ Y chromosome

23. _____ zygote

a. There are 46 of these threadlike structures in the nucleus of each cell.
b. This sex-determining chromosome can be inherited only from the father.
c. These molecules, found on chromosomes, contain "blueprints" for development.
d. The cells of normal females contain two of these.
e. This single cell results from the joining of sperm and ovum at conception.
f. Some traits, such as children's ability to learn language, can be described this way; they tend to follow the same developmental path, despite most environmental variations.
g. This refers to an alternative form of a gene; for example, the B form of the gene for blood type.
h. This term refers to a person's genetic endowment.

i.   A person's observable characteristics, developing through interaction between genes and environment.

j.   The genetic information available in a whole reproducing population is called this.

k.   When a child inherits an allele for type A blood from his mother and an allele for type O blood from his father, we use this term to describe his genotype for blood type.

l.   A child inherits an allele for type O blood from each parent; this term describes her genotype for blood type.

m.   This term refers to a less powerful allele that is not expressed when a more powerful allele is present.

n.   An allele whose effects show up phenotypically, even in the presence of another allele, is called this.

o.   This behavior may originally have evolved because mothers could not gather food and carry their babies at the same time.

p.   Two different alleles contribute to a trait; for example, type AB blood.

q.   Each chromosome is made of a single, double-stranded molecule of this substance.

r.   This describes the relationship between culture and biology in human evolution.

s.   These are useful in estimating the genetic and environmental contributions to a trait.

t.   They can pass a recessive gene to their offspring, although they show no signs of the characteristic themselves.

u.   In this process, certain traits become more common in the population, whereas others tend to disappear over time.

v.   This refers to the transmission of biological characteristics from one generation to the next.

w.   This refers to the ability of humans to build on the achievements of previous generations of people.

Key Terms II

Following are important terms introduced in Chapter 2. Match each term with the letter of the example that best illustrates the term.

1. _____ adoption study

2. _____ co-construction

3. _____ coevolution

4. _____ culture

5. _____ dizygotic twins

6. _____ ecological inheritance

7. _____ explicit instruction

8. _____ family study

9. _____ germ cells

10. _____ heritability

11. _____ imitation

12. _____ material tools

13. _____ mediation

14. _____ meiosis

15. _____ mitosis

16. _____ monozygotic twins

17. _____ mutation

18. _____ niche construction

19. _____ phenotypic plasticity

20. _____ social enhancement

21. _____ somatic cells

22. _____ symbolic tools

23. _____ twin study

a. These come in two varieties: sperm and ova.
b. This expresses the degree to which genetic factors influence the amount of variability in a trait.
c. Nearly all the body's cells are produced by this process of duplication and division.
d. These are all the cells in the body with the exception of the sperm and ova.
e. These result from the fertilization of two ova by two sperm.
f. Exposure to radiation can cause this change in the structure of the genetic material.
g. This method allows researchers to estimate the degree to which a particular trait is influenced by genes and environment.
h. This is the process through which sperm and ova contain 23 chromosomes, rather than 46.
i. In this, members of the same family are compared to assess their similarity for a particular trait.
j. This refers to the organization of people's activities through the use of tools.
k. This occurs, with respect to music, when a piano is present in a child's home.
l. This is an example: Because a child shows interest in music, she goes to concerts and is given access to instruments.
m. Writing and drawing are examples.
n. A trait that is easily influenced by the environment has a great deal of this characteristic.
o. This consists of tools that accumulate over time and are passed from one generation to the next.
p. These two individuals have exactly the same genotype.
q. This may involve studying genetically related individuals who are raised in different environments or genetically unrelated individuals who are raised in the same environment.
r. Two examples are a computer and a social practice, such as how birthdays are celebrated.
s. This reflects the fact that children's environments are shaped by the children themselves in conjunction with their parents and other people.
t. This refers to an individual learning a new behavior by watching others.
u. This term refers to the way biology and culture interact over time.
v. This term refers to the process through which modifications of the environment are passed from one generation to the next.
w. This procedure typically makes extensive use of symbolic communication.

Multiple-Choice Practice Questions

Circle the letter of the word or phrase that correctly completes each statement.

1. Researchers believe that culture
   a. does not exist in nonhuman animals.
   b. began to develop only after humans evolved their current physical form.
   c. developed concurrently with human physical evolution.
   d. Both a and b are correct.

2. Which way of passing on cultural knowledge is uniquely human?
   a. imitation
   b. explicit instruction
   c. social enhancement
   d. All these answers are correct.

3. The somatic cells of the body each contain
   a. 23 chromosomes.
   b. 23 pairs of chromosomes.
   c. 46 pairs of chromosomes
   d. 50 pairs of chromosomes.

4. An individual's phenotype
   a. represents his observable characteristics.
   b. results from the interaction of genetic and environmental influences.
   c. is unique, even compared to that of an identical twin.
   d. All these answers are correct.

5. A person who is genetically male receives, at conception,
   a. an X chromosome from his mother and a Y chromosome from his father.
   b. a Y chromosome from his mother and an X chromosome from his father.
   c. an X chromosome from each parent.
   d. a Y chromosome from each parent.

6. When two alleles for a trait are present but only one is expressed, we call the one that is not expressed
   a. dominant.
   b. codominant.
   c. recessive.
   d. complementary.

7. Which characteristic is an example of the codominance of alleles?
   a. type O blood
   b. female sex
   c. type AB blood
   d. red-green color blindness

8. Meiosis is
   a. the process by which the body's cells reproduce.
   b. the process by which the germ cells come to contain fewer chromosomes than the somatic cells.
   c. an error in gene replication.
   d. a polygenic trait.

9. If a child receives an allele for type A blood from her mother and an allele for type B blood from her father, she is _____ with respect to blood type.
   a. heterozygous
   b. recessive
   c. homozygous
   d. complementary

10. The total genetic material in a reproducing population is called the
    a. genotype.
    b. phenotype.
    c. range of reaction.
    d. gene pool.

11. _____ is a genetic disorder caused by an extra chromosome.
    a. Down syndrome
    b. Sickle-cell anemia
    c. Phenylketonuria
    d. All these answers are correct.

12. People who are heterozygous for the sickle-cell trait
    a. do not develop sickle-cell anemia.
    b. may have some symptoms under conditions of low oxygen.
    c. are more resistant to malaria than those without the gene.
    d. All these answers are correct.

13. Errors in gene replication, called _____, often have lethal results.
    a. meioses
    b. canalizations
    c. mutations
    d. recessive traits

14. _____ is an inherited disorder that can be treated through dietary intervention.
    a. Tay-Sachs disease
    b. Phenylketonuria (PKU)
    c. Klinefelter syndrome
    d. Muscular dystrophy

15. _____ traits tend to be resistant to environmental influence.
    a. Learned
    b. Canalized
    c. Inherited
    d. Psychological

16. Which of the following would be the best indicator that the environment had an effect on a particular characteristic?
    a. Identical twins are more similar than fraternal twins with respect to this characteristic.
    b. Siblings are more similar than unrelated people with respect to this characteristic.
    c. Adopted children are more similar to their adoptive siblings than to their biological siblings with respect to this characteristic.
    d. Fraternal twins and ordinary siblings are equally similar with respect to this characteristic.

17. When a characteristic has high heritability, this means that
    a. the amount of variability due to genetic factors is the same in any environment.
    b. a large amount of the variability in the population for this characteristic can be attributed to genetic factors.
    c. environmental interventions will have no effect on this characteristic.
    d. differences in this characteristic between different population groups are due entirely to genetic factors.

18. The trait of *lactose tolerance*—the ability of adults to digest fresh milk—
    a. occurs mainly in places where it conferred a survival advantage in the past.
    b. is now prevalent in nearly all human populations.
    c. is not a genetically based characteristic.
    d. only occurs among people of Northern European ancestry.

19. Most developmentalists view a child's environment as being
    a. constructed exclusively by the child.
    b. constructed by the adults surrounding the child.
    c. co-constructed by the child and others around the child.
    d. a product of the child's imagination.

Short-Answer Practice Questions

Write a brief answer in the space below each question.

1. What are some examples of material and symbolic tools in modern culture? How do children typically learn to use these tools?

2. Explain how behaviors—for example, the use of infant-directed speech—can become part of the genetic heritage of our species.

3. What does it mean to say that a trait is heritable? What are some ways to estimate heritability?

4. Sometimes, genes for disorders remain in the gene pool despite the adverse consequences to those who carry them. Explain why the sickle-cell gene remains in the population despite its cost in illness and premature death.

5. What are some reasons why siblings raised in the same family can be quite different from one another?

6. In what ways do children's genetic characteristics influence the kind of environments they inhabit? Give examples.

7. Describe how the behavior of people in a culture can make changes in the environment that will affect future generations.

Sources of More Information

Asimov, I. (1962). *The Genetic Code.* New York: New American Library of World Literature.
This book traces the research that led to the discovery of DNA.

Carson, R. A., & Rothstein, M. A. (Eds.). (1999). *Behavioral Genetics: The Clash of Culture and Biology.* Baltimore, MD: Johns Hopkins University Press.
In this edited volume, the authors focus on the science behind behavioral genetics and the ethical, legal, and social issues raised by work in this area.

Darwin, C. (1958). *The Origin of Species.* New York: New American Library of World Literature.
Charles Darwin's classic evolutionary account of the origin of human beings, originally published in 1859.

Dunn, J., & Plomin, R. (1990). *Separate Lives: Why Siblings Are so Different.* New York: Basic Books.
The authors tackle the question of how siblings, who share a great deal of genetic heritage, develop into quite different individuals.

Edelson, M. (2000). *My Journey with Jake: A Memoir of Parenting and Disability.* Toronto, Canada: Between the Lines.
A boy is born with a rare genetic disorder, and his mother describes the difficulties of caring for a severely disabled child.

Hamer, D., & Copeland, P. (1998). *Living with Our Genes: Why They Matter More Than You Think.* New York: Doubleday.
This book examines links between DNA and behavior and highlights the complex interactions between hereditary tendencies and environmental effects, as they influence such characteristics as body size, aging, addiction, and temperament.

Hassold, T. J., & Patterson, D. (Eds.). (1999). *Down Syndrome: A Promising Future, Together.* New York: John Wiley & Sons.
Medical, educational, developmental, and vocational issues are addressed in this book, which is aimed at giving the latest information to parents and others who work with children affected by Down syndrome.

Richards, J. E., & Hawley, R. S., (2005). *The Human Genome: A User's Guide* (2nd Ed.). Burlington, MA: Elsevier Science and Technology Books.
The authors—a professor of genetics and a health education writer—explore the discoveries of modern genetics and their relevance to such topics as cloning, inherited health problems, gene therapy, and mental illness.

Kitcher, P. (1996). *The Lives to Come: The Genetic Revolution and Human Possibilities.* New York: Simon & Schuster.
This book gives readers a philosopher's view of the ethical dilemmas that accompany new discoveries in the field of genetics.

What we learn from twins: The mirror of your soul. *The Economist,* January 3, 1998, 74–76.
This magazine article provides some interesting information about the history of twin studies and some of the political issues involved in research on the relative contributions of heredity and environment.

Answer Key

Answers to Key Terms I: 1.g, 2.r, 3.f, 4.t, 5.a, 6.p, 7.w, 8.q, 9.n, 10.c, 11.j, 12.h, 13.v, 14.k, 15.l, 16.o, 17.s, 18.u, 19.i, 20.m, 21.d, 22.b, 23.e.

Answers to Key Terms II: 1.q, 2.s, 3.u, 4.o, 5.e, 6.v, 7.w, 8.i, 9.a, 10.b, 11.t, 12.r, 13.j, 14.h, 15.c, 16.p, 17.f, 18.l, 19.n, 20.k, 21.d, 22.m, 23.g.

Answers to Multiple-Choice Questions: 1.c, 2.b, 3.b, 4.d, 5.a, 6.c, 7.c, 8.b, 9.a, 10.d, 11.a, 12.d, 13.c, 14.b, 15.b, 16.c, 17.b, 18.a, 19.c.

3

Prenatal Development and Birth

During the 9 months between conception and birth, rapid development transforms the human organism from a single cell to a baby capable of life outside the mother's body. Development proceeds through the processes of differentiation and integration: differentiation of one type of cell into many, and integration of bodily systems into a smoothly functioning whole.

At no time during the course of prenatal development is the developing organism completely buffered from the outside world. On the one hand, while still in the womb, the fetus registers signals from its sense organs, particularly those of balance and hearing. It may even learn to recognize familiar experiences. On the other hand, outside influences such as malnutrition, chemicals, and disease organisms may interfere with normal development.

Birth is a dramatic transition, both physically and behaviorally. It also marks the beginning of children's first social relationships, starting with their first face-to-face encounters with their parents. And finally, at birth, the beliefs and customs of the cultural groups into which children are born begin to shape their development in more direct ways. The influence of culture can be seen in the way preparations for childbirth are carried out—whether in a hut or in a hospital—in the rituals surrounding the process, and in the expectations with which the infant is greeted by parents and other members of the community.

Learning Objectives

Keep these questions in mind while studying Chapter 3.

1. Why do developmentalists consider it important to understand prenatal development?
2. What transformations occur as the one-celled zygote develops into a baby capable of surviving outside the mother's body?

3. How might the developing sensory abilities and motor capabilities of the fetus help to prepare it for postnatal life?
4. In what ways do environmental factors—for example, nutrition and maternal emotions—affect prenatal development?
5. How do teratogenic substances act to cause deviations from normal prenatal development?
6. What occurs during the birth process and how does it affect the newborn?
7. What are the risks to babies born prematurely or with low birth weight?

Chapter Summary

Birth is the culmination of a crucial period of development that begins at conception. The developing organism begins as a **zygote,** a fertilized ovum weighing only 15 millionths of a gram. As it develops into a newborn baby, changes occur in its physical form and also its interactions with the environment. During this time, the organism can be affected, positively or negatively, by influences such as maternal nutrition and health status. Many theorists regard development during the prenatal period as a model for development during later periods of life. Understanding prenatal development is important for this reason; in addition, it is important in helping to promote the birth of healthier babies.

I. THE PERIODS OF PRENATAL DEVELOPMENT

The fertilized ovum or *zygote,* containing genetic material in its nucleus, divides many times to form many different kinds of cells. During the approximately 266 days necessary for the zygote to develop from a one-celled organism to a newborn baby, it passes through three broad periods of development: the **germinal period, embryonic period,** and **fetal period.** Each period is characterized by distinctive patterns of growth and interaction with the environment.

A. The Germinal Period

The germinal period begins at conception and lasts for 8 to 10 days after conception, when the organism becomes attached to the wall of the uterus.

- During its journey through the fallopian tube, the zygote divides, through the process of *mitosis.* These initial mitotic divisions, called **cleavage,** begin about 24 hours after conception. In this process, cells divide at different times, rather than all together (**heterochrony**), which results in different parts of the organism developing at different rates (**heterogeneity**). Each of these early cells has the potential to grow into an embryo and develop into a baby. They are **totipotent stem cells;** that is, they have the flexibility to become any kind of cell in the body. Adults also have stem cells. They are called *multipotent stem cells* and are capable of becoming many different types of cells, although not every type of cell as during embryonic development.

- **Implantation** occurs when the developing organism, having moved further into the uterus, puts out tiny branches that burrow into the uterine wall and make contact with maternal blood vessels. If attachment is successful, this marks the transition between the germinal and embryonic periods of development.

B. The Embryonic Period

The embryonic period begins at implantation and continues for about 6 weeks. During this period, the basic organs take shape and the embryo begins to respond to direct stimulation. The nutrition and protection it receives from the mother allow it to grow rapidly.

- The membranes that will protect and nourish the developing embryo are the **amnion,** holder of the fluid that surrounds the embryo, and the **chorion,** which becomes the fetal portion of the **placenta,** an organ made of tissue from both the mother and the embryo. The placenta is linked to the embryo by the **umbilical cord.** The placenta acts as a barrier between the bloodstreams of mother and embryo, and as a filter that allows nutrients and oxygen to be delivered to the embryo and waste products to be carried away to the mother's bloodstream to be eliminated through her kidneys.
- The outer cells of the developing organism form the placenta and membranes. At the same time, the inner cell mass differentiates into three cell layers: the first to develop are the outermost or **ectoderm,** from which the skin and nervous system, among other things, develop; and the innermost or **endoderm,** which develops into the digestive system and lungs. Next, the **mesoderm,** which becomes the bones, muscles, and circulatory system, appears between these layers. How does a cell learn which type of cell it should become— skin, blood, or liver? It is thought that this occurs through **epigenesis,** the emerging of new forms through interaction of the previous forms with their immediate environment. A cell's environment consists of the surrounding cells, which exchange information and regulate each other's activities.

  Beginning during the prenatal period and continuing through adolescence, development occurs in **cephalocaudal** (from the head down) and **proximodistal** (from the midline outward) patterns. Table 3.1 of the textbook shows the timetable of development during the embryonic period. The pattern of development for all but the sexual organs is the same for all human embryos.
- For the first six weeks after conception there is no structural difference between genetically male and genetically female embryos; both have *gonadal ridges* from which the male and female sex organs will develop. Sexual differentiation for genetically male (XY) embryos begins in the seventh week of gestation with the formation of the testes, whereas sexual differentiation in genetically female (XX) embryos will not begin until several weeks later, when ovaries start to form. The rest of the process of sexual differentiation is controlled by hormones: in the presence of the male hormone testosterone, the external genitalia will be male; in the absence of testosterone, female genitalia will develop and a cyclical pattern of hormonal secretion will be established by the pituitary gland. Because an embryo can develop male or female characteristics, it sometimes happens that a

baby has sex organs with characteristics of both sexes; these babies are called *hermaph-rodites.*

C. The Fetal Period

The fetal period lasts from the eighth or ninth week of gestation until birth. At the start of the fetal period, all the basic tissues and organs exist in some form and the skeleton has begun to ossify. In the months that follow, the fetus increases in length from 1 1/2 inches to 20 inches and in weight from about .02 lb to about 7.1 lb. Important changes take place in the respiratory, nervous, and other organ systems during this time. Although it is protected and nourished by the mother's body, the fetus interacts with both the uterine environment and the outside world. Some influences are beneficial, whereas others are potentially harmful.

• Understanding the fetus's sensory capacities helps researchers determine how the environment affects its development.

  • About 5 months after conception, in response to functioning of the vestibular system of the middle ear, the fetus begins to develop a sense of balance and can sense changes in its mother's posture as it floats in the fluid-filled amniotic sac. This sense of motion is fully mature at birth.

  • At 26 weeks, fetuses respond to light. Toward the end of pregnancy, they may actually see light through the stretched wall of the mother's abdomen.

  • Fetuses are able to respond to sound at 5 to 6 months of gestation. The sound level inside the uterus has been measured at about 75 decibels. Fetuses can hear sounds originating outside the mother's body. The mother's voice is heard best, because it is transmitted from outside and also as vibrations inside the body. The fetus's heart rate may change in response to sounds.

  Researchers have found that, given a choice between hearing the mother's natural voice and her voice when filtered to sound as it would have sounded in the womb, newborn babies prefer to listen to the filtered version.

• As the fetus develops, it also becomes more active, engaging in more varied and coordinated movements. At 15 weeks, it performs all the movements observed in newborn infants. At 24 to 32 weeks, activity alternates with quiet periods. These periods of *inactivity* are believed to reflect the development of neural pathways that inhibit movement; that development results from maturation of higher regions of the brain.

  Research with other species suggests that fetal movement may be necessary for normal development to take place; for example, chick embryos paralyzed with drugs fail to eliminate excess neurons, a process that ordinarily accompanies neuromuscular development. As a result, their joints become fused. The human fetus makes breathing motions that are unnecessary for obtaining oxygen; however, these movements help to develop the muscles that will be necessary for respiration after birth.

• There is evidence that some learning takes place during the prenatal period. For example, one study showed that newborns appeared to recognize a story read to them repeatedly before birth and would modify their rates of sucking in order to produce the story. Later research found that fetuses come to prefer the sounds of their native language. They may learn through other sensory modalities as well, for example, smell and taste.

II. MATERNAL CONDITIONS AND PRENATAL DEVELOPMENT

Fetuses are indirectly affected by outside influences, through changes in the mother that are transmitted to them through the placenta.

A. Maternal Attitudes and Stress

Research by Henry David, based on a study carried out in Czechoslovakia in the 1960s and 1970s, lends support to the idea that a woman's attitude toward her pregnancy can affect the development of the fetus. Negative feelings, such as lack of acceptance of the pregnancy on the part of the mother, are associated with lower birth weight and more medical complications. Even a desired and planned pregnancy can increase stress on the mother. Mothers who are under stress or emotionally upset secrete hormones (adrenaline and cortisol) that pass through the placenta and affect the fetus's motor activity. These effects include a greater chance of premature delivery or low birth weight, and—according to one study—more aggressive behavior several years after birth.

B. Nutritional Influences

Adequate maternal nutrition during pregnancy is necessary for normal fetal development. Pregnant women need to consume between 2000 and 2800 calories per day in a diet that contains an adequate supply of vitamins (including folic acid) and minerals (including calcium and iron). Folic acid is necessary for the normal development of the fetus's **neural tube,** which will develop into the brain and spinal cord. It is important for women of childbearing age to ingest enough folic acid, starting before they become pregnant; this helps prevent *spina bifida* and *anencephaly,* serious neural tube defects. Most nonpregnant women of childbearing age do not get sufficient folic acid in their diets. A woman's culture influences her view of which foods are beneficial during pregnancy.

As demonstrated by the effects of severe famine—for example, in the siege of Leningrad during World War II—extreme malnutrition in early pregnancy results in greater numbers of central nervous system abnormalities, preterm births, stillbirths, and deaths at birth. Deprivation later in pregnancy leads to low birth weight and fetal growth retardation.

Less severe nutritional malnourishment can lead to low birth weight and miscarriage. Some evidence also exists that people who were undernourished as fetuses are at greater risk in later life for heart disease, strokes, and other illnesses. In addition, malnourished mothers are likely to live in impoverished environments and to have less access to education, sanitation, and medical care. Studies of the WIC program—a supplemental food program for low-income women, infants, and children—showed that women receiving supplemental food had fewer infants who died during infancy. Infants whose mothers received food supplements during late pregnancy did better on intellectual measures than those who did not receive supplements until after the infants were born. Similar results have been found in studies carried out in rural Guatemala and in Zanzibar. In many cases, poor maternal and fetal nutrition is accompanied by a variety of factors—including poor nutrition during childhood, lack of medical care, and little access to education—that, in combination, lead to higher rates of infant mortality and shortened life expectancies.

III. TERATOGENS: ENVIRONMENTAL SOURCES OF BIRTH DEFECTS

Teratogens are environmental agents—for example, drugs, radiation, infections, and chemical pollutants—that can kill the developing embryo or fetus or cause serious abnormalities.

Several principles apply to teratogenic effects:

1. The impact of teratogens on the developing organism depends on when exposure occurs. Exposure during the first 2 weeks may destroy the organism; after that time, exposure will affect whatever system is in the process of developing.
2. The effect of each teratogen is usually specific to a particular organ.
3. Not every developing organism will be equally affected by the same exposure to a teratogen.
4. Factors such as the mother's age and health can intensify or decrease the risk from exposure to a teratogen.
5. The greater the concentration of a teratogen to which the organism is exposed, the greater the risk.
6. Levels of a teratogen that can harm the developing organism may produce little or no effect on the mother.

A. Drugs

Most women in the United States take some form of medication during their pregnancies and a sizable minority use nonmedical drugs.

*   Prescription drugs can cross the placenta to affect the developing child. Some, such as thalidomide, cause major deformities; other common drugs have also been found to cause abnormalities in the developing fetus.
*   Caffeine, found in coffee, tea, and soft drinks, is not associated with malformations of the fetus; however, in large doses, it is associated with spontaneous abortion and low birth weight.
*   Tobacco smoking is associated with spontaneous abortion, stillbirth, and neonatal death; there is evidence that exposure to smoke is associated with lower levels of oxygen and higher levels of carbon monoxide in the blood of mother and fetus. The more cigarette smoke a fetus is exposed to, the less it weighs at birth.
*   Heavy consumption of alcohol during pregnancy can lead to serious abnormalities in infants, for example, **fetal alcohol syndrome,** which is associated with abnormalities of the brain, eyes, heart, and joints and with facial malformation. The effects of more moderate drinking can vary according to the amount and timing of exposure.
*   Marijuana use during pregnancy is associated with low birth weight and possibly with preterm delivery. However, in the United States, women who use marijuana during preg-

nancy have other risk factors, for example, being less educated and using other drugs; they also gain less weight and experience less prenatal care than nonusers.

- Cocaine use during pregnancy puts the mother at risk for heart attack, stroke, and seizures. The baby is at risk for prematurity, low birth weight, stroke, birth defects, postnatal irritability, lack of motor coordination, and learning problems. It is not clear to what extent later behavioral problems result from cocaine exposure itself or maternal risk factors—for example, the use of alcohol and other drugs or stressful life circumstances—that tend to accompany cocaine use during pregnancy.
- Methadone and heroin addiction on the part of mothers results in the birth of addicted infants who are at risk of being born prematurely and who have low birth weight and a tendency toward respiratory illnesses.

B. Infections and Other Conditions

Infections can be passed to an embryo or fetus across the placental barrier or during the birth process. Table 3.3 of the textbook describes some of these diseases.

- Rubella (German measles) can cause major developmental defects, including blindness, deafness, congenital heart disease, and mental retardation. The greatest risk occurs during the first 12 weeks of pregnancy. Rubella can be prevented through vaccination.
- Acquired immunodeficiency syndrome (AIDS) affects about 30 percent of babies whose mothers test positive for human immunodeficiency virus (HIV). A baby can become infected prenatally or during exposure to the mother's blood at birth. However, the chances of infection are reduced by as much as 50 percent if the mother takes the drug zidovudine (AZT) during pregnancy and at the time of delivery.
- Rh incompatibility can result in a mother forming antibodies that destroy the red blood cells of the fetus. Rh disease can be treated by blood transfusions; however, most cases are now prevented by an anti-Rh serum that prevents Rh-negative mothers from forming antibodies to their Rh-positive children's blood.
- Radiation exposure at high doses can lead to spontaneous abortion or prenatal death; it can also cause mental retardation. The effects of lower doses are not definitely known, but pregnant women who need to be x-rayed should inform their doctors that they are pregnant.
- Pollution by chemicals in air, food, and water can build up in the body and cause birth defects in unborn children. An example is Minimata disease, which occurred in Japan and was caused when mercury from water contaminated by industrial waste became concentrated in fish, which were, in turn, eaten by pregnant women. In one Brazilian city, severe air pollution from industrial plants was associated with the death of many babies whose brains failed to develop. In the United States, there is concern about risks to pregnant women who live near chemical dumps.

Table 3.4 of the textbook summarizes the important principles of prenatal development and illustrates them with examples.

IV. BIRTH

There are differences across cultures in the typical contexts in which an infant's birth takes place. However, in all cases, important changes take place at birth in the newborn's body and environment; now the baby must obtain oxygen by breathing and nourishment by sucking. At this time, the social relationship between parents and child also begins.

A. The Stages of Labor

Labor, the process that forces the fetus out of the mother's body, occurs approximately 266 days after conception and is customarily divided into three stages:

- During the first stage of labor, contractions of the uterus dilate or open the cervix—the opening of the uterus into the vagina. In a woman's first birth, this stage lasts about 14 hours.
- The second stage of labor begins when the baby's head enters the vagina and continues until the baby's head, then body, emerge from the mother's body.
- During the third stage of labor, the placenta and membranes are expelled.

B. Cultural Variations in Childbirth

The experience of giving birth depends, in part, on the traditions surrounding it in the culture in which the mother lives. These customs vary widely from culture to culture. For example, in some cultures, women are expected to give birth alone with no attendants; in others, one or more attendants assist the mother. In some cultures, it is customary to give birth in a hospital; in others, babies are born at home. The box "In the Field: Reclaiming Birth—Midwifery in the Inuit Villages of Northern Canada" describes a society in which women are returning to traditional practices that had been displaced for a time by a more medical model of childbirth.

C. Childbirth in the United States

In the United States today, 99 percent of babies are born in hospitals and 92 percent are delivered by a physician. Hospital-based birth can be safer in the event of complications and allows the use of drugs to relieve the pain of childbirth; also, most health insurance premiums will only cover the costs of births that take place in hospitals. However, medical intervention in normal, uncomplicated births is not without controversy.

- Drugs used to relieve the pain of childbirth include anesthetics, analgesics, and sedatives. These drugs may affect babies' breathing and sucking responses and other postnatal behavior. For women concerned about the adverse effects of drugs, educational classes can give an idea of what to expect during the birth process and teach alternative techniques—including breathing, relaxation, and suggest the presence of a supportive companion during labor—that can help to reduce the use of medication during labor and delivery.

- Medical interventions—for example, induced labor and cesarean section—are thought to occur more frequently than is medically necessary. In fact, these interventions have increased significantly since the 1970s. Alternative birthing arrangements, such as specialized birthing centers and the use of midwives, are associated with reductions in induced labor, the use of spinal anesthesia, and cesarean births.
- The stresses of labor and delivery may actually help babies adapt to postnatal life; cesarean-born infants are more likely to have breathing difficulties than those born vaginally. A hormonal surge during birth helps lung functioning and puts the newborn into a state of quiet alertness that may last up to 40 minutes.

V. THE NEWBORN'S CONDITION

Newborn babies weigh, on average, 7 to 7 1/2 pounds (5 1/2 to 10 pounds is the normal range) and are, on average, 20 inches in length.

A. Assessing the Baby's Viability

The neonate's physical and behavioral condition can be assessed using a variety of scales and tests:

- The **Apgar Scale** measures babies' heart rate, respiratory effort, muscle tone, reflex responsivity, and color at 1 and 5 minutes after birth. Total scores can range from 0 to 10; a score of less than 4 indicates poor condition and the need for immediate medical attention. The Apgar scoring system is shown in Table 3.5 of the textbook.
- The **Brazelton Neonatal Assessment Scale** assesses more subtle behavioral aspects of the newborn's condition. It tests reflexes, muscle tone, motor capacities, responsiveness to objects and people, and infants' ability to control their own behavior and attention. Scales like Brazelton's do well in pointing out babies who need medical intervention and assessment of development in the period following birth, but are less useful in predicting later characteristics—for example, intelligence or personality—from neonatal behavior.

B. Problems and Complications

Some babies are at risk for developmental problems. For example, they may have suffered oxygen deprivation or head injury during birth, or have trouble breathing on their own. In many cases, problems occur because babies are born prematurely and/or underweight.

- **Preterm,** or premature, infants are born at a **gestational age** of less than 37 weeks; the normal period of time between conception and birth is 37–43 weeks. Prematurity increased in the United States between 1990 and 2004; it now affects 12.5 percent of births. Although expert medical care now allows more premature babies to survive, they may have immature respiratory, digestive, and immune systems. The causes of preterm birth are not well understood; however, mothers who are poor, very young, in poor health, who smoke, or who are carrying multiple fetuses are more likely to give birth prematurely than those without these risk factors. However, more than half of all premature births are associated with no known risk factors.

- Newborns who weigh less than 5 1/2 pounds (2500 grams) are said to have **low birth weight.** Those who fall into the lowest 10 percent of weight for gestational age are said to be **small for gestational age.** Usually, they have experienced *intrauterine growth restriction,* which is associated with multiple births, maternal malnutrition, smoking or drug use, infections, chromosomal abnormalities, or abnormalities of the placenta or umbilical cord.

C. Developmental Consequences

A baby who is small at birth, whether preterm or not, is more likely to die or to suffer from a neurologically based developmental disability. Low-birth-weight babies frequently experience some decrease in coordination and in intellectual capacity. Premature babies of normal weight for their gestational ages are most likely to catch up with their full-term peers, although they may have problems with attention and visual-motor coordination during their school years. Those with low birth weights who grow up with socioeconomic disadvantages are at risk for developmental difficulties. However, premature and low-birth-weight babies who grow up under supportive environmental conditions are less likely to suffer negative effects.

VI. BEGINNING THE PARENT–CHILD RELATIONSHIP

Human infants are dependent for their well-being on their relationships with their parents. Love and caring between parents and child are not automatic; the bond develops over time. In any case, the events immediately after birth set the stage for future interactions.

A. The Baby's Appearance

In trying to understand the sources of attachment between parents and infants, some developmentalists have borrowed from ethology—the study of animal behavior and its evolutionary bases—the idea that the "babyness" of newborn infants' appearance leads adults to respond to them with caregiving behavior. Evidence exists that adults find the large heads, protruding cheeks, and large, low-set eyes of infants to be appealing. Research shows that, beginning at about the age of puberty, children switch from preferring to look at pictures of adults to preferring pictures of babies. There is also evidence that adults interact more frequently and lovingly with attractive babies than with those who are considered less attractive in appearance.

B. Social Expectations

From the time of birth, parents' reactions to their infants reflect their beliefs and expectations. The sex of the baby strongly affects their expectations. Boys may be described as "big" and girls as "cute" regardless of their actual appearance. Even ultrasound pictures of fetuses show this effect; parents rated female fetuses as softer, cuddlier, and more delicate than male fetuses. From the beginning, parents treat their infants in ways consistent with the community's ideas and knowledge about people and their future roles. The parent–infant relationship will serve as part of the foundation for children's future development.

Key Terms I

Following are important terms introduced in Chapter 3. Match each term with the letter of the example that best illustrates the term.

1. _____ amnion

2. _____ chorion

3. _____ cleavage

4. _____ ectoderm

5. _____ endoderm

6. _____ epigenesis

7. _____ gestational age

8. _____ heterochrony

9. _____ heterogeneity

10. _____ mesoderm

11. _____ neural tube

12. _____ placenta

13. _____ umbilical cord

14. _____ zygote

a. This term refers to a membrane that develops into the fetal component of the placenta.
b. This is the layer of cells from which the lungs and digestive system develop.
c. The unevenness seen between the levels of development of different parts of an embryo is an example of this.
d. The layer of cells from which the bones and muscles are formed is called this.
e. A thin but tough membrane that contains the fluid surrounding the embryo is called this.
f. Getting sufficient folic acid in the diet helps in its normal development.
g. The skin and central nervous system develop from this layer of cells.
h. This organ, made from tissues of both the mother and the embryo, helps the embryo obtain nourishment and dispose of wastes.
i. The idea that new forms arise during development through the interaction of existing forms with the environment is known as this.
j. This results from the union of sperm and egg cells.
k. The amount of time that has passed since the fertilization of an ovum has occurred is called this.
l. This structure links the embryo to the placenta.
m. The processs that occurs about 24 hours after conception, when the zygote divides into two daughter cells that, in turn, each divide into two daughter cells, is called this.
n. This refers to the fact that not all cells divide at the same rate during embryonic development.

Key Terms II

Following are important terms introduced in Chapter 3. Match the term with the letter of the example that best illustrates the term.

1. _____ Apgar Scale

2. _____ Brazelton Neonatal Assessment Scale

3. _____ cephalocaudal pattern

4. _____ embryonic period

5. _____ fetal alcohol syndrome

6. _____ fetal period

7. _____ germinal period

8. _____ implantation

9. _____ low birth weight

10. _____ preterm

11. _____ proximodistal pattern

12. _____ small for gestational age

13. _____ teratogens

14. _____ totipotent stem cells

a. The period of prenatal development, lasting about 6 weeks, during which the body's basic organs take shape is called this.

b. Birth that occurs before the thirty-seventh week of gestation is called this.

c. In this process, the developing organism attaches itself to the wall of the uterus.

d. The period of prenatal development that begins at conception and ends when implantation occurs is called this.

e. This is illustrated by the fact that the embryo's arms begin to form earlier than its legs.

f. These come from the environment and harm the developing fetus by causing deviations in development.

g. The period of prenatal development during which the organ systems develop sufficiently to allow the developing organism to survive outside the mother's body is called this.

h. Examples are that the upper arm develops before the forearm and the forearm before the hand.

j. Newborns with this characteristic may have experienced intrauterine growth restriction.

k. An assessment of the baby's physical condition at 1 and 5 minutes after birth is named this.

l. An underdeveloped brain, heart disease, and malformations of the face are some indicators of this.

m. Babies have this if they weigh less than 5 1/2 pounds at birth.

n. This evaluates newborns' neurological condition by testing their behavior.

o. That each of these cells is capable of growing into a human baby is called this.

Multiple-Choice Practice Questions

Circle the letter of the word or phrase that correctly completes each statement.

1. During the prenatal period, the one-celled _____ develops into a fully formed baby.
   a. ovum
   b. blastocyst
   c. zygote
   d. embryo

2. The germinal period of development begins at conception and ends when
   a. the organism divides into two cells.
   b. the organism is implanted in the uterine wall.
   c. the major organ systems are formed.
   d. the heart begins to beat.

3. The fluid-filled _____ protects and supports the developing embryo.
   a. amnion
   b. placenta
   c. blastocyst
   d. zona pellucida

4. The bones and muscles of the developing organism are formed from which layer of the inner cell mass?
   a. endoderm
   b. mesoderm
   c. ectoderm
   d. trophoblast

5. During prenatal development, the embryo's arms
   a. are formed earlier than the legs.
   b. are formed at the same time as the legs.
   c. are formed later than the legs.
   d. are formed later than the hands.

6. In the absence of testosterone during prenatal development, the external genitalia will be _____.
   a. male
   b. undifferentiated
   c. both male and female
   d. female

7. Studies of fetal hearing indicate that
   a. fetuses are capable of hearing, but the uterine environment is very quiet, so there is little to hear.
   b. fetuses "hear" only by feeling vibrations on their body surfaces, not with their ears.
   c. fetuses hear many sounds from outside their mothers' bodies, and can discriminate between them.
   d. fetuses do not hear sounds from the world outside, as the background noise level in the uterus is too high to allow other sounds to come through.

8. Researchers believe that the movements made by fetuses
   a. serve no particular developmental purpose.
   b. are necessary for normal development of their muscles and joints.
   c. are attempts to communicate with their mothers.
   d. only occur when their mothers are relaxed and resting.

9. Research shows that women who are under stress during pregnancy
   a. secrete hormones that affect their fetuses' behavior.
   b. give birth to larger babies than women who experience peaceful pregnancies.
   c. give birth to babies who are placid and regular in their bodily functions.
   d. experience no special problems or advantages in their pregnancies.

10. Which of the following can cause birth defects?
    a. alcohol
    b. radiation
    c. environmental pollutants
    d. All these answers are correct.

11. Abnormalities of the central nervous system, prematurity, and death of the baby are most strongly associated with severe malnutrition
    a. during the first trimester of pregnancy.
    b. during the second trimester of pregnancy.
    c. during the third trimester of pregnancy.
    d. only if it occurs during the entire course of the pregnancy.

12. Exposure to a teratogen during prenatal development
    a. always leads to fetal death.
    b. affects whatever system is developing at the time of exposure.
    c. affects all fetuses with comparable exposure in the same way.
    d. does not affect the fetus at exposure levels that are safe for the mother.

13. The baby emerges from the mother's body at the end of
    a. the first stage of labor.
    b. the second stage of labor.
    c. the third stage of labor.
    d. the fourth stage of labor.

14. The main disadvantage to the use of obstetric medications is that
    a. they are not effective in relieving the pain of labor.
    b. although they do not affect the fetus, they may adversely affect the mother.
    c. they enter the bloodstream of the fetus and may cause adverse effects.
    d. in order to use them, it is necessary to give birth in a hospital.

15. The "stress" hormones that babies produce during labor are thought to
    a. help their circulation and respiration adjust to life outside the womb.
    b. be the basis for psychological birth trauma.
    c. prevent them from making a smooth adjustment to postnatal life.
    d. have no real effect on them.

16. The _____ evaluates the baby's physical condition at 1 and 5 minutes after birth.
    a. Brazelton Neonatal Assessment Scale
    b. PKU test
    c. Bayley Mental and Motor Scale
    d. Apgar Scale

17. Women who _____ are more likely than others to give birth prematurely.
    a. are of middle-class socioeconomic status
    b. are carrying more than one fetus
    c. are in their twenties
    d. have no known risk factors

18. Which is *not* a sign of "babyness," as Konrad Lorenz described it?
    a. small head in proportion to body
    b. round cheeks
    c. large eyes
    d. high forehead

19. Babies who _____ are more likely than others to have long-lasting developmental problems in later years.
    a. are preterm
    b. are small for gestational age
    c. are from homes that are impoverished
    d. share all these characteristics

20. Parents tend to describe their newborns as
    a. "easy" if they are girls and "difficult" if boys.
    b. "big" if they are boys and "cute" if girls.
    c. "big" and "beautiful" regardless of sex.
    d. "resembling their mothers" regardless of sex.

Short-Answer Practice Questions

Write a brief answer in the space below each question.

1. What are the major features of the germinal, embryonic, and fetal periods of prenatal development?

2. Explain how the timing of exposure to a teratogen determines its effect on development. What other factors influence the effects of teratogens?

3. Based on information about the sensory capacities of the fetus, how do you imagine its environment inside the uterus?

4. How does prenatal sexual differentiation occur in males? In females?

5. How does malnutrition affect prenatal development? Why is it difficult to determine the effect of nutritional deprivation alone on development?

6. What are the developmental consequences of preterm delivery and low birth weight? What factors affect the long-term outlook for babies with these conditions?

7. What happens during the process of birth? How do these events affect the baby?

8. How does the appearance of a newborn baby affect the behavior of parents and other adults?

9. What are some positive and negative aspects of parents' tendencies to have expectations about their newborns on the basis of the infants' sex?

Putting It All Together

As discussed in Chapter 1, developmentalists interpret the facts they collect in terms of several major questions about development:

- Is development continuous or do stagelike changes take place?
- What are the roles of genetic factors and environmental forces in development?
- What are the sources of individual differences?

Using what you know about prenatal development, find an example of each of the following as it occurs during the prenatal period:

- stages of development

- continuous change

- critical (or sensitive) periods

- genetic influence

- effects of the environment

- cultural influences

Sources of More Information

Azar, B. (December 1997). Behaviors of a newborn can be traced to the fetus. *APA Monitor, 28,* 16.
Research on rats helps developmental researchers decipher the role of fetal behavior in preparing for postnatal life.

Azar, B. (December 1997). Learning begins even before babies are born, scientists show. *APA Monitor, 28,* 15.
This article describes some of the clever methods researchers have developed to study fetal learning.

Kitzinger, S. (2003). *The Complete Book of Pregnancy and Childbirth.* New York: Knopf.
This is a comprehensive discussion of pregnancy and the process of childbirth, aimed at helping the pregnant woman to understand what occurs and what to expect.

Lamaze, F. (1987). *Painless Childbirth: The Lamaze Method.* Lincolnwood, IL: NTC Contemporary Publishing Co.

A popular method of preparing for childbirth is explained by the physician who brought it from the former Soviet Union to France.

Nilsson, L., & Hamberger, L. (2003). *A Child Is Born.* 4th ed., rev. and updated. New York: Delacorte Press.
A photographer and an obstetrician discuss prenatal development and birth, using in utero photographs and ultrasound.

Pasquariello, P. S. (Ed.). (1999). *The Children's Hospital of Philadelphia Book of Pregnancy and Child Care.* New York: John Wiley & Sons.
This book covers topics relating to pregnancy, birth, the newborn baby, and health and development in children up to 5 years of age.

Profet, M. (1997). *Pregnancy Sickness: Using Your Body's Natural Defenses to Protect Your Baby-to-Be.* Reading, MA: Addison-Wesley.
This book takes the view that pregnancy sickness serves the purpose of protecting the embryo during its most vulnerable period. Suggestions are included for managing pregnancy sickness and avoiding teratogens.
Vaughn, C. (1998). *How Life Begins.* New York: Bantam, Dell Publishing.
This is a readable discussion of prenatal development in a scientific context, written by a science journalist.

Answer Key

Answers to Key Terms I: 1.e, 2.a, 3.m, 4.g, 5.b, 6.i, 7.k, 8.n, 9.c, 10.d, 11.f, 12.h, 13.l, 14.j.

Answers to Key Terms II: 1.k, 2.n, 3.e, 4.a, 5.l, 6.g, 7.d, 8.c, 9.m, 10.b, 11.h, 12.j, 13.f, 14.o.

Answers to Multiple-Choice Questions: 1.c, 2.b, 3.a, 4.b, 5.a, 6.d, 7.c, 8.b, 9.a, 10.d, 11.a, 12.b, 13.b, 14.c, 15.a, 16.d, 17.b, 18.a, 19.d, 20.b.

4

The First Three Months

During the first few postnatal months, infants are mainly adjusting to life outside their mothers' bodies, and parents are adjusting their lives to accommodate their new offspring. Infants are born with all their sensory systems operating and a number of well-developed behavior patterns that allow them to respond to the world. However, a great deal of development occurs during early infancy. Some changes in infants' capacities seem to be the result of maturation of their nervous systems. For example, several reflexes present at birth, such as involuntary grasping, disappear during the first weeks or months. But learning also plays a role, and other reflexes are modified by use, becoming part of more complex behaviors, as when rooting, sucking, swallowing, and breathing become integrated with one another (and with maternal behaviors as well) in nursing.

Cultural variations in the ways parents organize their infants' experiences exert some influence on development. For example, infants from cultures—such as that of the United States—in which they are expected to sleep all night without waking to feed will, in fact, learn to sleep through the night sooner than infants from cultures in which this is not an important expectation. But at the end of the first 3 months, it is possible to see how changes at all levels—biological, behavioral, and social—have moved infants to a new level of ability to engage with the world.

Learning Objectives

Keep these questions in mind while studying Chapter 4.

1. What sensory and response capabilities are present at birth, and how does development of the central nervous system allow infants to expand their behavioral capabilities?
2. In what ways does experience with the environment affect maturation of the nervous system?

3. What learning processes are infants able to use in order to respond to occurrences in their environments?
4. What are some examples of increasing behavioral organization in infants?
5. How does temperament affect the experiences infants have and how they react to them?
6. How do changes in infants' feeding and sleeping patterns during the first months after birth help them become coordinated with the schedules of their families?
7. How do cultural practices affect the way infants' environments are arranged?

Chapter Summary

I. PHYSICAL GROWTH

During the first 3 months after birth, infants gain about 6 pounds and grow more than 4 inches in length; they also gain about an inch in head circumference.

A. Measuring Body Growth

Infants' physical growth is typically evaluated using **growth charts** that show averages—and deviations from the averages—for weights, heights, and other measures; these are compiled by studying large samples of normal infants. Studies have shown that it is normal for breast-fed babies to gain weight more slowly during the first year than those who are formula-fed. A large international study conducted by the World Health Organization (WHO) found that babies everywhere, regardless of ethnicity or socioeconomic status, show comparable patterns of growth, so long as they are raised in healthy environments.

B. Growth of the Skull

The primary determinant of head growth is brain development. The infant skull has seven flat bones that are relatively soft and elastic, separated by **fontanels**—also known as "soft spots." These allow the infant's head to change shape during the birth process and later to expand during periods of rapid brain development. Infants' heads may be temporarily flattened from spending a great deal of time on their backs before they are able to move around freely. This has become more common as parents have begun putting babies to sleep on their backs, as discussed in the box "Sudden Infant Death Syndrome." Various cultures have purposely changed the shape of infants' skulls in order to indicate status within the family and community.

II. BRAIN DEVELOPMENT

Before babies are born, their brains and central nervous systems support basic sensory and motor functions. At birth, the brain contains most of the cells it will have; however, it will continue to grow, becoming four times larger than it was in the newborn infant. The next section will discuss the nerve cells that transmit information, which are called **neurons.**

A. Neurons and Networks of Neurons

Each neuron has an **axon,** the main protruding branch that carries messages to other cells in the form of electrical impulses, and **dendrites** through which it receives information from other cells. Messages are carried from one neuron to another by a chemical secreted by the sending neuron; this **neurotransmitter** bridges the gap (called a **synapse**) between the axon of the transmitting neuron and a dendrite of the receiving neuron. The combination of a sending and a receiving neuron is the simplest example of a neuronal network.

The brain grows in size after birth partly because of increases in **synaptogenesis**—the formations of new connections among neurons—made possible by increases in the number of dendrites and axon terminals, as shown in Figure 4.4 of the textbook. It also becomes larger because of myelination, a process in which the axons of neurons become covered with **myelin,** a fatty coating that insulates them and allows them to transmit impulses anywhere from 10 to 100 times faster than before.

B. The Structure of the Central Nervous System

As shown in Figure 4.5 of the textbook, the central nervous system contains three major sections: the **spinal cord** extends down the back and contains the spinal nerves that carry messages between the brain and specific areas of the body; the **brain stem** at the top of the spinal cord, which controls breathing, sleeping, and elementary reactions such as blinking and sucking; and the **cerebral cortex,** which is divided into two hemispheres, each of which has four lobes, separated by deep grooves and specialized for different functions. The *occipital lobes* are for vision; the *temporal lobes* for hearing and speech; the *parietal lobes* for spatial perception; and the *frontal lobes* for the control and coordination of the other cortical areas, allowing for more complex forms of behavior and thought. The human cortex also has large "uncommitted" areas, allowing the brain to change in response to the experiences children encounter as they develop (that is, to demonstrate *plasticity*). At birth, the spinal cord and brain stem are the most highly developed areas of the central nervous system; the cerebral cortex is relatively immature and is not well connected to the lower-brain areas. As the cortex matures and becomes more efficiently connected to the brain stem and spinal cord, the infant's abilities expand.

C. Experience and Development of the Brain

Development of the brain, like development of behavior, comes about through interaction of the organism with the environment. Some processes of brain development are referred to as **experience-expectant.** These seem to anticipate experiences that infants will encounter in any normal environment. Examples of these experiences are encountering visual light/dark borders or hearing the sounds of human language. Evidence for these processes is found in the **exuberant synaptogenesis** that occurs during several points of development, resulting in many more synapses than would be required by the organism's experiences. Those synapses that are not used will die off selectively in a process called **synaptic pruning** that occurs both prenatally and then periodically until early adulthood. Although experience-expectant synapses are created before they are needed, in **experience-dependent** brain development, synapses are generated in response to an individual's specific experiences. This was demonstrated in a study of rats by Mark Rosenzweig and his colleagues. The subjects were housed in either a standard laboratory environment or in an enriched environment with a variety of playthings. Those in the enriched environment had larger and heavier brains with more synaptic connections and larger amounts of neurotransmitters; they also performed better on tasks such as maze learning.

III. SENSING THE ENVIRONMENT

Developmentalists have disagreed about the extent to which newborn infants are able to perceive and understand the world and the extent to which their sensory capacities are the result of biology or are dependent on experience.

A. Methods of Evaluating Infant Sensory Capacities

All the sensory systems of full-term newborns are functioning. However, not all systems develop at the same rate (heterochrony); therefore, some capacities are more mature than others (heterogeneity). Developmentalists study infants' sensory capacities by observing their reactions to stimuli—for example, does a child turn his or her head in the direction of a sound? Sometimes, two stimuli are presented at once; in order for infants to show a preference for one stimulus over the other, then they must be able to distinguish between the two. Another common method relies on infants' tendency to pay less and less attention to a repeatedly presented stimulus (**habituation**); if the stimulus is changed in a way that makes it seem new to the infant, he or she will once again pay attention (**dishabituation**).

B. Hearing

As discussed in Chapter 2, fetuses respond to sounds outside the mother's womb.

Newborn infants turn their heads toward the sources of sounds, startle when they hear loud noises, and can distinguish—and prefer—the human voice compared to other sounds. They are attracted to the sounds of language, in particular the exaggerated sounds of "motherese," also called "baby talk" or "infant-directed speech." Also, as demonstrated by Peter Eimas and his colleagues, using a habituation procedure, young infants are able to perceive distinctions between the basic speech sounds called **phonemes,** which are the smallest categories in speech that carry meanings. They can even distinguish phonemes that do not occur in the language spoken around them. For example, Japanese infants, in contrast to Japanese adults, perceive the phonemes /r/ and /l/ as different even though they do not differ in the Japanese language.

C. Vision

Infants' vision is not fully developed at birth. The lens of the eye and the retinal cells, and the neural pathways that relay information to the brain are not yet mature. Also, the movements of the two eyes are not yet well-coordinated. Newborns are quite nearsighted, with an acuity that has been estimated as in the range of 20/300 to 20/600. However, they can see fairly clearly objects at a distance of 1 foot, about as far away as their mothers' faces are during nursing. At 2–3 months, infants can coordinate the vision of both eyes. By the time they are crawling, at about 7 or 8 months of age, their acuity is close to that of adults.

- Newborns actively scan their environments. Marshall Haith and his colleagues found that they engage in *endogenous* eye movements, which originate in the neural activity of the brain and occur even in the dark. Newborns also demonstrate *exogenous* looking, which is stimulated by the external environment, for example, by changes in brightness that are associated with the edges and angles of objects.

- Newborns have most of the physiological ability to perceive color. However, they have trouble discriminating between two colors that are equally bright. By about 2 months of age, their color vision approaches adult levels.

- As demonstrated by Robert Fantz, newborn babies prefer to look at patterned figures rather than plain ones. By 2 months of age, they demonstrate the ability to recognize the three-dimensionality of objects and the boundaries between them. Movement and vocalization appear to play important roles in object perception, and infants' vision is best under conditions of high contrast—for example, a black cat on a white chair. Gordon Bronson, testing the scanning abilities of 2-week-old infants, found that they tended to scan only the high-contrast portions of simple figures. However, by 3 months of age, their scanning had become much more sophisticated and better controlled.

- Studies by Robert Fantz in the early 1960s demonstrated that newborns could distinguish a schematic face from a facelike figure in which the features had been scrambled. More recent work has shown that this only occurs when the schematic face has more elements in the top half, as seen in real faces. Also, early studies by Fantz and others used stationary stimuli. More recently, other investigators, using moving, naturalistic stimuli, have shown that infants only 9 minutes old will turn toward a moving schematic face rather than a scrambled one and that infants 2–7 hours old can distinguish their mothers' faces from the face of a stranger, even after a 15-minute delay.

D. Taste and Smell

Newborns have the ability to discriminate tastes and odors and show strong preferences for things that taste and smell sweet. A sweet taste also has a calming effect on crying babies and can help them cope with aversive situations. Newborns produce distinct facial expressions similar to those of adults in response to different flavors. Babies have been indirectly exposed to a variety of flavors from their mothers' diets before birth, as a result of swallowing amniotic fluid. After birth, breast-fed babies are exposed to flavors of the maternal diet that appear in their mothers' breast milk. For example, Menella and her colleagues showed that infants who had been exposed to carrot flavor in amniotic fluid or breast milk reacted more positively later on to carrot-flavored cereal. Similarly, the flavor of formula consumed by formula-fed infants can influence their food preferences several years later.

Newborns also can discriminate among a variety of odors. When tested a few minutes after birth, they show a preference for maternal breast odors. They also react strongly to unpleasant odors (presented on a swab under the nose) and smile at sweet smells. Infants' responses to unpleasant tastes and smells are adaptive, in the sense that they have the effect of reducing contact with the substances causing the tastes or smells; for example, wrinkling the nose reduces the intensity of an unpleasant odor.

E. Intermodal Perception

Outside the laboratory, infants perceive objects and events with more than one sensory system. In fact, at birth they may already be prepared to perceive that stimuli from different sensory modalities go together. An example of **intermodal perception** is infants' recognition that the sight of their mothers and the sounds of their mothers' voices go together. Research has indicated that hearing a mother's voice actually helps the infant learn to recognize her face. Infants' early sensory capacities are summed up in Table 4.1 of the textbook.

IV. THE ORGANIZATION OF BEHAVIOR

Infants are born with a number of inborn behaviors that allow them to respond adaptively to the environment. By 3 months of age, as a result of biological and cultural processes, they will be able to engage in new forms of organized behavior; these will expand their capacities for acting on the objects and interacting with the people in their world.

A. Reflexes

Newborns are equipped with an array of **reflexes**—well-integrated, involuntary responses to specific types of stimulation. Table 4.2 of the textbook describes some of the reflexes present at birth. Some reflexes remain throughout life (for example, the eyeblink reflex); others disappear over time (for example, the sucking reflex). Some reflexes serve an obvious purpose—for example, the rooting and sucking reflexes are components of nursing. Others—the Moro reflex, for example—serve no observable purpose. Damage to the central nervous system can be diagnosed when a reflex is absent, when it persists beyond the time when it should have disappeared, or when it reappears after an injury.

B. From Reflex to Coordinated Action

Reflexes are the building blocks for **action**—complex and coordinated behaviors. Nursing is a good example of an action that arises during early infancy. At birth, the reflexes used in feeding—rooting, sucking, swallowing, and breathing—are not yet smoothly coordinated. By 6 weeks, however, the components of nursing occur in an efficient, integrated sequence. As it is described by *dynamic systems theory,* nursing emerges as the component behaviors interact over time, become increasingly coordinated, and finally unify into a complex system of action. The box "In the Field: Baby Friendly Hospital Care" highlights the importance of caregivers' efforts in promoting behavioral development in infants.

Although it is easy to see the connection between early feeding reflexes and the development of nursing, disagreement exists among developmentalists about the relationship between the early "stepping reflex" and the later action of walking. The stepping reflex disappears at about 3 months; walking appears as a voluntary behavior at approximately 1 year of age. One point of view, held by Philip Zelazo, holds that, when the brain undergoes reorganization as the cerebral cortex develops rapidly during the first months after birth, the lower-level stepping reflex disappears, only to reappear in a new form as a voluntary behavior under cortical control. On the other hand, Esther Thelen and her colleagues argue that early stepping disappears, not because of changes in the cortex, but because of changes in the baby's weight and muscle mass that make the legs too heavy for the muscles to lift. This point of view is supported by evidence that stepping reappears when infants are supported in water and their weight is less as a result of the increase in buoyancy. Thelen's work is an example of the dynamic systems approach; walking is viewed as a complex form of behavior that emerges from the interaction of a variety of less complex parts.

C. Reaching

Except for getting their fingers to their mouths, newborn infants' contact with objects appears purely accidental. However, research by Claus von Hofsten has shown that they engage in *prereaching,* a form of visually initiated reaching in which infants reach in the direction of an object but are unable to coordinate reaching and grasping movements. At about 3 months of age, with development of the visual and motor areas of the cortex, *visually guided reaching* emerges; now, infants can make use of feedback from their own movements in order to get their hands close to an object and can open their fingers in anticipation of grasping it. Amy Needham and her colleagues showed that infants' development of reaching and grasping could be accelerated by giving them support in the form of Velcro-covered mittens that could be used to grasp Velcro-covered objects.

D. Piaget's Theory of Developing Action

As discussed in Chapter 1, Piaget viewed the *schema* as the most basic form of understanding; schemas develop through *adaptation,* which is a twofold process involving *assimilation* and *accommodation.*

Piaget referred to infancy as the **sensorimotor stage;** in this stage, adaptation mainly consists of coordinating sensory perceptions and simple motor responses. Piaget identified six substages within the sensorimotor stage, as shown in Table 4.3 of the textbook. Substages 1 and 2 occur during the first few months and are described in this chapter; the others will be discussed in Chapter 5.

- In Substage 1 (birth to 1 or 1 1/2 months), infants mainly learn to coordinate and control their first schemas, the reflexes present at birth.
- Substage 2 (from about 1 or 1 1/2 months to 4 months) is characterized by the **primary circular reaction:** infants now repeat, for the pleasure of it, actions that are centered on their own bodies, such as sucking their fingers, waving their hands, or kicking their feet. These actions are called circular because they lead back to themselves, serving to prolong

interesting events. They undergo *differentiation,* becoming increasingly more fine-tuned and flexible, and *integration,* as separate actions become coordinated into new behavior patterns. Piaget considered primary circular reactions to be the first sign of cognitive development.

E. Learning Theories of Developing Action

Some theorists, in accounting for the emergence of new forms of behavioral organization, emphasize the role of **learning**—a relatively permanent change in behavior brought about when infants make associations between behavior and events in the environment. Types of learning that occur throughout life are *habituation* (discussed earlier in this chapter), *imitation* (which will be discussed in Chapter 6), *classical conditioning,* and *operant conditioning.*

- Through **classical conditioning,** previously existing behaviors come to be elicited by new stimuli. Classical conditioning was first described by Russian physiologist Ivan Pavlov. In his studies with dogs, a tone served as a **conditional stimulus (CS),** which was paired with food in the dog's mouth—an **unconditional stimulus (UCS).** This UCS invariably caused salivation—an **unconditional response (UCR).** After a number of pairings, presentation of the CS alone caused the dog to salivate—a **conditional response (CR)** had been learned. Figure 4.20 of the textbook illustrates classical conditioning.

    It appears that, through classical conditioning, infants can learn expectancies about connections between events in their environments. For example, a co-worker of Pavlov showed that a baby could learn to open its mouth and make sucking motions in response to the sound of a bell that was previously paired with the sight of a glass of milk. Classical conditioning has been demonstrated in infants within hours of birth if the infants are alert and the stimuli used are biologically relevant.

- Whereas classical conditioning explains how infants come to build expectancies about connections between events, **operant conditioning**—in which behaviors are shaped by their consequences—gives rise to new and more complex behaviors. Actions that produce rewarding consequences will be repeated; those that do not will tend to not be repeated. A consequence that results in the greater likelihood of a behavior being repeated is called *reinforcement.* Rovee-Collier and her colleagues showed that infants could learn to make a mobile move by making kicking motions. The interesting visual effect served as a positive reinforcer for the kicking.

    Evidence that learning is important in the development of behavioral organization comes from research showing that even very young infants can remember what they learned from one experimental session to the next; this ability improves markedly during the first few months after birth.

V. TEMPERAMENT

Developmentalists have noted that infants are born with individual differences in how they respond to their environments. These differences are related to **temperament**—emotional and behavioral characteristics that are fairly consistent across situations and stable over time. Alexander Thomas,

Stella Chess, and their colleagues identified a set of key traits of temperament, discussed in Table 4.4 of the textbook. On the basis of these traits, they found that babies could be classified as *easy* (playful, adaptable, and regular in biological functions), *difficult* (irritable, negative toward new experiences), and *slow to warm up* (low in activity level and needing some time to adapt to new situations). Different categories of temperament have been developed by other researchers; for example, Mary Rothbart and her colleagues devised a child behavior questionnaire that creates a profile based on each child's levels of *reactivity* (characteristic level of arousal), *affect* (dominant emotional tone), and *self-regulation* (control over what one attends and reacts to).

It is agreed that genetic factors are important in temperament. Stephen Suomi's research with monkeys uncovered a gene in which one allele is associated with a highly reactive temperament while a different allele is associated with a calmer temperament. And human studies have found evidence that temperamental traits such as irritability, persistence, and flexibility show stability over time.

Cross-cultural comparisons have demonstrated some differences in temperament between ethnic and national groups. For example, Chinese children were found to be less active than American children; this may be a cultural difference, because high levels of activity and impulsiveness are discouraged by Chinese parents.

Are adjustment problems in childhood or adolescence related to temperament in infancy? There is some indication that temperamental traits reflecting early fearfulness, withdrawal distress, and lack of adaptability are linked to later problems with anxiety, depression, and social withdrawal. However, most studies do not find strong correlations between measures of temperament at different ages.

A. Becoming Coordinated with the Social World

Infants all over the world depend for their survival on responsive caregivers; they also need to be able to coordinate their own actions with those of their caregivers. When babies and parents coordinate their schedules—for example, for eating and sleeping—babies fit smoothly into the lives of their families and the life patterns of their communities. The box "Sleeping Arrangements" reveals some of the ways in which parents of various cultures accomplish this goal.

B. Sleeping

Peter Wolff, studying newborns' activity patterns, found that they display seven different states of alertness, shown in Table 4.5 of the textbook, in four of which they are asleep or nearly asleep. Each of these levels of arousal is accompanied by different brainwave patterns.

Newborns sleep about 16 1/2 hours per day during the first week; this is down to just under 14 hours per day by the end of 4 months. However, their sleep comes in many short periods. As they grow older, sleeping and waking periods become longer and begin to coincide with adult day/night schedules.

Both cultural expectations and brain maturation affect how quickly babies adopt adultlike sleep cycles. Infants in industrialized countries sometimes cannot adapt as quickly to sleeping at night and being awake during the day as their parents would like. The box "Sudden Infant Death Syndrome" discusses the effects of brain maturation and sleeping practices on the occurrence of **sudden infant death syndrome (SIDS)**.

C. Feeding

Nursing is a behavior that requires coordination between infant and mother. The mother most learn to hold the baby in a way that makes it easier for the baby to grasp the nipple; as discussed earlier, the baby must coordinate sucking, swallowing, and breathing. Mothers have been observed to make "preadapted" responses such as jiggling the breast or bottle during pauses in sucking so as to prolong a feeding session.

Feeding is also affected by cultural practices. For example, in some cultures babies are breast-fed for 2 years or more, a practice that helps to space births and thus protect babies from **kwashiorkor,** a form of protein-calorie malnutrition that may occur when a child is deprived of breast milk following the birth of a younger sibling. Culture also affects the schedule on which infants are fed. For example, today pediatricians in the United States tell mothers to feed their babies when they think the babies are hungry; however, during the 1920s through the 1940s, mother were advised to feed their infants only every 4 hours, even if they showed signs of hunger. This advice was followed mainly by less experienced mothers.

If fed on demand, newborns prefer to feed about every 3 hours; most babies are able to go 4 hours between feedings by the time they reach 2 1/2 months of age. By 7–8 months of age, babies are feeding about four times per day, an approximation of the adult eating schedule. No difference has been found between the growth rates of babies fed on demand and those fed on a strict schedule.

D. Crying

Crying tells parents that something is wrong. At first, crying is coordinated by structures in the brain stem; it is several months before the cortex becomes involved, at which point "voluntary" crying becomes possible. In infants all over the world, crying reaches a peak at about 6 weeks of age, then decreases in frequency at about 12 weeks.

From an evolutionary perspective, crying promotes caregiving when infants are hungry, in pain, or separated from the caregiver. In fact, infants cry less in cultures whose caregiving behaviors involve rapid responses to infant cries, as well as frequent breastfeeding and cosleeping with infants at night.

Adults react to infants' cries with increased heart rate and blood pressure, and even among nursing mothers with milk flow. Adult listeners can distinguish among different kinds of cries and between normal cries and the higher-pitched cries of "at risk" babies.

It is sometimes difficult to tell exactly why an infant cries. Some infants who cry excessively are said to have *colic,* an unexplained medical condition associated with prolonged crying that is unpredictable and hard to soothe.

VI. SUMMING UP THE FIRST 3 MONTHS

During the first 3 months after birth, infants change remarkably in the organization of their behaviors and their coordination with the behavior of their caregivers. These changes have their roots in biology (for example, maturation of the central nervous system) and in the physical and sociocultural environment, and bring newborns to a new threshold of cognitive, social, and emotional development.

Key Terms I

Following are important terms introduced in Chapter 4. Match each term with the letter of the example that best illustrates the term.

1. _____ action

2. _____ axon

3. _____ dendrites

4. _____ experience-dependent

5. _____ experience-expectant

6. _____ exuberant synaptogenesis

7. _____ fontanels

8. _____ growth chart

9. _____ intermodal perception

10. _____ kwashiorkor

11. _____ myelin

12. _____ neurons

13. _____ primary circular reaction

14. _____ reflexes

15. _____ sensorimotor stage

16. _____ temperament

17. _____ visual acuity

a. This is the time of life during which developments in behavior primarily involve coordination between motor behaviors and sensory circumstances.

b. These are used by pediatricians to evaluate children's physical development.

c. This disorder may occur when a mother stops nursing a baby due to the birth of a younger sibling.

d. A baby who sees its hand pass across its field of vision finds this interesting, and then repeats the movement over and over again is an example.

e. Nursing is one example of this type of complex, coordinated behavior.

f. This improves greatly during the first 8 months after birth.

g. This process gives infants more neural connections than they really need; those that are not used will eventually disappear.

h. These allow infants' skulls to expand in response to brain growth.
i. These well-integrated but involuntary responses represent much of the newborn's behavior.
j. This substance coats nerve fibers, allowing nerve impulses to travel more efficiently.
k. This is the main protruding branch of a neuron along which messages are transmitted.
l. This involves the formation of neural connections in advance of need.
m. Without these structures, neurons could not receive messages from neighboring cells.
n. This involves the formation of neural connections in response to experience.
o. Knowing that a sound goes with a particular visual image is an example.
p. This is another word for "nerve cells."
q. An example of this is "slow to warm up."

Key Terms II

Following are important terms introduced in Chapter 4. Match each term with the letter of the example that best illustrates the term.

1. _____ brain stem
2. _____ cerebral cortex
3. _____ classical conditioning
4. _____ conditional response
5. _____ conditional stimulus
6. _____ dishabituation
7. _____ habituation
8. _____ learning
9. _____ neurotransmitter
10. _____ operant conditioning
11. _____ phonemes
12. _____ spinal cord
13. _____ synapse
14. _____ synaptic pruning
15. _____ synaptogenesis
16. _____ unconditional response
17. _____ unconditional stimulus

a. An infant who learns to suck a pacifier in order to activate a mobile above her crib is an example.
b. A baby makes sucking movements with his mouth when he sees his nursing bottle approaching is an example.
c. This part of the nervous system controls vital functions such as breathing and inborn reflexes.
d. This part of the nervous system carries messages between the brain and the spinal nerves.
e. Through this process, infants learn to anticipate events rather than simply react to them.

f.   This stimulus automatically elicits some response (as a puff of air in the eye elicits blinking).

g.   This kind of change in behavior comes about because of an infant's experiences of events in the environment.

h.   This is the name for the gap between neurons, across which nerve impulses must travel.

i.   In Pavlov's study, a tone that signaled food was about to be presented came to be called this.

j.   This substance aids in the transmission of impulses from one neuron to the next.

k.   This part of the nervous system allows infants to integrate new sensory information with memories of previous experiences.

l.   This process is one of the factors responsible for growth in the size of the brain.

m.   A response to a particular stimulus that automatically occurs (as when a baby turns his head in the direction of a touch on the cheek) is called this.

n.   These are responsible for the difference in sound between "pear" and "bear."

o.   A newborn who stops paying attention to the washing machine is demonstrating this response pattern.

p.   When neural connections are not needed, they are eliminated through this process.

q.   A baby who has stopped paying attention to the radio and perks up when the station is changed is demonstrating this response pattern.

Multiple-Choice Practice Questions

Circle the letter of the word or phrase that correctly completes each statement.

1. _____ are protuberances on a neuron that can receive electrical impulse from other neurons.
   a.   Axons
   b.   Cell bodies
   c.   Dendrites
   d.   Neurotransmitters

2. The _____ controls vital functions such as breathing and sleeping.
   a.   cerebral cortex
   b.   cerebellum
   c.   brain stem
   d.   spinal cord

3. "Myelination" refers to
   a.   a process of brain growth through the formation of new neurons.
   b.   the formation of a fatty sheath around nerve fibers.
   c.   a structural part of brain development that is nearly complete at birth.
   d.   the formation of reflex arcs in the spinal cord.

4. Rosenzweig and his colleagues found that rats that were raised in a stimulating environment with playthings and activities
   a. were similar, in development of brain and behavior, to control rats raised in standard laboratory cages.
   b. developed more brain complexity than control rats, but did not learn any faster than control rats.
   c. did not differ from control rats in brain development, but were better at learning mazes and other tasks.
   d. developed more complex brains than control rats, and were also better at learning mazes and other tasks.

5. On which would a newborn best be able to focus?
   a. his mother's face while he nurses
   b. a mobile hanging over the far end of his crib
   c. a person standing across the room
   d. All these aanswers are correct.

6. Studies of how young infants react to speech sounds have shown that 2-month-olds
   a. cannot distinguish between closely related phonemes such as /pa/ and /ba/.
   b. can distinguish only among phonemes that occur in the language they hear spoken around them.
   c. can distinguish among phonemes even if they do not occur in the language spoken around them.
   d. can distinguish only among phonemes that they can pronounce.

7. Newborns prefer to look at stimuli that are
   a. plain rather than patterned.
   b. facelike, with scrambled features.
   c. facelike and moving in front of them.
   d. Newborns like each of the stimuli equally well.

8. When newborns are exposed to odor stimuli,
   a. they show no particular reaction.
   b. they turn their heads toward maternal breast odors.
   c. they wrinkle their noses when exposed to foul odors.
   d. Both b and c are correct.

9. The _____ reflex involves flinging out the arms, then hugging them back to the center of the body.
   a. grasping
   b. Moro
   c. swimming
   d. Babinski

10. Nursing
    a. is present at birth in the same form as seen in older infants.
    b. develops greater efficiency and coordination during the first weeks of life.
    c. is composed of several reflexes that are and remain separate from one another.
    d. takes a longer time in older infants than in newborns.

11. According to Esther Thelen and her colleagues, babies' stepping reflex
    a. disappears because of reorganization of the brain during the transition from involuntary to voluntary behavior.
    b. disappears because of changes in a baby's weight and muscle mass that make stepping difficult.
    c. disappears because babies are not given the opportunity to practice stepping.
    d. never disappears, but instead directly turns into voluntary walking.

12. Which of the following might be a primary circular reaction?
    a. An infant opens his mouth for milk when he sees his mother approach.
    b. An infant repeatedly brings her hand to her mouth and briefly sucks her fingers.
    c. A baby learns to ignore the sound of the highway outside his window.
    d. A newborn copies his mother when she opens her eyes wide in a surprised expression.

13. When an infant turns her head, she is given a taste of sugar water. After a series of trials, she turns her head consistently. This is an example of
    a. operant conditioning.
    b. classical conditioning
    c. imitation.
    d. habituation.

14. Through _____, babies' existing behaviors come to be elicited by new stimuli.
    a. operant conditioning
    b. imitation
    c. classical conditioning
    d. habituation

15. Infants who are regular in biological functions, playful, and adaptable have been labeled "easy" with respect to
    a. motor development.
    b. temperament.
    c. personality.
    d. emotion.

16. The age at which infants begin to "sleep through the night"
    a. is entirely determined by the level of maturity of their nervous systems.
    b. varies among infants but is, on average, the same for babies in all cultures.
    c. is influenced by cultural practices and also by maturation.
    d. is determined entirely by cultural practices.

17. Which of the following is associated with higher rates of sudden infant death syndrome?
    a. maternal smoking
    b. breastfeeding
    c. putting babies to sleep on their backs
    d. All these are associated.

18. Babies' cries usually cause adults to
    a. react with increased heart rate and blood pressure.
    b. avoid contact with the babies.
    c. react with decreases in heart rate.
    d. react with signs of depression.

19. According to a study of newborns, when newborn babies are fed "on demand," they prefer to feed
    a. every hour.
    b. every 2 hours.
    c. every 3 hours.
    d. every 4 hours.

Short-Answer Practice Questions

Write a brief answer in the space below each question.

1. Which of infants' sensory processes are the most mature at birth? Which undergo the most developmental change during infancy?

2. What types of visual stimuli do newborns prefer to look at? What changes take place in their looking behavior over the first few months of life?

3. How is *plasticity* demonstrated in the development of an infant's central nervous system?

4. What do developmentalists mean by *temperament*? What evidence exists that it is influenced by genetics? By culture?

5. How do both mother and infant contribute to the development of efficient nursing?

6. How do infants form expectancies through classical conditioning? Describe a situation in which this might actually occur.

7. Describe several methods used by developmental researchers to study the sensory abilities of newborns.

8. Discuss differences across cultures in expectations about infants' adoption of a typical adult sleep/wake cycle. What differences in behavior emerge?

Putting It All Together

People of different cultures vary in their opinions about how childbirth and the rearing of children should be accomplished. *From Chapters 3 and 4, find several examples illustrating the way differences in parents' beliefs and expectations result in varying experiences for their infants.*

Sources of More Information

Brazelton, T. B., & Sparrow, J. A. (2006). *Touchpoints: Birth to Three,* 2nd ed. Reading, MA: Perseus Books.
This book, which covers the period from birth to 3 years of age, includes material on feeding, crying, and temperament as well as general developmental issues and problems.

Ginsburg, H. P., & Opper, S. (1988). *Piaget's Theory of Intellectual Development,* 3rd ed. Englewood Cliffs, NJ: Prentice-Hall.
This is a readable presentation of Piaget's work and theory, aimed at undergraduate-level students.

Gopnik, A., Meltzoff, A. N., & Kuhl, P. K. (2001). *The Scientist in the Crib: What Early Learning Tells Us about the Mind.* New York: William Morrow.
The authors tackle questions about how babies come to make sense of the world around them.

Montagu, A. (1986). *Touching: The Human Significance of the Skin.* New York: HarperTrade.
The author describes the importance of tactile interaction for human development.

Pryor, K., & Pryor, G. (2005). *Nursing Your Baby,* 4th ed. New York: HarperCollins.
This book provides a comprehensive and readable discussion of breastfeeding, including how to make it work for working mothers.

Wolf, C. (1998). *On the Safe Side: Your Complete Reference to Childproofing for Infants & Children.* Wichita, KS: Whirlwind Publishing Company.
This book deals with one of the major adjustments that must be made by families with new babies—making the home safe for infants and young children.

Answer Key

Answers to Key Terms I: 1.e, 2.k, 3.m, 4.n, 5.l, 6.g, 7.h, 8.b, 9.o, 10.c, 11.j, 12.p, 13.d, 14.i, 15.a, 16.q, 17.f.

Answers to Key Terms II: 1.c, 2.k, 3.e, 4.b, 5.i, 6.q, 7.o, 8.g, 9.j, 10.a, 11.n, 12.d, 13.h, 14.p, 15.l, 16.m, 17.f.

Answers to Multiple-Choice Questions: 1.d, 2.c, 3.b, 4.d, 5.a, 6.c, 7.c, 8.d, 9.b, 10.b, 11.b, 12.c, 13.a, 14.c, 15.b, 16.c, 17.a, 18.a, 19.c.

5 Physical and Cognitive Development in Infancy

CHAPTER

At no time after birth does development occur so quickly as in the first two years. During their first 24 months, infants become larger and stronger; physically, they move from relative helplessness to independent locomotion. They develop increasing control over their bodies, as reflected in "gross motor" skills such as walking and running, "fine motor" skills such as scribbling with crayons, and the ability to feed and dress themselves and to control elimination.

Infants' growing cognitive abilities parallel the development of their motor skills. New developments in thought allow them to reflect on what has happened in the past and to set goals for the immediate future. Infants become faster in processing sensory information and, at the same time, are able to pay attention for progressively longer periods of time. Improvements in memory allow them to retain more of what they learn; in play, older infants can imitate things they have seen others do.

There is disagreement among researchers as to how much young infants know about the properties of the physical world. What is not in doubt is that, with growth and experience, infants become better able to demonstrate a conceptual understanding of gravity, causation, number, object permanence, and categorization.

These physical and cognitive changes interact in infants' development during infancy and—as will be seen in later chapters—also affect their growing ability to communicate and their relationships with their caregivers and the other people in their lives.

Learning Objectives

Keep these questions in mind while studying Chapter 5.

1. How do biological changes that occur during infancy allow infants to develop locomotion, coordinated reaching and grasping, and other voluntary motor behavior?

2. What are some of the ways in which environmental and cultural factors influence the development of children's motor and cognitive skills?

3. Why is there disagreement among developmentalists as to how much knowledge about the world is present from birth and how much has to be learned through experience?

4. How do developmental researchers attempt to arrange the environment so as to determine what infants know, even though the infants are too young to express their knowledge?

5. How do the different methods used to elicit infants' abilities affect researchers' estimates of the ages at which these abilities appear?

6. How much can infants remember? How do improvements in memory relate to growth in other cognitive skills?

Chapter Summary

Changes in babies' motor and cognitive abilities between 3 months and 2 years depend on changes in the physical structures of their bodies and brains. During this period, they learn to move around on their own and become adept at manipulating objects; they also begin to imitate others, to remember what they have observed, and to communicate using language.

I. PHYSICAL GROWTH

A large number of physical changes occur between 3 months and 2 years of age, as shown in Figure 5.1 of the textbook. These include changes in body size and proportions, growth of muscles and bones, and development of the brain.

A. Size and Shape

Most babies grow about 10 inches and triple their weight during the first year—averaging 28–30 inches in height and 20–22 pounds. During the second year, they continue to grow substantially, though at a slower rate, gaining on average 5 pounds and 4 inches, to reach an average of 27 pounds and 34 inches. The growth rate continues to taper off until a growth spurt in adolescence.

Babies' bodies grow differentially; by 12 months, their heads account for a smaller and their legs a greater proportion of overall length than they did at birth. This lowers their center of gravity and makes walking easier. During the second year, they lose the potbellies that are typical of younger infants and develop a more streamlined appearance. Growth norms, such as those shown in Figure 5.4 of the textbook, are derived by averaging the measurements of large numbers of children; the growth of individual children is affected by many factors, such as genetics, diet, and socioeconomic status.

B. The Musculoskeletal System

Infants' bones start to ossify, or harden, beginning with those of the hands and wrists. Their muscles become longer and thicker, another development that prepares them for walking.

Although boys tend to be larger than girls, girls mature faster than boys. By the time of birth, the skeletons of female newborns are 3 to 6 weeks more mature than those of male newborns. By puberty, girls will lead boys in physical maturity by 2 years.

II. BRAIN DEVELOPMENT

As discussed in Chapter 4, a baby's brain develops through *experience—expectant* and *experience-dependent* processes, allowing it to respond both to species-universal experiences and to the experiences of the particular environment in which the child lives. Developmentalists are especially interested in learning more about (1) the relationship between brain development and the onset of new skills and abilities, and (2) the extent to which experiences (or deprivation of experiences) affect brain development and function.

A. Brain and Behavior

The brain develops at different rates in different regions. The cortex is of special interest because it is associated with voluntary (as opposed to reflexive) behavior, abstract thought, problem solving, and language.

When babies are between 7 and 9 months of age, the **prefrontal area** of the cortex begins to function in a new way; this allows infants to have greater ability to regulate and inhibit their actions. Now they appear able to "stop and think." Imaging techniques have revealed that myelination of language-related areas of the cortex occurs just before toddlers have a characteristic spurt in vocabulary growth. And myelination of the neurons linking the prefrontal cortex and frontal lobes to the brain stem allows interaction between thinking and emotion. Toward the end of infancy, increased branching of cortical neurons results in greater interconnection; brain areas that were previously at different levels of maturation now reach similar levels of development. With most of the structure that will someday support adult behavior already in place, the brain's growth continues at a slower pace until adolescence.

B. Brain and Experience

As discussed in Chapter 4, through the processes of *exuberant synaptogenesis* and *synaptic pruning,* children's everyday experiences affect the development of the brain's structures and functions. A by-product of research in this area has been a billion-dollar market for development-enhancing products aimed at infants and small children. The box "Bringing Up Brainy Babies" discusses whether such products are useful.

Of greater concern is the effect of early deprivation on later development. For example, during the 1990s, many families from Western Europe and North America adopted children who had been living under conditions of physical, intellectual, and social deprivation for prolonged periods of time in Romanian orphanages. Were these children able to recover and develop normally? Researchers found that those who were adopted before 6 months of age seemed to recover fully; in contrast, those adopted after 6 or more months in the orphanages were significantly intellectually impaired. Because a great deal of brain development takes place between 6 and 24 months after birth, it is likely that these children lacked essential experiences during a time when the brain is especially sensitive to the effects of experience (a *sensitive period* or time of greater *plasticity*). Brain imaging of a group of adopted orphans revealed deficits in the functioning of areas of the limbic system that are related to motivation and emotion; animal studies have shown these areas to be particularly vulnerable to the effects of stress.

III. MOTOR DEVELOPMENT

Between 3 and 24 months of age, infants undergo dramatic change both in **fine motor skills,** which involve the control and coordination of small muscles, such as those of the fingers and eyes, and **gross motor skills,** which involve large muscles, such as those used in locomotion.

A. Fine Motor Skills

Fine motor skills allow infants to grasp and manipulate objects, and to begin to feed and dress themselves. A summary of milestones in fine motor development is shown in Figure 5.5 of the textbook.

- *Early Skills.* Babies begin to gain voluntary control over reaching and grasping movements at about 3 months of age. During the next several months, their movements become quicker and more accurate. By 9 months, their grasping motions are well integrated and automatic, and parents need to be sure their homes are "baby-proofed." By 12 months, babies can pick up small objects using thumb and fingers, hold a spoon, and drink from a cup.

  As they gain control over their hands, babies appear to perceive that different objects lend themselves to different ways of interaction—for example, rattles lend themselves to being shaken, soft toys to being stroked.
- *Later Skills.* Fine motor coordination increases during the second year of life. By 2 years of age, infants can throw a ball, turn the pages of a book, use safety scissors, string large beads, and build a block tower. They can also hold a cup without spilling the contents and feed themselves with a spoon. In addition, they can dress themselves in clothes without complicated fastenings.

B. Gross Motor Skills

Locomotion, the ability to move around on their own, gives babies more opportunities to explore the environment. It also serves to decrease babies' dependence on their caregivers. Although wide variation exists in the ages at which infants reach the milestones associated with locomotion (shown in Figure 5.9 of the textbook), they all move through the same sequence of development.

- *Creeping and Crawling.* Newborns engage in a pushing movement, controlled by subcortical reflexes, that can propel them forward. This reflexive pushing disappears at about 2 months of age and is not replaced by coordinated crawling on hands and knees until 5 or 6 months later. By 8 to 9 months of age, infants can crawl skillfully on flat surfaces; this allows them to explore the environment in a new way.

  Once crawling allows infants greater freedom to explore, they begin to display a wariness of heights, typically between 7 and 9 months of age. Research by Joseph Campos and his colleagues, using the "visual cliff," has demonstrated that it is infants' experience in moving around on their own that leads to this fear of heights.

- *Walking.* Walking allows babies to cover more distance and to use their hands to carry and manipulate objects while moving around. They are able to walk at the point at which they can coordinate the component movements—standing upright, shifting their weight, alternating their legs, and balancing; they also must have sufficient muscle strength. Walking involves not only the development of motor skills but also increased sensitivity to perceptual input from the environment.

C. The Role of Practice in Motor Development

Is practice necessary for the development of early motor skills? Wayne and Margaret Dennis discovered that Hopi infants raised traditionally (strapped to cradle boards), on average, walked no later than those raised by less traditional parents. This suggested that practice is not necessary for the development of walking.

However, other observations from various cultures suggest that giving babies practice in specific motor skills—walking, for example—causes them to learn these skills at somewhat earlier ages. It is also sometimes true that restricting practice of a skill may delay its onset. For example, modern North American infants spend most of their time on their backs and little time in a prone (face down) position. This has resulted in a delay of the onset of crawling by as much as two months. Infants of the Ache, a people living in the Paraguayan rain forest, learn to walk nearly a year later than North American infants, due to lack of opportunities to practice in the dense forest. However, once they are allowed to move about on their own, Ache children spend their time in complex play activities; then, their motor skills become extremely well developed.

D. Control of Elimination

Changing expectations about children's control of elimination are discussed in the box "In the Field: The Diaper-Free Movement." Although it is possible to teach children to eliminate on the toilet as early as the first year, voluntary control of elimination seems to be a function of maturation. Some children can remain dry during the day by the time they are 2 years old, while many do not achieve complete daytime dryness until later. Nighttime dryness is more difficult and is not achieved until children are 3 1/2 to 4 years old. Successful toilet training is important because it allows children greater independence.

IV. COGNITIVE DEVELOPMENT: THE GREAT DEBATE

Developmentalists disagree about how the development of thinking progresses during the first two years after birth. Piaget's view was that intelligence during this period is sensorimotor, and that it is not until a shift at the end of infancy that the child is able to represent the world mentally; at this point, the infant's mind could be described as *conceptual*. Other developmentalists believe that cognitive development is more continuous and that even very young infants possess the beginnings of a conceptual system.

A. Sensorimotor Development

As discussed in Chapter 4, Piaget viewed development as arising from children's own actions on the world. In referring to the earliest period of development as the sensorimotor stage, Piaget emphasized his belief that, during this period, children acquire knowledge through motor actions directed at the immediate environment and guided by the sensory organs. During the first two substages, infants learn to control and coordinate reflexes and to begin to modify and repeat behaviors, centered on their own bodies, that lead to pleasant or interesting results.

B. Reproducing Interesting Events (Substage 3)

In substage 3 (4 to 8 months), babies perform **secondary circular reactions,** in which they repeat actions that cause interesting results in the outside environment—for example, kicking at a mobile in order to see the dangling objects move. Piaget saw this as an indication that babies are beginning to view objects as more than an extension of their own actions.

C. The Emergence of Intentionality (Substage 4)

In substage 4 (8 to 12 months), babies become able to engage in behaviors directed toward reaching a goal (an example of **intentionality**). For example, a baby may sweep a cushion out of the way (one schema) in order to reach for and grasp a stuffed toy (a second schema). At this point, goal-oriented behavior is only directed at objects and people that the baby can perceive directly.

D. Exploring by Experimenting (Substage 5)

In the fifth substage, **tertiary circular reactions,** 12- to 18-month-old children explore the world in more complex ways by systematically varying the actions they use to reach their goals. Piaget called this more systematic behavior "experiments in order to see." However, he concluded that infants in this substage are not yet able to mentally plan, organize, and imagine the consequences of their actions and must still perform them physically.

E. Representation (Substage 6)

According to Piaget, 18- to 24-month-old children literally "re-present" the world to themselves mentally. These first mental symbols are called **representations.** Using representations allows babies to plan solutions to problems before carrying them out. They are now able to imagine objects not present, imitate past events (**deferred imitation**), engage in **symbolic play** (pretend or fantasy play), and solve problems more systematically and less by trial and error.

Children all over the world have been observed to progress through the same sequence of sensorimotor behavior. Piaget's procedures have even been standardized for evaluating the development of at-risk children. However, some researchers do not agree that infants cannot represent objects to themselves until the end of the sensorimotor stage. They argue that infants have representational *competence* that they cannot express in *performance* on traditional Piagetian tests.

V. CONCEPTUAL DEVELOPMENT

According to Piaget, infants who do not yet form representations do not yet understand the world conceptually; they need cues from the perceptual features of objects in the immediate environment. However, there is some evidence that infants who have still not reached the end of the sensorimotor stage do have the capacity to understand the world in more abstract terms.

A. Understanding the Permanence of Objects

Piaget believed that infants are not born with a sense of **object permanence**—the understanding that objects continue to exist when they are out of sight—but gradually develop it during the sensorimotor period. Even after babies actively begin to search for hidden objects at about 8 months of age, he noted, they tend to search for an object in a place where they have observed it before—even if they have just seen it hidden in a different place! Piaget called this pattern of responding the **A-not-B error.** Piaget believed that it was not until late in the second year of life that infants could keep an absent object in mind and also mentally reason about the absent object. This notion has generated a great deal of research.

   1. Alternative Explanations of Infants' Difficulties
      Some developmentalists attribute the A-not-B error to limitations on infants' memory or motor skills rather than to a failure to represent objects mentally.
      • A series of studies by Adele Diamond suggests that babies' limited ability to remember impairs their performance on hidden object tests. Thus, for example, they may search for an object in a new location if they are allowed to reach for it immediately; if, however, a delay is introduced, they quickly forget the object's lo-

cation and become confused. The older the infant, the longer the delay that he or she can tolerate before the location of the object is forgotten. So, while 7 1/2-month-old infants would forget an object's location after a delay of 2 seconds, 9-month-olds could wait 5 seconds, and 12-month-olds were able to withstand a delay of 10 seconds.

- Infants also tend to repeat behavior patterns; this is called *perseveration.* Diamond believed that infants' tendency to engage in motor perseveration is another reason they search for an object in a location where they have seen it previously. Infants also may engage in *capture errors,* in which they continue using a previously successful solution in new situations.

2. Alternative Approaches to Measuring and Understanding Object Permanence
Some developmentalists have proposed methods for measuring infants' understanding of object permanence that do not require the infants to engage in active searching. If infants are capable of representational thought at or near the time of birth, it should be possible to demonstrate it with these methods.

- *Violation of Expectations Method.* Infants are known to look longer at events that violate their expectations. In the **violation of expectations method,** they are shown a possible event and an impossible event. For example, Renée Baillargeon and her colleagues habituated infants to an event in which a carrot passed behind a screen and came out on the other side. When the carrot was a tall carrot, it would be visible as it passed behind a window on its way across the rear of the screen; when the carrot was a small carrot, it would not be visible. On some test trials (the "possible" event), the small carrot passed behind the screen and was not visible in the window before reappearing on the other side. On other trials (the "impossible" event), the tall carrot followed the same path but was not visible in the window, as it should have been. Did infants look longer at the impossible event? Baillargeon found that even infants of 2 1/2 months looked longer at the impossible event; she concluded that they were already able to form mental representations and had done so during the habituation trials.
- *Dynamic Systems Approach.* Esther Thelen and her colleagues view object permanence as they do action in any context: as an instance of interaction among infants' experiences with objects, memories of those experiences, current motor skills, and the demands of the task at hand. In this view, infants do not make a transition from sensorimotor to conceptual thought; instead, they develop in their ability to coordinate the systems involved in sensorimotor and conceptual intelligence.
- *The Role of Experience.* Jeanne Shinskey and Yuko Munakata investigated the process through which infants build mental representations of objects (rather than asking *when* they have the capacity to do so). They hypothesized that infants' representations strengthen as the infants gain experience with the objects; therefore, they might have a stronger sense of object permanence for familiar objects than for novel objects. To test this, Shinskey and Munakata conducted a study in which

7-month-olds had the opportunity to reach for a familiar object or a novel object under differing conditions. They found that whereas under normal lighting conditions the infants preferred to reach for a novel object, when the room was darkened, they preferred to reach for the familiar object. Presumably, the infants had a stronger sense of the familiar object's location; this would support the idea that their representation of the familiar object was stronger.

B. Understanding Other Properties of the Physical World

Infants understand other things about the properties of objects. For example, Renée Baillargeon and her colleagues have demonstrated that 4 1/2-month-olds evidently expect objects to obey the law of gravity; they stared longer at a block that appeared to be suspended in midair than at one supported by another block.

Other studies have found that 4-month-olds understand objects cannot move through a solid physical obstruction. Also, if an object is inside a container, infants understand that it will move to another location when the container is moved.

C. Reasoning about Objects

Piaget theorized that even when young children are aware of the physical properties of objects, they are not yet able to reason about them. This idea has also generated research.

- *Counting.* Karen Wynn investigated counting in 4-month-olds by using the procedure pictured in Figure 5.19 of the textbook. The infants stared longer at an impossible situation that depicted two dolls when there should have been one, or one doll when there should have been two. Infants also seem to be able to match numbers between sensory modalities. For example, when listening to a recording of three voices, they look longer at a video that shows three faces than one that shows only two. On the other hand, Leslie Cohen and Kathryn Marks found that infants would look longer at a familiar display, no matter how many objects it contained.
- *Cause–Effect Relationships.* Alan Leslie and his colleagues have argued that their research demonstrates 6-month-old infants possess an appreciation of physical causality. They measured this by habituating infants to computer displays in which a square bumped a second square and the second square moved (showing causality); when shown a similar display in which the second square moved only after a delay, they stared longer at this apparently noncausal event. However, Lisa Oakes and Leslie Cohen found that, when they replaced the squares with realistic objects, 6-month-olds seemed overwhelmed and no longer responded on the basis of causality. It can be argued from this that infants are still in the process of learning to infer causality and can only display their knowledge under favorable circumstances.
- *Categorizing.* Categorizing is the process of seeing similarities in different objects and events. For example, all cats are similar to each other in some ways and different from dogs. The ability to categorize is highly developed in adults and helps us to take knowledge learned in one situation and apply it in another. When does categorization emerge

in children? Quinn and Eimas determined that 3-month-olds were able to learn quickly how to categorize cats and dogs; for example, after seeing a series of images of cats, they looked longer at a picture of a dog than at that of a new cat. When young infants form categories, corresponding changes occur in the electrical activity of their brains.

On what basis do infants form categories: on perceptual similarities alone or on more abstract, conceptual features? This relates to the question raised earlier regarding the extent to which infants' knowledge is perceptual and sensorimotor, and the extent to which it is abstract and conceptual.

There is some evidence that, toward the end of the first year, infants become able to form conceptual categories—that is, to categorize on the basis of such features as what things do and how they have come to be a certain way. Jean Mandler and Laraine McDonough found that whereas 7-month-old babies responded to models of birds and airplanes, which were perceptually similar, as if they were the same, 9- to 11-month-olds responded to them as members of separate categories. This suggests a developmental shift from perceptual to conceptual categorization, although at an earlier age than theorized by Piaget. Further evidence for conceptual categorization derives from another Mandler and McDonough study involving generalized imitation. They found that 9- and 11-month-old infants who saw an adult perform an action—for example, giving a toy dog a drink—were more likely to imitate the action with an object from the same category (giving a toy bunny a drink) than with an object from a different category (giving a truck a drink).

Controversy still surrounds the basis of categorization by infants, with some researchers believing that perceptual similarity remains the most important and others believing that, by the end of the first year, infants can form genuine conceptual categories. Leslie Cohen and his colleagues have advanced the view that young infants form categories on the basis of specific object features but that, around 10 months of age, they become able to process relationships among these features. In any case, by the end of infancy, babies are capable of using categories to organize their behavior in relation to the objects around them.

VI. THE GROWTH OF ATTENTION AND MEMORY

The ability to attend to and remember aspects of the environment is important in learning to understand object permanence, causality, and the other properties of objects discussed earlier.

A. Developing Attention

As shown in Figure 5.24 of the textbook, by measuring infants' heart rates it is possible to distinguish four phases of attention:

- *Phase I: Stimulus Detection Reflex.* This is indicated by a brief slowing, then quickening of the heart rate, and indicates the baby's initial awareness of a change in the environment.
- *Phase II: Stimulus Orienting.* The heart rate slows down as the baby's attention becomes fixed on the stimulus.

- *Phase III: Sustained Attention.* The heart rate remains slow as the baby processes the stimulus. The whole body may become still and it is more difficult to distract the baby with a new stimulus. Sustained attention is a voluntary state that corresponds to *paying attention.*
- *Phase IV: Attention Termination.* The heart begins to return to prestimulus levels; the baby may still be looking at the stimulus, but is no longer processing its information.

Three-month-olds can only sustain their attention for 5 to 10 seconds; their ability to focus attention improves over the course of infancy. At the same time, infants become faster at processing information. A 2-year-old needs far less time than a 1-year-old to process the information in a simple pattern; thus, the 2-year-old may actually spend less time looking at it. In contrast, 2-year-olds spend more time than younger infants in attending to complex stimuli.

B. Developing Memory

During the first year, infants improve in their ability to remember what they learn. Carolyn Rovee-Collier and her colleagues found that when 2-month-olds were taught to move a mobile attached to a string by kicking their legs, they remembered their training for 24 hours but had forgotten it after a 3-day delay; 3-month-olds remembered their training for about a week. Six-month-olds did even better, remembering their training after a 2-week delay. If given a brief visual reminder, the infants could remember much longer. A study in which 6- to 18-month-old infants learned to make a train move, shown in Figure 5.27 of the textbook, revealed similar results: as infants grow older, a steady increase occurs in the length of time they can recall their experiences.

Because of the steady improvement they have observed in infants' memory over the first year, Rovee-Collier and her colleagues consider this development to be a continuous process that does not involve any new principles of learning or remembering. However, other researchers believe that just as categorization seems to shift from a perceptual to conceptual basis at 6 to 9 months of age, memory undergoes a qualitative shift at about the same time. According to this view, the shift involves moving from reliance on **implicit memory**—the ability to *recognize* experiences—to **explicit memory**—the ability to *recall* ("call to mind") objects and events without a clear reminder. Explicit memory is of special interest because it requires a conscious representation of something not present to the senses.

VII. IMPLICATIONS

During the first two years, infants undergo huge physical and cognitive changes. In the nervous system, myelination of neural pathways allows development of voluntary behavior and more integrated functioning of the different brain areas. Infants' motor abilities improve; they learn to walk and to manipulate and explore objects. At the same time, their growing abilities to form representations of objects, people, and events allows them to develop skills such as symbolic play, imitation, and language, which will be discussed in later chapters.

Key Terms

Following are important terms introduced in Chapter 5. Match each term with the letter of the example that best illustrates the term.

1. _____ A-not-B error

2. _____ deferred imitation

3. _____ explicit memory

4. _____ fine motor skills

5. _____ gross motor skills

6. _____ implicit memory

7. _____ intentionality

8. _____ locomotion

9. _____ object permanence

10. _____ prefrontal area

11. _____ representations

12. _____ secondary circular reactions

13. _____ symbolic play

14. _____ tertiary circular reactions

15. _____ violation of expectations method

a. A child, sitting in a high chair, repeatedly drops peas onto the floor. Sometimes holding his arm straight out, sometimes to the side, he varies the position from which each pea is dropped is an example.
b. To achieve this, babies must be able to integrate the movements of many parts of their bodies.
c. This occurs during the recognition of things that have been experienced before.
d. According to Piaget, this appears in infants' behavior during sensorimotor substage 4.
e. An example is when a 7-month-old boy learns to pull the ring his parents have dangled over his crib, causing a music box to play. He pulls it over and over again.
f. This part of the brain is important in the growth of infants' ability to regulate their own behavior.
g. An example is when Allison watches her brother operate a new toy, and later in the day performs the same actions on the toy.
h. Ben, a 10-month-old, immediately whisks his mother's handkerchief off a squeeze toy after his mother has covered it. Ben is showing this
i. The small muscles of the eyes and hands are used in these.
j. An example is when Gia watches her mother hide a toy under the sofa cushion, and then looks for it first under the blanket where her mother hid it the last time.
k. Jessica is making use of these when she thinks about the family pets when they are out of the room.
l. These involve use of the large muscles of the body.
m. Infants are habituated to an event; then they are presented with both possible and impossible variants of the event. The infants have been exposed to this.

n. An example is when Paul places pebbles in a bowl, stirs them around, and serves "soup" to his teddy bear.

o. This occurs when a 1-year-old is able to recall something without needing a clear reminder.

Multiple-Choice Practice Questions

Circle the letter of the word or phrase that correctly completes each statement.

1. What, if any, changes occur in infants' body proportions during the first year of life?
   a. The head becomes a larger proportion of total body length.
   b. The head becomes a smaller proportion of total body length.
   c. The head and body maintain the same relative proportions.
   d. The head and body each maintain the same overall size.

2. The _____—a part of the brain involved in voluntary behavior—undergoes important development between 7 and 9 months after birth.
   a. cerebellum
   b. brain stem
   c. prefrontal cortex
   d. hippocampus

3. Toward the end of infancy, brain development is characterized by
   a. an increase in myelination.
   b. growth in the length and complexity of neurons.
   c. increased interaction among different areas of the brain.
   d. All these answers are correct.

4. Cross-cultural observations of the development of infants' motor skills show that
   a. infants of all cultures reach early motor milestones at the same ages, regardless of differences in childrearing practices.
   b. the amount of practice a child gets may cause motor milestones to be reached earlier or later than would otherwise occur.
   c. early motor milestones cannot be reached earlier through practice; however, they can be delayed by restricting movement.
   d. restriction of practice has a permanent negative effect on the acquisition of motor skills.

5. By _____, most children have enough control over elimination to remain consistently dry while asleep.
   a. 1 year of age
   b. 2 years of age
   c. 3 years of age
   d. 4 years of age

6. According to Piaget, during the last few months of the first year, infants are learning to
    a. modify their basic reflexes.
    b. make interesting experiences, centered on their own bodies, last.
    c. make interesting events in the outside world last.
    d. engage in actions in order to reach a goal.

7. In substage 5, tertiary circular reactions, children begin to
    a. repeat interesting action sequences without variation.
    b. carry out actions in thought rather than physically.
    c. vary the action sequences they use to reach a goal.
    d. imitate objects and events that are not present.

8. Which is an example of symbolic play?
    a. using a banana as a telephone
    b. making cookies out of play dough
    c. serving a doll a coffee cup of sand
    d. All these answers are correct.

9. Children begin to demonstrate fear of heights
    a. immediately after birth.
    b. as soon as they are carried by their parents.
    c. after they have experienced moving around on their own.
    d. at the end of the sensorimotor stage of development.

10. The ability to bring to mind objects and events experienced in the past is called
    a. recognition.
    b. explicit memory.
    c. deferred memory.
    d. implicit memory.

11. Engaging in _____ imitation requires children to be able to represent objects and events to themselves.
    a. deferred
    b. symbolic
    c. sensorimotor
    d. secondary

12. Piaget considered the A-not-B error to be an indication that
    a. infants tend to perseverate in their motor responses.
    b. infants do not remember the location of objects for more than a few seconds.
    c. infants cannot yet reason systematically about objects.
    d. infants are not yet able to make the motor responses necessary in order to search for hidden objects.

13. Which is true of babies' memory during the first year?
    a. Babies steadily improve in the length of time they can remember a learned behavior.
    b. Babies can remembered learned behaviors much longer if they are given a "reminder" before retesting.
    c. Babies' memory for learned behaviors is as good at 3 months as it is at 12 months of age, provided that the correct testing procedures are used.
    d. Both a and b are correct.

14. Researchers using _____ have concluded that even young infants have some understanding of the physical properties of objects.
    a. Piaget's tasks
    b. the violation-of-expectations method
    c. brain imaging techniques
    d. infants' verbal responses

15. Which did researchers consider to be an example of conceptual categorization?
    a. A baby responds the same way to toy birds and toy airplanes.
    b. A baby responds differently to cats and dogs.
    c. A baby responds the same way to a flower mobile and a bird mobile.
    d. A baby responds differently to two rattles.

16. In a study aimed at investigating babies' awareness of number, Karen Wynn found that 4-month-olds when shown a display with one doll where there should have been two
    a. looked longer than when the display contained the expected two dolls.
    b. looked for less time than when the display contained the expected two dolls.
    c. looked for the same amount of time as they did when the display contained the expected two dolls.
    d. refused to look at the display because they were afraid of the dolls.

17. Who would generally look longer at a complex stimulus display?
    a. a 3-month-old
    b. a 12-month-old
    c. a 2-year-old
    d. Children of all these ages will look for about the same amount of time.

18. Some researchers believe that babies shift at 7 to 9 months of age from relying exclusively on _____ memory to being capable of _____ memory.
    a. implicit; explicit
    b. sensorimotor; representational
    c. explicit; implicit
    d. symbolic; abstract

Short-Answer Practice Questions

Write a brief answer in the space below each question.

1. In what ways do changes in infants' central nervous systems correspond to changes in their motor and cognitive abilities?

2. What do cross-cultural studies tell us about the roles of nature and nurture in the development of motor skills?

3. What types of evidence have led researchers to believe that infants may believe in the continued existence of hidden objects even though they fail to search for them?

4. What are some of the ways we can tell that children have begun to mentally represent things to themselves?

5. Describe the difference between recognition and recall. How do researchers measure each in infants?

6. Describe two different methods you could use to test whether a 9-month-old infant can engage in conceptual categorization.

Putting It All Together

In this section, you will need to put together information from Chapters 4 and 5 to get a more complete picture of development throughout infancy.

To review Piaget's substages of sensorimotor development, here are some behaviors that Piaget observed his own children performing during the sensorimotor stage. *Match each behavior with the substage in which you would expect it to occur.*

Substages

1. Control and coordination of reflexes
2. Primary circular reactions
3. Secondary circular reactions
4. Goal-oriented behavior
5. Tertiary circular reactions
6. Representation

_____ Laurent strikes at a pillow to lower it, then reaches over it to grasp a box of matches.

_____ Laurent repeatedly brings his hand to his mouth in order to suck his fingers.

_____ Lucienne sees her father hide a chain inside a slightly open matchbox. She looks at the opening, opens and shuts her mouth several times, and finally reaches a finger to slide open the box and grasp the chain.

_____ Laurent becomes quicker at finding his mother's nipple when it touches him anywhere on his face.

_____ Laurent lifts toys and lets them fall, varying his arm position each time.

_____ Lucienne, lying in her bassinet, sees a doll hanging above her and kicks it. The doll sways, and Lucienne attempts to kick it again and again.

Try to think of another example of infant behavior that would illustrate each substage.

Sources of More Information

American Academy of Pediatrics. (1998). *Caring for Your Baby and Young Child: Birth to Age 5,* rev. ed. New York: Bantam Books.
This is a guide to the care of young children and contains a great deal of information about physical and cognitive developmental milestones.

Brazelton, T. B. (1983). *Infants and Mothers: Differences in Development,* rev. ed. New York: Dell.
The author follows the progress of an active baby, a quiet baby, and an average baby through the first 12 months of life.

Brazelton, T. B. (1989). *Toddlers and Parents: A Declaration of Independence,* rev. ed. New York: Delacorte, 1989.
This book describes individual differences among toddlers and discusses the developmental tasks children face during later infancy.

Caplan, F. (Ed.). (1995). *The First Twelve Months of Life: Your Baby's Growth Month by Month.* New York: Bantam Books.
This guide looks at the month-by-month physical, cognitive, and social changes that take place during an infant's first year.

Caplan, F., & Caplan, T. (1998). *The Second Twelve Months of Life.* New York: Berkeley Publishing Group.
This book describes the development of mental, motor, and language skills, month by month, during the second year.

Shatz, M. (1995). *A Toddler's Life: Becoming a Person.* New York: Oxford University Press.
A developmental psychologist describes, in the tradition of Piaget's observations, her grandson Ricky's development, from 15 months to 3 years of age.

Uzgiris, I., & Hunt, J. M. (1989). *Assessment in Infancy: Ordinal Scales of Psychological Development.* Champaign, IL: University of Illinois Press.
This book describes a standardized instrument, based on Piaget's research on sensorimotor development, that is used for assessing development in infancy.

Answer Key

Answers to Key Terms: 1.j, 2.g, 3.o, 4.i, 5.l, 6.c, 7.d, 8.b, 9.h, 10.f, 11.k, 12.e, 13.n, 14.a, 15.m.

Answers to Multiple-Choice Questions: 1.b, 2.c, 3.d, 4.b, 5.d, 6.d, 7.c, 8.d, 9.c, 10.b, 11.a, 12.c, 13.d, 14.b, 15.b, 16.a, 17.c, 18.a.

Answers to Putting It All Together: 4, 2, 6, 1, 5, 3.

6 Social and Emotional Development in Infancy

During infancy, children develop socially and emotionally in important ways. Developing greater control over their emotions, they use smiling, crying, and pouting to help them coordinate their behavior with that of their mothers and other caregivers. During the first year, infants become attached to their caregivers and distressed when they leave. Although older infants are still dependent on caregivers for support when coping with unfamiliar situations, they are learning to predict and understand their periodic absences and returns. The formation of a secure attachment between infant and caregiver is advantageous for the child's later social development.

Increasing facility with language helps infants make their needs better known as they learn to recognize familiar words, use words to request things, and, later, comment on their own activities.

Physical, cognitive, social, and emotional growth interact over time, allowing infants to develop greater degrees of autonomy and self-direction. Between 18 and 24 months, their behavior begins to reveal a sense of "selfhood," including the appearance of self-conscious emotions such as pride and embarrassment. By the end of infancy, parents the world over notice their children are demonstrating increasing self-awareness and recognize that they have attained a new level of development.

Learning Objectives

Keep these questions in mind while studying Chapter 6.

1. What explanations have been proposed to account for infants' expression of emotions?
2. What evidence exists that caregivers and infants can share moods? What is the physiological basis for this?
3. How do developmentalists measure attachment between infants and their caregivers? How do different theoretical orientations explain attachment?

4. What factors influence the variations in patterns of attachment behavior seen in different infants?
5. How do infants develop in their ability to produce and understand language?
6. What new behaviors lead developmentalists to conclude that, about the time of their second birthday, children develop a sense of "self"?

Chapter Summary

I. THE NATURE OF INFANT EMOTIONS AND EMOTIONAL EXPRESSIONS

Developmentalists ordinarily define emotions in terms of the following features:

- Physiological reactions such as changes in heart rate, breathing, and hormonal functioning
- Communication of internal states of feeling to others through facial expressions, vocalizations, and other behaviors
- Cognitive effects on how we interpret what is happening to us
- Action (for example, laughing, crying, withdrawing) resulting from the experience of the emotion

Technically, **emotion** is defined as a *feeling state that involves distinctive physiological responses and cognitive evaluations that motivate action.* Emotions vary in intensity, in the time and course of their occurrence, and in the ability of the person experiencing the emotion to control its expression. The control and modulation of emotional expressions are called **emotion regulation.**

A. Theories of Emotional Development

The **basic emotions**—joy, fear, anger, surprise, sadness, and disgust—seem to be expressed in similar ways in all cultures. This supports their status as universal adaptive responses that are generated by—and, in turn, contribute to—our biological and cultural evolution.

There are two controversies about how emotions develop. (1) Are infants' basic emotions already similar to those of adults at birth, or do infants become more capable of feeling these emotions over time? (2) Do emotions other than those considered basic (shame, guilt, pride, for example) emerge full-blown at specific periods of development, or do they emerge from more global positive and negative feeling states? Several perspectives on emotional development differ with respect to these questions.

- According to the **theory of gradual differentiation,** infants, at birth, are only capable of expressing general positive or negative emotional reactions: contentment or distress. This view emphasizes *discontinuity* of emotional expression; thus, a newborn's crying expresses distress, whereas that of an older infant expresses a more specific feeling such as anger or sadness.
- According to the **differential emotions theory,** proposed by Carroll Izard and his colleagues, the basic emotions are biologically innate and culturally universal. Thus, these emotions are present at birth in adultlike form, and the emergence of other emotions in

infancy and childhood, as well as the ability to regulate emotions, is associated with development of the prefrontal cortex.

- A third view regards infants' emotions as **ontogenetic adaptations** that have evolved because they contribute to survival and development. This perspective focuses on the circumstances under which infants experience particular emotions and the ways infants' emotional expressions affect interactions with their caregivers. For example, infants' early smiles are *endogenous*—responses to internal, physiological fluctuations. Between 1 and 2 months, infants smile in response to perceptual stimulation; finally, at 2 to 3 months of age, infants' smiles become truly social, responding to others' smiles and eliciting them in turn.

B. Infant Emotions and Social Life

Infants' emotions become coordinated with those of their caregivers in face-to-face interactions called **primary intersubjectivity;** in these interactions, the mother and baby display a kind of emotional sharing in which each recognizes and shares the emotional state of the other. Sometimes, this kind of interaction can break down—for example, when the mother suffers from depression. In laboratory studies, researchers have investigated what happens when the emotional connection between babies and their interactive partners is interrupted.

- One way to manipulate social interaction in the laboratory is the *still-face method,* in which—after a few minutes of normal interaction—a mother is cued to maintain a still face and to stop responding to the baby. In the *delayed-transmission method,* a mother and infant interact naturally, seeing and hearing one another through audiovisual monitors; then, the mother's responses are delayed to make them out of synch with the infant's behavior. Both of these methods result in negative emotional responses from infants as young as 2 months of age.
- Infants of depressed mothers act differently in the still-face procedure; while they avert their eyes (as infants normally do) from their mother's still face, they do not protest or fuss. This suggests that they have learned to disengage from unresponsive interactions with their mothers.
- Evidence from laboratory studies suggests that infants have a need to be emotionally connected to others. According to Harriet Oster, this may account for the common infant behavior of pouting. Examination of the pouting expression suggests that it is not a component of crying; also, it is directed at a social partner. Oster considers pouting to be an effort to regulate distress and maintain the social contact that crying would disrupt. Oster points out that, as observed by Darwin, some of our most characteristic facial expressions are related to crying and to our attempts to control crying.

C. Intersubjectivity and the Brain

How does the brain contribute to the experience, expression, and regulation of emotions in infancy? Research by Giacomo Rizzolatti, an Italian neuroscientist, with monkeys resulted in the discovery of **mirror neurons,** brain cells that fire when an animal sees or hears another perform an action, just as though the animal were itself performing the action. Humans also have mirror neuron systems. Andrew Meltzoff and Jean Decety have argued that innate processes, including mirror neurons, account for the observed ability of newborn infants to imitate certain facial expressions and movements. They note that adults in many cultures play imitative games with children and suggest that imitation plays an important role in forming emotional connections with others. Infants not only imitate others; they pay attention when adults imitate them. By 14 months of age, cognitive and social processes moderate the neurological basis of imitation and infants will engage in games of mutual imitation with adults for 20 minutes or more.

II. THE INFANT–CAREGIVER EMOTIONAL RELATIONSHIP

As babies begin to move around on their own, they need to be able to learn about the world while, at the same time, avoiding its hazards. The development of attachment, an emotional bond between children and their caregivers, helps provide a balance between exploration and safety. This bond becomes evident between 7 and 9 months of age, and undergoes changes during the course of infancy and beyond.

Developmentalists cite four signs of attachment in infants and young children:

1. They seek to be near the primary caregivers.
2. They show distress if separated from their caregivers.
3. They are happy when reunited with the caregivers.
4. They orient their actions to the caregiver.

A. Explanations of Attachment

Because children in all cultures begin to show distress at separation from their caretakers at about 7 to 9 months of age, it has been suggested that attachment is a universal feature of development. Theorists have suggested several different explanations for why attachment occurs.

- *Freud's Drive-Reduction Explanation.* Sigmund Freud's theory emphasizes the importance of **biological drives**—states of arousal such as hunger and thirst—that urge the organism into action in order to satisfy essential needs. Satisfying the needs leads to pleasure. Freud proposed that infants become attached to those who help them satisfy these drives. In particular, children become attached to their mothers, who satisfy their need for nourishment. A problem with this explanation is that research has not shown attachment to result from reduction of the hunger drive. Studies conducted with infant rhesus monkeys by Harry Harlow and his co-workers found that, contrary to the drive-reduction hypothesis, bodily contact and the comfort it provides are more important than nourishment in fostering attachment. The infant monkeys in their study became attached to terry-cloth-covered substitute mothers in preference to wire-bodied ones, even when only the wire "mothers" provided them with food.
- *Bowlby's Ethological Explanation.* The work of John Bowlby had its roots in his observations of children who had been separated from their families during World War II and cared for in institutions. He found that children separated from their mothers exhibited fear, then

despair and depression, and finally **detachment,** a state of indifference. Bowlby's explanation, influenced by the work of ethologists, emphasizes the way that attachment provides a balance between infants' need for safety and their need to explore the environment. Bowlby's explanation finds more support from Harlow's infant monkey studies than Freud's did. When confronted with an unfamiliar, frightening stimulus—for example, a drum-beating mechanical teddy bear—a baby monkey would run to its terry cloth mother for comfort. Afterward, from the safety of the "mother," it would begin to explore the object that had seemed so frightening a short time before. However, although soothing tactile sensations provided the infant monkeys with a sense of security, this was not sufficient for healthy social development; monkeys who became attached to nonliving surrogates did not learn how to behave socially with other monkeys and acted either indifferently or abusively toward them. Under normal circumstances, primary intersubjectivity developed through interaction with a responsive caregiver provides a foundation for emotional and social development.

B. Phases of Attachment

Bowlby believed that attachment develops through four phases during the first 2 years of life. In each phase, infants take on more responsibility for maintaining the balance of the attachment system.

1. *The "Preattachment" Phase* (birth to 6 weeks). Infants remain in close contact with their caregivers; during this phase, they do not become upset when left with an unfamiliar caregiver.
2. *The "Attachment-in-the-Making" Phase* (6 weeks to 6–8 months). Infants show the first signs of wariness toward unfamiliar people and begin to exhibit clear preference for their familiar caregivers.
3. *The "Clear-Cut Attachment" Phase* (6–8 to 18–24 months). This phase is characterized by **separation anxiety** when the caregiver leaves. The caregiver becomes a **secure base** from which the infant can explore, returning occasionally for reassurance.
4. *The "Reciprocal Relationship" Phase* (18–24 months and older). The child is more mobile and spends increasingly longer periods away from the caregiver; now caregiver and child share responsibility for maintaining the equilibrium of the attachment system. In humans, this phase lasts for several years.

Attachment helps infants to feel secure during periods of separation from their caregivers. In Bowlby's view, the attachment relationship serves as an **internal working model** that children construct from their experiences and that they can use to guide their future interactions with caregivers and others.

C. Patterns of Attachment

What kinds of infant–caregiver interactions lead to the development of healthy social relationships? On the basis of observations in Africa and in the United States, Mary Ainsworth concluded that there are consistent, distinct patterns of mother–infant interaction. Most mother–infant pairs seemed to work out a comfortable relationship by the third year of the child's life; however, others had relationships characterized by persistent tension and difficulty in regulating joint activities. Ainsworth and her colleagues studied attachment in a laboratory procedure called the **strange situation,** in which children were left with a strange adult in an unfamiliar room, left entirely alone, and, finally, reunited with their mothers. The researchers were interested in how infants made use of their mothers as a secure base, how they reacted to the stranger, and how they reacted to the mother upon her return.

Several patterns of attachment behavior have been identified:

- In **secure attachment,** the pattern found in about 65 percent of middle-class children in the United States, infants are upset when their mothers leave and unlikely to be consoled by the stranger; however, they are quickly reassured when their mothers return. This pattern reflects a healthy balance between children's desire to be in close contact with the mother and their desire to explore the environment.

- In **avoidant attachment,** found in about 23 percent of cases, infants appear indifferent to their mothers and—if they become distressed when their mothers leave—are as likely to be consoled by the stranger as by their mothers; these infants may ignore their mothers when they return.

- Children who exhibit **resistant attachment,** approximately 12 percent of middle-class children in the United States, are upset from the start in the strange situation. They are distressed when their mothers leave, but struggle to resist comfort from them when they return.

- Some children's behavior is described as **disorganized attachment.** These children seem to have not developed a coherent method for dealing with the stress of the strange situation. They may exhibit inconsistent behavior such as screaming while their mothers are gone but silently moving away from them when they return.

Research on attachment has tended to focus on infants and their mothers. However, as discussed in the box "Attachment to Fathers and Others," when fathers are the primary caregivers, infants are just as securely attached to them as to their mothers. Do infants cared for in day care centers develop secure attachments to their parents? This question is taken up in the box "Out-of-Home Care: A Threat to Attachment?" A large U.S. study indicated that extensive out-of-home care during infancy has slight negative effects on children's attachment relationships, social behaviors, and intellectual development; however, the effects are weaker than those of insensitive mothering or the family's socioeconomic status. Providing a strong foundation for children's emotional and social development is of great importance; thus, researchers are interested in the causes and possible consequences of the patterns of attachment just identified.

D. The Causes of Variations in Patterns of Attachment

Research on patterns of attachment has focused on three types of contexts that influence the responsiveness and sensitivity of the care infants receive:

- *The Family Context.* Many studies show that, as first reported by Mary Ainsworth and as found in studies by Michael Lamb and his colleagues, infants whose mothers are sensitive to their needs are more likely to behave in a securely attached manner. Infants whose caregivers are abusive or insensitive are more likely to be insecurely attached. Maternal depression, low socioeconomic status (SES), and other factors that increase stress on parents are associated with insecure attachment. However, the correlation between sensitivity and attachment is not a strong one, showing there are other factors linking parental behaviors to attachment that are not yet understood.

- *Institutional Contexts.* Children who have spent their early lives in orphanages may find it difficult to form loving relationships with others because they have experienced prolonged social-emotional deprivation. In extreme cases, they may develop Reactive Attachment Disorder (RAD), a serious disorder involving inappropriate social relating, discussed in the box "In the Field: Children with Reactive Attachment Disorder." Children who had been severely deprived in Romanian orphanages were found to adjust well to life in Canadian homes if they were adopted before 4 months of age. However, if they spent 8 months or longer in orphanages, they showed residual effects of their experiences, including less secure attachment to their adoptive parents. Barbara Tizard and Jill Hodges studied children raised in high-quality residential nurseries in England. These children suffered no physical deprivation, but because they were cared for by large numbers of nurses, they had no opportunity to form close attachments to their adult caregivers. However, when the children were adopted, between 2 and 8 years of age, they were nearly always able to form attachments with their adoptive parents. Those returning to their biological families fared less well, perhaps because their parents gave them less attention; the older they were when returned to their parents, the less likely that mutual attachment developed. The problem of providing adequate care for orphaned children is ongoing. Currently, more than 12 million children in sub-Saharan Africa alone are living as orphans because they have lost their parents to the HIV-AIDS epidemic.

- *Cultural Contexts.* Sharp disagreement surrounds the effect of cultural variations on the attachment process. One view is that attachment is a universal feature of development and that the interactions which nourish it are the same across cultures. Another view is that notions of sensitive caregiving are culturally specific and that there are important cultural variations in attachment. Evidence for both views exists. For example, Abraham Sagi and his colleagues found that communally raised infants in Israeli *kibbutzim,* when tested in the strange situation, were more often resistant and less frequently rated as securely attached than kibbutz children who slept in their parents' homes at night. Vivian Carlson and Robin Harwood, examining maternal sensitivity in mothers from the United States and Puerto Rico, observed that Puerto Rican mothers exerted more control over their infants. This was behavior that, in U.S. mothers, would be judged "insensitive" and associated with less secure attachment. However, maternal control is consistent with Puerto Rican cultural values and the infants of controlling Puerto Rican mothers were not judged to be insecurely attached. Thus, although attachment is a universal phenomenon, it is possible that its development, and the caregiving behaviors that foster it, may vary depending on the community into which children are being socialized. Figure 6.10 of the textbook shows variations in patterns of attachment found in studies in a variety of cultures.

E. Attachment Patterns and Later Development

How important is secure attachment in infancy to later emotional well-being? Alan Sroufe and his colleagues reported that, at age 3 1/2, children who had been judged securely attached in infancy were more curious, played more effectively with other children, and maintained better relationships with their teachers than children who had been judged insecurely attached in infancy. At 10 and again at 15 years of age, the securely attached children were found to be more socially skilled, more self-confident, more open in expressing their feelings, and to have more friends.

In a 20-year longitudinal study, conducted by Everett Waters and his colleagues, 72 percent of participants received the same attachment classification as adults that they had received as infants.

According to some researchers, whether an individual's attachment classification remains constant over time depends on how well the person's *internal working model,* built up in infancy, functions over time and across situations. Inge Bretherton hypothesizes that the model will guide behavior as long as the child's expectations concerning others' behavior and reactions are met; however, it may change or be replaced in response to experiences that disconfirm the child's expectations, or in response to major transformations in the child's environment. Traumatic events and other negative life experiences can have a large and lasting effect on children's attachment status.

III. THE CHANGING NATURE OF COMMUNICATION

Between 9 and 12 months of age, infants and their caregivers begin to display a new form of connection—**secondary intersubjectivity**—allowing infants and caregivers to share feelings about events beyond themselves, for example, pleasure at seeing a familiar object or event.

A. Social Referencing

An important example of secondary intersubjectivity is **social referencing,** a form of communication in which babies' reactions to unusual situations are affected by their caregivers' facial expressions—the caregivers' reactions tell them whether they should feel apprehensive or reassured. Baby girls are more likely than baby boys to be wary of objects that make their mothers appear worried. Perhaps in consequence, mothers use more intense expressions when communicating with boys. Between 9 and 12 months of age, infants' social referencing becomes more selective. Tricia Striano and Phillipe Rochat found that 7-month-olds, when confronted by a remote-controlled barking dog, "checked" repeatedly with the adult even when the adult did not look at them. In contrast, 10-month-olds stopped looking at the adult if the adult did not glance at them when the dog barked; they appeared to know that they could get information from the adult only when the adult was paying attention to them.

B. Gaze-Following and Pointing

Whereas a 5-month-old does not follow his or her mother's gaze when the mother looks to one side, a 6- or 7-month-old, if the situation is clear and simple, will follow the mother's gaze or pointing finger to see what she is looking at. This ability to look in the direction in which a caregiver gazes or points increases rapidly between 10 and 12 months.

C. The Beginnings of Language Comprehension and Speech

Once babies move around on their own, new forms of vocal communication allow mothers and babies to remain coordinated even when out of sight of one another.

As early as 4 months of age, babies can recognize their own names; by 6 months, they apparently recognize names for familiar objects. According to Roberta Golinkoff and her colleagues, when babies hear a familiar word (for example, their name, or "mommy" or "daddy"), **perceptual scaffolding** occurs, in which the familiar word serves as an anchor for learning the words that immediately precede or follow it. By 9 months, babies begin to understand common expressions such as "Wave bye-bye." The ability to understand language precedes the ability to produce it. Production of language has its roots in the cooing sounds that babies begin to make at 10 to 12 weeks of age. Soon, babies coo and gurgle in response to the voices of others and will even take part in cooing "conversations" when their own sounds are imitated.

Babbling (involving consonant-vowel combinations) begins at about 7 months of age, as a form of vocal play. Babbling is controlled by the brain's left hemisphere, demonstrating that the areas which support language are already active. Early babbling involves practicing sound combinations found in all languages and is the same in all cultures; however, by 9 months, babies begin to drop from their babbling sounds that do not belong to the language they hear every day. In *jargoning,* which begins toward the end of the first year, babies begin to babble with the stress and intonation of the language they are learning and to repeat short utterances in particular situations, as if they have a meaning. By 12 months of age, babies can understand about a dozen simple phrases and say several words themselves.

Deaf infants engage in vocal babbling only if they have residual hearing. In signing homes, however, they babble with their hands.

IV. A SENSE OF SELF

By the time they are 6 months old, infants seem to have an intuitive sense of themselves as people. Locomotion provides them with further experience of their separateness from their caregivers; then, they learn that they can share experiences with others, especially through the use of language.

A. Self-Recognition

Gordon Gallup found that chimpanzees could learn to recognize their images in a mirror and make use of them to find spots of dye that had been surreptitiously painted on their heads. In contrast, a wild-born macaque monkey did not learn to recognize itself despite many hours of exposure to the mirror. A similar procedure has been used with human infants from 3 to 24 months of age. Before 3 months of age, infants show little interest in their mirror images. Beginning at about 4 months of age, infants will touch a mirror image if something interesting is reflected there. Ten-month-olds can use a mirror image to find a toy being lowered behind their backs. However, it is not until approximately 18 months that children begin to identify their own images in the mirror. At that age, if a red spot is applied to a child's nose, he or she will try to touch the spot after seeing it on the mirror image.

B. The Self as Agent

Between 18 and 24 months, about the time that children start to use two-word utterances, they begin to describe their own actions in their speech. Now they see themselves as agents exerting power over their environments.

C. The Emergence of Self-Conscious Emotions

In addition to the six basic emotions displayed at or soon after birth (joy, fear, anger, surprise, sadness, and disgust), at some time after 8 months of age, infants experience certain **self-conscious emotions** such as embarrassment, pride, shame, guilt, and envy. These emotions are linked to children's emerging ability to evaluate their behavior in terms of other people's expectations. So, toddlers may display pride in a new ability or shame at having failed to live up to adult standards.

At the end of infancy, there is a recognizable change in children as a result of their increasing self-awareness, sensitivity to adults' standards, awareness of their own abilities, and ability to create plans of their own. This change, which occurs at about the age of 2, is characterized by children's growing sense of autonomy.

V. DEVELOPING TRUST AND AUTONOMY

As discussed in Chapter 1, Erik Erikson conceived of infancy as divided into two stages. In the first, **basic trust versus mistrust,** the infant determines if the world is either a safe place to explore or a threatening one. Erikson believed that the infant's sense of trust was fostered by warm and responsive parenting; in contrast, unresponsive, insensitive, or disorganized parenting could lead to mistrust of people and the environment.

During their second year, infants enter the second stage, **autonomy versus shame and doubt.** In it, they develop a sense of themselves as either competent or not competent to accomplish tasks. Now they want to do many things for themselves without help. According to Erikson, babies develop confidence in their abilities when their parents structure the environment so that they can be successful in their early efforts; if parents are too controlling or fail to allow them to demonstrate competence, babies' efforts to achieve may be stymied by feelings of doubt and shame.

VI. IMPLICATIONS

During infancy, infants exert their innate biologically based capacities to express their emotions and share them with their social partners. Because their social interactions are influenced by the values and practices of their culture, they serve to draw infants into the lives of others and into participation in the community.

Key Terms

Following are important terms introduced in Chapter 6. Match each term with the letter of the example that best illustrates the term.

1. _____ attachment

2. _____ autonomy versus shame and doubt

3. _____ avoidant attachment

4. _____ babbling

5. _____ basic emotions

6. _____ basic trust versus mistrust

7. _____ biological drives

8. _____ detachment

9. _____ differential emotions theory

10. _____ disorganized attachment

11. _____ emotion

12. _____ emotion regulation

13. _____ internal working model

14. _____ mirror neurons

15. _____ ontogenetic adaptations

16. _____ perceptual scaffolding

17. _____ primary intersubjectivity

18. _____ resistant attachment

19. _____ secondary intersubjectivity

20. _____ secure attachment

21. _____ secure base

22. _____ self-conscious emotions

23. _____ separation anxiety

24. _____ social referencing

25. _____ strange situation

26. _____ theory of gradual differentiation

a. According to Erikson, this is the challenge children confront during the first year of life.
b. This is a phase of development that, according to Erikson, occurs during the second year of life.
c. Hunger and thirst are examples of these.
d. An example is when Suzanne turns her gaze toward the front door, and Brian, her 8-month-old, also stares in that direction.
e. Pride and embarrassment are examples of these.
f. A 1-year-old who plays by himself in the living room, but comes into the kitchen periodically to make contact with his mother is an example.

g. An infant takes part in an experimental study in which her mother leaves her alone in an unfamiliar room, and a strange adult tries to comfort her until her mother returns is an example.

h. A 1-year-old who screams when he notices that his mother has left the room is an example.

i. A 2-year-old who is able to predict her mother's coming and going on the basis of past experiences of being separated from and reunited with her is an example.

j. In children displaying this pattern, a stranger is just as effective at comforting a child as his or her own caregiver would be.

k. This pattern of attachment is the most common among middle-class infants in the United States.

l. These include anger, pleasure, and surprise.

m. This may happen in children who have been separated from their parents for a long time.

n. A baby who plays with language sounds ("ba-ba-ba-ba-ba") is an example.

o. This view is supported by cross-cultural work showing the universality of human facial expressions.

p. Their presence may be what makes it possible for newborns to imitate certain facial expressions of adults.

q. This involves a distinctive physiological response, serves to communicate our feelings to others, is affected by cognition, and is a source of action.

r. These have evolved because they contribute to infants' survival and development.

s. In an Israeli study, this pattern was found more often among babies who slept in communal nurseries than among those who slept in their parents' homes.

t. This development helps children balance their need for safety and their need to explore the environment.

u. We engage in this when we try to modulate and control our feelings and their expression.

v. This term refers to a coordination of mood between infant and caregiver.

w. An example is when a nurse on entering the examination room greets a 10-month-old girl, and the infant glances at her mother's face, then smiles at the newcomer.

x. This term describes how a familiar word can serve as an anchor for learning new words.

y. According to this view, babies are born experiencing only general emotional states that are elaborated over time.

z. Children displaying this pattern seem to lack a coherent method for dealing with the stress of separation from their caregiver.

Multiple-Choice Practice Questions

Circle the letter of the word or phrase that correctly completes each statement.

1. Which of the following is a "basic emotion"?
   a. mistrust
   b. fear
   c. embarrassment
   d. All these are basic emotions.

2. Harriet Oster has suggested that _____ help(s) infants to regulate their distress while maintaining social contact.
   a. pouting
   b. tantrums
   c. maintaining a still face
   d. separation anxiety

3. Between the ages of 7 and 9 months, infants begin to act _____ people and objects or situations that are unfamiliar.
   a. attracted to
   b. attached to
   c. indifferent to
   d. afraid of

4. Which of the following is *not* a sign of attachment to the mother during the first year of life?
   a. The child cries when his mother leaves the room.
   b. The child follows his mother around the house.
   c. The child is perfectly happy to be left by his mother.
   d. The child is happy when his mother returns after a separation.

5. Which of the following is an example of *primary intersubjectivity*?
   a. A child turns her gaze toward the door when her mother looks that way.
   b. Seeing his mother's look of alarm, a child cries when approached by a large dog.
   c. A child takes turns smiling at his mother and being smiled at in return.
   d. A child is upset when he is left with a babysitter while his parents go out.

6. John Bowlby's explanation of attachment emphasizes the role of attachment in
   a. satisfying biological drives.
   b. building trust between infant and caregiver.
   c. promoting the development of object permanence.
   d. balancing safety and exploration.

7. Harry Harlow found that his infant monkeys that were raised by artificial substitute mothers
   a. always became attached to the wire mother, whether they were fed by the wire mother or by the cloth mother.
   b. always became attached to the cloth-covered mother, whether they were fed by the cloth-covered mother or by the wire mother.
   c. always became attached to the mother substitute, wire or cloth, that fed them.
   d. did not derive comfort from either kind of artificial mother.

8. In Mary Ainsworth's "strange situation," _____ children calm down quickly and resume playing when their mothers return after a brief separation.
   a. securely attached
   b. avoidant
   c. resistant
   d. All these answers are correct.

9. Which can cause interference with *primary intersubjectivity* between mother and infant?
   a. a laboratory procedure in which the mother maintains an unmoving facial expression
   b. maternal depression
   c. delayed video transmission of a mother's responses to her infant
   d. All these answers are correct.

10. According to Erik Erikson, around 2 years of age, children become involved in dealing with which of the following issues?
    a. trust
    b. autonomy
    c. separation anxiety
    d. bonding with parents

11. Babies use the process of *perceptual scaffolding* to learn
    a. where others are looking.
    b. the meanings of new words.
    c. to anticipate when the caregiver will return after an absence.
    d. to recognize their mirror images.

12. Children show signs of recognizing their mirror images
    a. starting shortly after birth.
    b. at about the time they develop separation anxiety.
    c. at about the time they begin to describe their own actions.
    d. at about the time they begin preschool.

13. _____ is a form of vocalization that has the intonation and stress of actual utterances.
    a. Cooing
    b. Babbling
    c. Jargoning
    d. One-word speech

14. Self-recognition has been observed in which of the following?
    a. adolescent chimpanzees
    b. macaque monkeys
    c. 3-month-old infants
    d. All these answers are correct.

15. Which of the following is an example of a self-conscious emotion?
    a. embarrassment
    b. anger
    c. sadness
    d. All these answers are correct.

Short-Answer Practice Questions

Write a brief answer in the space below each question.

1. Distinguish the *theory of gradual differentiation* and the *differential emotions theory* as explanations of babies' development. How do both differ from the view of emotional expressions as *ontogenetic adaptations*?

2. Discuss the role of imitation in the development of *intersubjectivity*. What role is the *mirror neuron* system likely to play in this?

3. Describe the phases of attachment to caregivers demonstrated by infants. What developmental and evolutionary purposes are served by parent–infant attachment?

4. What kinds of long-lasting effects result when infants lack consistent, responsive caregiving because they are in institutional care? Are formerly deprived children able to form attachments to adults after infancy? Discuss the research evidence.

5. Discuss the interaction among the following behaviors during infants' second year of life: self-recognition, describing their own actions in speech, and measuring themselves against adult standards. How does this interaction lead to a change in the way adults perceive the child at the end of infancy?

Putting It All Together

Looking back at Chapters 4 and 5, discuss how the development of attachment is related to changes in babies'

- gross motor development.

- memory and reasoning ability.

- resolution of the issues of *basic trust versus mistrust* during the first year and *autonomy versus shame and doubt* during the second year of life.

Sources of More Information

Ames, L., Ilg, F., & Haber, C. (1980). *Your Two-Year-Old.* New York: Dell Publishing.
The authors describe typical 2-year-old behavior in the tradition of Gesell's approach, which emphasizes the role of nature in development.

Bowlby, J. (1988). *A Secure Base: Parent-Child Attachment and Healthy Human Development.* New York: Basic Books.
A discussion of attachment and its role in child rearing by one influential researcher in the field.

Carpenter, M., Nagell, K., & Tomasello, M. (1998). Social cognition, joint attention, and communicative competence from 9 to 15 months of age. *Monographs of the Society for Research in Child Development, 63*(4), Serial No. 255.
This is a monograph describing research on the development of infants' social-cognitive skills.

Erikson, E. (1998). *The Life Cycle Completed: Extended Version.* New York: W.W. Norton.
This is a discussion of Erikson's psychosocial theory of development.

Singer, D., & Singer, J. (1992). *The House of Make-Believe: Children's Play and the Developing Imagination.* Cambridge, MA: Harvard University Press.
This book traces play from birth through adulthood, beginning with its roots in the activities of infants and toddlers.

Walden, T. A., & Ogan, T. A. (1988). The development of social referencing. *Child Development, 59,* 1230–1240.
This study examines the course of development of social referencing in infants from 6 to 22 months of age.

Zucker, K. J. (1985). The infant's construction of his parents in the first six months of life. In *Social Perception in Infants,* Tiffany Field & Nathan Fox (Eds.). Norwood, NJ: Ablex.

Answer Key

Answers to Key Terms: 1.t, 2.b, 3.j, 4.n, 5.l, 6.a, 7.c, 8.m, 9.o, 10.z, 11.q, 12.u, 13.i, 14.p, 15.r, 16.x, 17.v, 18.s, 19.d, 20.k, 21.f, 22.e, 23.h, 24.w, 25.g, 26.y.

Answers to Multiple-Choice Questions: 1.b, 2.a, 3.d, 4.c, 5.c, 6.d, 7.b, 8.a, 9.d, 10.b, 11.b, 12.c, 13.c, 14.a, 15.a.

7

Language Acquisition

One of the most amazing accomplishments of children's preschool years is their rapid acquisition of language. With language, children can make their needs known more clearly and can state their opinions; they also become able to learn more easily from the experiences of others, including those of people who lived generations earlier.

Despite its importance for human beings, language development has yet to be thoroughly explained by developmentalists. No single theory is able to account for all the known facts; however, biological, sociocultural, and cognitive accounts can each explain certain aspects of language acquisition.

As Elizabeth Bates has expressed it, language acquisition may be thought of as learning "to do things with words." In order to be able to do things with words, children must learn to produce the sounds and master the grammatical rules of the language they are learning; they must also learn to select words and constructions that will best express what they want to say.

What experiences must children have in order to learn a language? Certainly, they must be exposed to the language itself. Adults provide children with informal language instruction during the course of socializing them as members of the family and community. And while adults in some cultures engage in more deliberate teaching, such is apparently not necessary for children to communicate in this uniquely human way.

Learning Objectives

Keep these questions in mind while studying Chapter 7.

1. What are the two important keys necessary for language acquisition?
2. What basic biological features are necessary in order for children to be able to acquire language?
3. What is the role of the social environment in children's language acquisition? When children lack social input, what are the effects on language?

4. What are the phonological, semantic, grammatical, and pragmatic domains of language acquisition?
5. How do biological, sociocultural, and cognitive approaches contribute to our understanding of language acquisition?

Chapter Summary

Children's language abilities undergo explosive growth during the period from 2 to 6 years of age.

I. THE POWER OF LANGUAGE

Many species make communicative sounds and gestures, but human language is the most powerful and flexible. As discussed in previous chapters, newborn infants show a preference for human speech over other types of sounds. They are capable of differentiating between *phonemes*—the basic sound categories of language—even those that do not occur in the language they hear spoken around them.

Although initially newborns' only means of vocal communication are facial expressions and crying, their repertoire soon expands to include *cooing,* followed by *babbling* and *jargoning,* as discussed in Chapter 6. At the same time, babies become more skilled at interacting with their social partners. *Primary intersubjectivity,* the face-to-face interaction that appears at about 3 months of age, is accompanied by smiles and vocalizations. It is followed, between the ages of 9 and 12 months, by *secondary intersubjectivity;* now, babies and their social partners can communicate about people, objects, or activities that are the focus of their joint attention. Table 7.1 of the textbook shows the early milestones of language development and the approximate ages at which they are reached.

II. KEYS TO THE WORLD OF LANGUAGE

In order to have access to the world of language, two "keys" are necessary: (1) the biological structures and systems to support language and (2) participation in a language-using community.

A. The Biological Key to Language

Researchers have tackled the question of biological prerequisites in two ways: by inquiring whether other species can comprehend and produce language; and by studying the role of specific brain structures and processes in supporting language acquisition.

• To what extent is the ability to learn language unique to humans? Chimpanzees raised in human families do not learn speech, although they learn to comprehend many spoken words. Chimps have been taught to use manual language and to communicate through symbols on a keyboard. In particular, Sue Savage-Rumbaugh, Duane Rumbaugh, and their colleagues have had a great deal of success with Kanzi, a Bonobo ape. Bonobos have learned to use language to make requests and comments, and can construct two-word utterances. They achieve the ability to produce and comprehend language at roughly the level of 2-year-old human children. However, in contrast to the language learning of human children, they accomplish this only through intensive teaching.

- Adults who suffer damage to the left side of the brain develop *aphasia,* a deficit in the ability to either produce language (*Broca's aphasia*) or comprehend it (*Wernicke's aphasia*); this suggests a localization of language function in the left hemisphere. In fact, in adults, damage to the left hemisphere is far more likely to result in aphasia than damage to the right hemisphere. Neuroimaging studies have shown that Broca's area plays an important role in processing complex sentences (for example, "The song that the boy sang pleased the teacher"); these types of sentences are beyond the processing abilities of nonhuman species. Simple sentences activate an evolutionarily older part of the brain that we share with other primates.

   There is evidence that infants' brains are predisposed to process language in the left hemisphere. For example, when 5-month-old babies babble, their mouths open more on the right side, which is controlled by the left hemisphere of the brain. However, as shown in Figure 7.2 of the textbook, children who suffer damage to the left hemisphere around the time of birth do not lose their ability to acquire language; the greater plasticity of their developing brains allows areas of the right hemisphere to take over language functions.

B. The Environmental Key to Language

Interaction with other people appears crucial for normal language acquisition. For example, Genie, a girl who lived in forced isolation from age 2 to age 13, never acquired more than the basics of language after she was rescued and placed in a family environment. Genie had not had the opportunity to hear other people use language or to make her own attempts to communicate using language; both are important for language acquisition.

- In order to learn about language deprivation in a context that does not involve abuse, affecting all aspects of development, researchers have studied the deaf children of parents who do not know sign language. These children have restricted language experience but otherwise participate normally in family activities. They often learn to communicate in "home sign," a kind of communication through pantomime that they develop themselves. Susan Goldin-Meadow and her colleagues have found that home sign develops the basic features of language, including multiple-part utterances and complex sentence structure. Similar patterns were observed among deaf children of Mandarin-speaking parents in Taiwan. The box "Children Creating a Language" describes the way Nicaraguan sign language developed from what were originally the home signs of a group of deaf children.

   Although home sign can develop into a reasonably complex communication system, it does not develop the more subtle aspects of language that can only be acquired by exposure to accomplished language users. Without additional stimulation, children's language development stalls. Likewise, a hearing child raised by deaf parents, who was neither spoken nor signed to, was found to experience language development at about the same level as the deaf children of nonsigning parents. It seems that children who grow up in an impoverished language environment during the first years of life can develop the rudiments of language, so long as they have someone to communicate with; to fully acquire language, they require a richer linguistic environment.

- Children are exposed to a variety of language-learning environments. For example, some are exposed to more than one language at a time, as discussed in the box "Learning Two Languages." Studies of children learning two languages at once have found that they reach language acquisition milestones at about the same time as monolingual children.
- Adults in different cultures vary in the amount of talk that they direct toward infants. North American mothers direct a great deal of speech toward them, in contrast to mothers from cultures such as the Mayan of Mexico and the Walpiri of Australia. Kaluli mothers in New Guinea use explicit instruction to teach words to their children; similar practices have been observed among Samoans and among working-class mothers in Baltimore, Maryland. Many adults also use **infant-directed speech** (*motherese* or *baby-talk*) when speaking to infants. This is characterized by a high-pitched voice, exaggerated shifts in intonation, simplified vocabulary, and emphasis on the boundaries between meaningful parts of an utterance. Eric Thiessen and his colleagues found that 8-month-olds hearing a string of nonsense words with the pitch and intonation of infant-directed speech could learn the words better than babies hearing them in a more monotone presentation. Table 7.2 of the textbook shows typical simplifications used by U.S. adults when speaking to their children; evidence exists that the complexity of adults' speech to children is related to the complexity of the children's speech.
- Parents also tend to expand on and reformulate children's utterances into more adultlike and grammatically correct versions. Researchers disagree as to whether this deliberate feedback has any effect on children's language development. There is agreement, though, that children's vocabulary development is affected by the amount of language that they hear.

III. THE BASIC DOMAINS OF LANGUAGE ACQUISITION

Phonological development involves learning how to segment strings of speech sounds into meaningful units. It is also necessary to understand the meanings of the words and their combinations; this is called **semantic development.** In order to interpret utterances, it is also necessary to understand **grammar,** the rules for putting words together and sequencing them in sentences. Finally, **pragmatic development** involves learning the social and cultural conventions that govern the way language is used in particular contexts. In practice, these four domains of language work together as a unified system.

A. Phonological Development

It takes children several years to master the pronunciation of the sounds of their native language. Sometimes, mastering pronunciation is complicated by malformations such as cleft lip or palate, as discussed in the box "In the Field: A Speech-Language Pathologist in Vietnam." While children are learning, they compensate for difficulties in pronunciation by leaving out parts of words (saying "ca" when "cat" is meant) or by using the same sound pattern for several similar-sounding words (for example, "bubba" for "baby," "button," and "bub-ble"). In order for children to attend to and pronounce different sounds, the sound differences must be associated with differences in meaning, as /l/ and /y/ in "lard" and "yard." Some-times, two sounds are different in one language but not in another; for example, English speakers hear "boat" and "vote" as distinctly different, whereas Spanish speakers do not. Children must also learn to cope with the fact that words often contain more than one **mor-pheme** or meaning-bearing part. For example, the word "transplanted" is made up of three morphemes: "trans," "plant," and "ed"; "horses" is made up of two: "horse" and "s." Chil-dren learn to apply their knowledge of morphemes to figure out the meanings of new words.

B. Semantic Development

The first real words appear late in the first year and acquire meaning through a joint effort be-tween children and their adult listeners.

- As shown in Figure 7.4 of the textbook, wide variation exists in the rate at which children acquire new words. On average, they say their first words around the time of their first birthday. They can utter about 10 words by 13 to 14 months of age. However, their *recep-tive vocabularies* are larger; when children can say 10 words, they understand approxi-mately 100 words. By 17 to 18 months, children can use about 50 words. This rises to 300 words by the time they reach 2 years of age. Children's first words mainly name fa-miliar objects, especially those on which they can act. Words naming objects that change and move (cars or animals) are more likely to be named than those that are stationary (trees and houses). Nouns account for about half of the words in 2-year-olds' vocabular-ies. They also make use of relational words that refer to changes in state or location ("gone," "here," or "no"). In addition, Allison Gopnik and Andrew Meltzoff found that, beginning at about age 2, children used words ("Hooray!" or "uh-oh") to comment on their successes and failures; this supports the idea, discussed in Chapter 6, that children of this age are sensitive to social expectations.
- Young children's word errors reveal much about their language development. **Overexten-sion** occurs when children apply a word too broadly—for example, calling all animals "doggie." Some typical overextensions are shown in Table 7.3 of the textbook. **Underex-tension** refers to a too narrow application of a word—for example, using the word "cat" to only refer to one particular cat.
- How does children's early vocabulary undergo such a rapid *growth spurt*? Elsa Bartlett and Susan Carey found that preschool children learned the name of an unfamiliar color after one experience in which their teacher introduced the name of the color into class-room conversation. This process—in which children form a quick idea of a word's mean-ing—is called **fast mapping.** Fast mapping has been observed in children as young as 15 months of age. It does not occur in younger babies because they are not yet adept at using social cues to infer a speaker's intention. For example, Shannon Pruden and her col-leagues found that when an experimenter named an object, 10-month-olds tended to apply the name not to the object the experimenter was looking at, but to the object they them-selves found most interesting.

- Soon after they begin to name objects, children start to use figurative language such as **metaphor**—use of a word that draws a comparison between two unrelated things which are similar in some way. The ability to use metaphor—and to understand the metaphors used by others—develops throughout childhood.

C. Grammar Development

Toward the end of infancy, grammar appears in children's speech as they begin to form utterances of two or more words. Now, they can express concepts such as possession and nonexistence and create different meanings by changing the order of the words.

- We know that children have some grasp of grammatical rules early in language development. For example, they are able to use word order to help them interpret sentences that are grammatically correct but contain nonsense words. They can also use grammar to figure out the meaning of new words—a process called **syntactic bootstrapping.** We also see children's awareness of grammatical rules reflected in their speech errors; if Jennifer says "Johnny camed late," we learn that she knows the "ed" sound is used when indicating actions that have already taken place.
- The length of 2- and 3-year-olds' sentences in terms of "mean length of utterance" (MLU), measured in morphemes, increases rapidly, as shown in Figure 7.6 of the textbook, along with their vocabularies and grammatical abilities. Children come to make greater use of **grammatical morphemes** (such as "a" and "ing"), which create meaning by showing the relations between sentence elements. Children are sensitive to grammatical morphemes by the time they begin to produce multiword utterances. The sequence in which they actually appear in children's speech is roughly constant among children learning English. Table 7.4 of the textbook shows the order in which English-speaking children typically acquire these elements of language. The appearance of grammatical morphemes in speech is an indication that children distinguish between nouns and verbs, as they apply correctly the grammatical morphemes appropriate to each.

D. Pragmatic Development

Children often engage in inappropriate language behavior—for example, interrupting adults in the middle of a conversation—because they do not yet understand *pragmatics,* which include the social and cultural conventions for language use. These rules may differ across cultures.

- Utterances can be thought of as **conversational acts,** actions that achieve goals through language. Even children's earliest utterances may be regarded as **protoimperatives,** intended to engage another person to achieve a goal (for example, holding up a cup and saying "more"), or **protodeclaratives,** which serve as ways of referring to things (for example, pointing to a dog and saying "doggie"). Even 2-year-olds are able to understand and respond to indirect commands ("Is the door shut?") as requests for action rather than information. And 3-year-olds can use several different grammatical forms to achieve the same goal.

- As children grow more adept at conversation, they also become more able to tell stories or *narratives*. When Peterson and McCabe asked children to talk about memorable events, they found that typically the children would structure the narrative as a **chronology**—a sequence of events. As the children get older, they are influenced by their culture's way of telling stories, a process called **cultural modeling.**

IV. EXPLANATIONS OF LANGUAGE ACQUISITION

For most of the twentieth century, theories of language acquisition fell into two broad categories, emphasizing either nature or nurture. Today, theorists agree that both biology and the environment are important for language acquisition.

A. Biological Explanations

A maturational explanation of language acquisition was proposed by linguist Noam Chomsky, who has suggested that the ability to acquire language is innate and language is not learned in the same way as other kinds of behavior. Instead, he considers the capacity to comprehend and generate language to be a special property of the human brain. Chomsky has hypothesized that children are born with a **language acquisition device (LAD),** programmed to recognize the rules of whatever language they are exposed to. When young children are acquiring language, they often are very resistant to grammatical correction, lending some support to the biological point of view that language acquisition does not depend on specific teaching. Obviously, the environment plays a role, for example, in determining which language a child learns to speak.

B. Social and Cultural Explanations

Some developmentalists emphasize the close link between the sociocultural environment and children's acquisition of language.

Jerome Bruner has highlighted the importance of **formats**—socially patterned adult–child activities such as "peek-a-boo" and bedtime routines. The formatted activities within which children acquire language provide a **language acquisition support system (LASS),** the environmental complement to Chomsky's LAD.

Interactions with others help children learn word meanings. For example, Michael Tomasello and his colleagues found that mothers talking to young children tended to refer to objects that were already the focus of the child's and mother's attention, making it easier for the children to figure out the referents of new words. It also appears that explicit rewards for learning language are not necessary; children's built-in reward for using new words is their greater ability to communicate.

C. Cognitive Approaches

According to cognitive approaches to understanding language acquisition, children's language development results from development in their thinking and information-processing abilities. For example, at 18 months of age, children can reason about hidden objects and show increasing awareness of social standards; at the same time, they begin to comment on absent objects and describe their own activities in words. Preschoolers' conversational skills also reflect their cognitive development. They may engage in **collective monologues** in which they each voice their own thoughts without taking into consideration what the other speaker is saying. Such interactions result from young children's *egocentrism;* in time they give way to **true dialogue,** in which the utterances of one speaker take into account what the other speaker has said.

- If language acquisition is *not* primarily driven by biology, how do developmentalists explain how children acquire grammatical rules? According to Elizabeth Bates and her colleagues, the mastery of grammatical structures can derive from vocabulary growth combined with children's attempts to express more complex thoughts. Research has found a correlation between vocabulary size and the grammatical complexity of children's utterances, as shown in Figure 7.8 of the textbook.
- How do cognitive impairments influence children's language development? Children with Down syndrome, who have moderate to severe mental retardation, can hold conversations but do not produce or understand grammatically complex speech. This suggests that normal cognitive functioning is necessary for normal language. However, children with Williams syndrome also have mental retardation but possess better language skills than those with Down syndrome; this suggests that some aspects of language may develop independently of general cognitive functioning.

V. RECONSIDERING THE KEYS TO LANGUAGE

Questions about how children learn to produce and understand language are still only partially answered. Perhaps, as Jerome Bruner has suggested, language results from the union of the LAD and the LASS. And although explicit instruction appears unnecessary for early language acquisition, it plays a more important role as children grow older and receive specialized instruction in specific skills that will prepare them for adult life in their culture.

Key Terms

Following are important terms introduced in Chapter 7. Match each term with the letter of the example that best illustrates the term.

1. _____ chronology

2. _____ collective monologues

3. _____ conversational acts

4. _____ cultural modeling

5. _____ fast mapping

6. _____ formats

7. _____ grammar

8. _____ grammatical morphemes

9. _____ infant-directed speech

10. _____ language acquisition device (LAD)

11. _____ language acquisition support system (LASS)

12. _____ metaphor

13. _____ morphemes

14. _____ overextension

15. _____ phonological development

16. _____ pragmatic development

17. _____ protodeclaratives

18. _____ protoimperatives

19. _____ semantic development

20. _____ syntactic bootstrapping

21. _____ true dialogue

22. _____ underextension

a. These involve using language to accomplish goals.

b. This is the way children form a quick idea of a word's meaning when they hear it in a structured situation.

c. An 18-month-old does this when he applies the word "doggie" to all four-legged animals.

d. An example is when a toddler says "More!" while holding up her cup.

e. Young children often use this simple structure when telling stories.

f. This is the hypothetical structure that underlies children's ability to acquire language, according to linguist Noam Chomsky.

g. A child is doing this when she uses the word "dog" only for images of dogs rather than real dogs.

h. Some examples are "ing," "the," and "ed."

i. These rules determine the ordering of words in sentences and the ordering of parts within words.

j. A verbal exchange in which young children each speak without paying attention to what the other is saying is called this.

k. This term refers to using one's knowledge of grammar to help figure out what a new word means.

l. Jerome Bruner uses this term to refer to the totality of the events within which children are led to acquire language.

m. Learning that it is appropriate to speak more formally to teachers than to family members is an example.

n. The ritualized routines of bedtime are examples of these.

o. A person using this speaks in a high-pitched voice and simplifies his or her speech in many ways.

p. A conversation between two people in which each takes into account what the other person has said is called this.

q. This is the unit used in calculating a child's "mean length of utterance" (MLU).

r. An example is saying "He has a cold heart."

s. Learning to segment speech sounds into meaningful units of language is called this.

t. These are used early in language development to help establish joint attention and sustain a dialogue.

u. This refers to the process of learning the meanings of words and combinations of words.

v. These are ways of telling stories that are specific to a particular culture.

Multiple-Choice Practice Questions

Circle the letter of the word or phrase that correctly completes each statement.

1. Chimpanzees raised in human environments
    a. communicate with sounds but not with gestures.
    b. have successfully learned the rudiments of human vocal language.
    c. have learned to communicate in simple ways using nonvocal languages.
    d. have demonstrated language development comparable to that of 4-year-old children.

2. Damage to which of the following regions of the brain results in a type of aphasia in which people are capable of producing language, but produce utterances that do not make sense?
    a. the prefrontal area
    b. Wernicke's area
    c. Broca's area
    d. the motor cortex

3. The aspect of language that deals with the ordering of words in sentences and the ordering of parts within words is called
    a. pragmatics.
    b. phonetics.
    c. semantics.
    d. grammar.

4. Children who suffer brain damage to the left hemisphere at birth
    a. never develop the ability to use or comprehend language.
    b. learn to comprehend language but not to produce it.
    c. localize language functions in the right hemisphere.
    d. learn to produce language at the level of normal 2-year-olds.

5. Susan Goldin-Meadow found that deaf children whose hearing parents did not sign to them
    a. developed a simple form of signing on their own.
    b. became mentally retarded.
    b. learned on their own to speak orally.
    d. never developed any form of language.

6. The speech of American adults to young children
   a. is not significantly different from their speech to adults.
   b. is more repetitive, but otherwise similar to their speech to adults.
   c. is slower, but otherwise similar to their speech to adults.
   d. is simpler, with higher pitch and clearer pronunciation, than their speech to adults.

7. The sounds that are meaningful in a particular language are called
   a. morphemes.
   b. graphemes.
   c. phonemes.
   d. protodeclaratives.

8. Which of the following utterances contains five morphemes?
   a. "Kitty!"
   b. "John is eating an apple."
   c. "She jumps rope fast."
   d. "Bobby, have some gum."

9. Which of the following is an example of "overextension"?
   a. using the word "bird" for both a parakeet and a baby chick
   b. calling a cow "doggie"
   c. using the word "eeow" to refer to all cats
   d. saying "fis" instead of "fish"

10. Most of children's earliest vocabulary consists of
    a. nouns used to name objects.
    b. grammatical morphemes.
    c. verbs used to describe actions.
    d. adjectives used to describe things.

11. The experiment by Elsa Bartlett and Susan Carey, in which preschool children learned the name of a new color, illustrates the role of _____ in language acquisition.
    a. holophrase
    b. grammatical morphemes
    c. explicit teaching
    d. fast mapping

12. Children's ability to understand and use metaphor starts at about the time they
    a. first begin to produce sounds.
    b. begin to name objects.
    c. begin elementary school.
    d. reach adolescence.

13. Grammatical morphemes
    a. are rules for ordering words in sentences.
    b. are the same in all languages.
    c. are likely to appear in all children's speech in about the same order.
    d. do not appear in children's speech until the end of the preschool period.

14. A toddler is using a "protodeclarative" when she
    a. points to a dog and says, "doggie."
    b. hands a cup to her mother and says, "more."
    c. says "yes" when her mother asks, "Is the door shut?"
    d. looks at her mother when a stranger says, "Hello."

15. When young children are asked to tell a story about an experience, their account is typically in the form of
    a. a dialogue.
    b. a metaphor.
    c. a fantasy.
    d. a chronology.

16. Which of the following theorists has hypothesized a language acquisition device (LAD) that is programmed to recognize universal linguistic rules?
    a. Jean Piaget
    b. Lev Vygotsky
    c. Elizabeth Bates
    d. Noam Chomsky

17. According to Piaget, toddlers' conversations take the form of "collective monologues" because
    a. they do not have large enough vocabularies to carry on dialogues.
    b. they are not yet able to take account of another's viewpoint.
    c. they need to be instructed in the rules of conversation.
    d. their receptive language skills lag behind their ability to speak.

18. Elizabeth Bates found which relationship between the complexity of children's grammar and the size of their vocabularies?
    a. The larger children's vocabularies, the less complex the grammar they use.
    b. The larger children's vocabularies, the more complex the grammar they use.
    c. Grammatical complexity and vocabulary are both related to age, but are not related to one another.
    d. No relationship exists between grammatical complexity and vocabulary until children are at least 4 years of age.

Short-Answer Practice Questions

Write a brief answer in the space below each question.

1. Discuss the evidence that the human brain is specialized for language acquisition.

2. What similarities and differences are there between language as it is learned by human children and by nonhuman primates?

3. To what experiences must children be exposed in order to acquire language? What happens if these requirements are not met?

4. In what ways do parents in various cultures arrange the environment in order to support infants in learning to understand language?

5. How is the language acquisition of bilingual children similar to and different from that of children learning a single language?

6. How do children use their knowledge of grammar to help them interpret the meaning of new words?

Putting It All Together I

Match each milestone in language development with the age at which it occurs. You may want to refer back to material in earlier chapters.

_____ 1. Children can perceive the categorical sound distinctions used in all the world's languages.

_____ 2. Children's language typically contains overextensions.

_____ 3. Children's conversations take the form of collective monologues.

_____ 4. Children begin to practice consonant-vowel combinations.

_____ 5. Children's vocalizations take on the intonation and stress patterns that characterize the language they are learning.

_____ 6. Children respond to others' voices with cooing and gurgling sounds.

a. at birth
b. at about 12 weeks of age
c. at about the middle of the first year
d. toward the end of the first year
e. at 2 years of age
f. during the preschool period

Putting It All Together II

Match up the facts about language development with the approach that most strongly explains them. Refer back to previous chapters when necessary.

_____ 1. Babies can distinguish categorical differences between phonemes.

_____ 2. Children's earliest "words" usually do not have clear meanings and must be interpreted by adults.

_____ 3. Children acquire much of their early vocabularies by repeating the names they hear others give to objects.

_____ 4. Deaf babies begin to "babble" manually at about the same time as hearing babies begin to babble.

_____ 5. Changes in some of children's early sensorimotor accomplishments—for example, self-recognition and object permanence—appear to be related to changes in the ways they use words.

_____ 6. Grammatical complexity of children's utterances is related to the size of their vocabulary.

_____ 7. Compared with nonhuman primates, children pick up human language quite easily.

a. nativist theories
b. social and cultural explanations
c. cognitive approaches

Sources of More Information

Bialystock, E. (2001). *Bilingualism in Development: Language, Literacy and Cognition.* New York: Cambridge University Press.
The author explores how growing up bilingual affects language acquisition, cognition, and educational performance.

Boysson-Bardies, B. (1999). *How Language Comes to Children: The First Two Years.* Cambridge, MA: MIT Press.
A French psycholinguist explains the course of language development during the first two years of life.

Hart, B., & Risley, T. (1995). *Meaningful Differences in the Everyday Experience of Young American Children.* Baltimore, MD: Brookes Publishing.
The authors, who work in the social learning tradition, report on a study that demonstrates how the amount of language interaction between parents and children translates into differences in children's later achievement.

Lenneberg, E. (1969). On explaining language. *Science, 164*(3880), 635–643.
A classic discussion of the biological underpinnings of language development that demonstrates varying approaches to the study of language acquisition need not be antagonistic.

Pepperberg, I. (2000). *The Alex Studies: Cognitive and Communicative Abilities in Grey Parrots.* Cambridge, MA: Harvard University Press.
The subject of much of this research is an African Grey parrot named Alex; one of the most interesting aspects of the work is how language is acquired by interacting with others and by watching them interact with one another.

Pinker, S. (1994). *The Language Instinct.* New York: HarperCollins.
The author, working in the tradition that emphasizes nature over nurture, regards language as an evolutionary adaptation used by humans for communication.

Savage-Rumbaugh, S., Shanker, S., & Taylor, T. (1998). *Apes, Language and the Human Mind.* New York: Oxford University Press.
This volume presents information on language learning by Kanzi, a bonobo, and its implications for understanding how human language has evolved.

Answer Key

Answers to Key Terms: 1.e, 2.j, 3.a, 4.v, 5.b, 6.n, 7.i, 8.h, 9.o, 10.f, 11.l, 12.r, 13.q, 14.c, 15.s, 16.m, 17.t, 18.d, 19.u, 20.k, 21.p, 22.g.

Answers to Multiple-Choice Questions: 1.c, 2.b, 3.d, 4.c, 5.a, 6.d, 7.c, 8.c, 9.b, 10.a, 11.d, 12.b, 13.c, 14.a, 15.d, 16.d, 17.b, 18.b.

Answers to Putting It All Together I: 1.a, 2.e, 3.f, 4.c, 5.d, 6.b.

Answers to Putting It All Together II: 1.a, 2.b, 3.b, 4.a, 5.c, 6.c, 7.a.

8 CHAPTER

Physical and Cognitive Development in Early Childhood

Although they now can represent things to themselves, children between 2 and 5 years of age often display thinking abilities that appear strangely uneven. Their reasoning may be perfectly logical when applied in familiar contexts, but startlingly illogical in less familiar domains.

Piaget's account of thinking during early childhood has been the starting point for several explanations of preschoolers' development, and the phenomena he observed, including egocentrism, precausal reasoning, and appearance/reality confusions, continue to be of interest to contemporary developmentalists. Competing approaches also attempt to explain development; these approaches focus either on information-processing, privileged domains, or the way culturally organized activities support children's thought.

At the start of early childhood, children can walk well, feed themselves with a spoon, and turn the pages of a book. By the time they begin kindergarten, they can skate or ride a scooter, get dressed without help, and even print simple letters. Similar development takes place in their thinking skills. Young children need to learn many things about the world around them, including that stones cannot melt, that there is a real person behind a clown costume, and that other people will probably assume a box with a picture of candy on its cover is really a box of candy, whether it is or not.

Learning Objectives

Keep these questions in mind while studying Chapter 8.

1. What kinds of changes take place in children's brains and bodies during the preschool years?
2. What are the characteristics of preschool children's thinking, according to Piaget? Does children's thinking invariably illustrate these characteristics?

3. What factors contribute to improvements in children's thinking during early childhood, according to information-processing approaches?

4. What evidence exists for privileged domains in children's cognitive development? How do different approaches explain domain-specific development?

5. How does a child's culture serve to organize his or her exposure to events and how does this affect the child's ability to reason about them?

6. Under what circumstances does young children's cognitive development appear to be a continuous process? Under what conditions does it appear stagelike?

Chapter Summary

Children in the 2- to 5-year-old age range are uneven in their performance on intellectual tasks—sometimes logical and sometimes illogical, sometimes reasonable and sometimes irrational. Some theorists regard development as stagelike and discontinuous; they tend to see this unevenness of performance as unimportant. According to this view, children's underlying *competence* is said to be at a particular level, but with variations in *performance* depending on how a task is presented or the child's familiarity with it. In contrast, theorists who view development as continuous consider the unevenness of children's performance to be evidence that development occurs through gradual increases in various psychological mechanisms such as short-term memory capacity.

I. PHYSICAL AND MOTOR DEVELOPMENT

Children's bodies and brains grow at a slower rate during early childhood than they did during infancy.

A. Motor Development

Children's motor abilities develop rapidly during early childhood, as shown in Table 8.1 of the textbook. At 2 years of age, they can already run and go up and down stairs without help; at 3 years, they can ride a tricycle. Four-year-olds can throw a ball overhand. At this point, they demonstrate high **motor drive**—that is, they take great pleasure in their ability to control their bodies and enjoy practicing their motor skills whenever possible. By 5 years of age, children can hop and skip, skate, and ride a scooter. Their fine motor skills undergo similar development: they progress from using a spoon and turning the pages of a book at 2 years of age to dressing themselves without help, drawing, using scissors, printing letters, and even tying their own shoes by 5 years of age.

B. Health

With slower growth in early childhood, children's appetites diminish somewhat and they may become finicky about food; nonetheless, they need to eat enough nourishing food for good health. Young children may also get less sleep than they need, which can cause them to be overly emotional and have trouble concentrating.

- Pediatricians recommend that young children sleep 12 to 15 hours in a 24-hour period (including naps). However, according to Christine Acebo and her colleagues, 2- to 5-year-olds typically get less than 9.5 hours of sleep per day. Most children in their study woke often at night, particularly those from low-income families. The effects of sleep deprivation on young children are not yet known.

- In many areas of the world, children are breast-fed at least into the third year of life. However, in most industrialized countries, they are weaned by 2 years of age. Growth patterns in the early years have implications for later physical development. For example, children who are overweight between 2 and 4 years of age are five times more likely to be overweight in adolescence than those of normal weight during early childhood. There is also risk associated with being underweight early in life, as revealed by a Finnish study. The researchers found that the people at greatest risk of cardiovascular disease as adults were those who were underweight during the first two years of life and later underwent a period of rapid weight gain during early and later childhood. A similar pattern has been revealed in a study of children in China, India, Guatemala, Brazil, and the Philippines. These countries have been experiencing an increase in calories, fats, and sugars in children's diets; this is accompanied by higher risk for diabetes and heart disease when the children reach adulthood.

- In many regions of the world, more than 40 percent of preschool children experience stunted growth because of inadequate nutrition; in the United States, 11 percent of families are considered **food insecure**—lacking sufficient food to ensure good health—and 4 percent are considered "food insecure with hunger." Children's nutrition is also affected by parental attitudes toward food and body image stereotypes. For example, parents may want their sons to be "big and strong," while preferring their daughters to be thin.

C. Brain Development

By age 5, children's brains have attained 90 percent of their adult weight. Much of the growth results from *myelination*, especially in the areas of the frontal cortex that are involved in planning and regulating behavior. Neurons become longer and develop more branches, allowing new connections between different brain areas. At the same time, *synaptic pruning* continues as unused synapses are eliminated.

Unevenness in both the levels of maturity of brain areas and the myelination of connections between areas can account for some of the unevenness seen in young children's performance on cognitive tasks; higher levels of performance can be expected to occur when a task calls on brain systems that are already highly developed. When areas are not yet well developed or connected, interesting errors in performance may occur. For example, 18- to 30-month-olds typically commit **scale errors** in which they fail to take into account information about an object's size. Thus, they may try to fit a large peg into a small hole or to fit themselves into a doll-sized chair. Culture plays a role in early childhood brain development. Culturally important activities promote *experience-dependent* synaptic proliferation in children's brains, thus influencing which areas are likely to undergo development.

II. PREOPERATIONAL DEVELOPMENT

According to Piaget's theoretical framework, once children have completed the sensorimotor sub-stages, they are able to engage in representational thinking. By 7 to 8 years of age, they will be capable of **mental operations** such as logically combining, separating, and transforming information. During the **preoperational stage,** cognitive development can be viewed as a process of overcoming the limitations that stand in the way of logical thinking, outlined in Table 8.2 of the textbook.

A. Centration

The greatest limitation to preoperational thinking, Piaget hypothesized, is the tendency toward **centration**, the focusing of attention on one aspect of an object or a problem while ignoring others. The key to cognitive growth beyond the preoperational stage is **decentration,** the ability to pull away from focusing on one aspect of an object or problem in order to consider multiple aspects of it. This mental distancing allows the development of **objectivity,** which Piaget regarded as the most important goal of cognitive development. Piaget viewed all of cognitive development, from infancy through adolescence, as a march toward objectivity, an aspect of scientific reasoning. However, in preschool children, centration results in several common errors of reasoning: egocentrism; confusing appearance and reality; and precausal reasoning.

- Piaget believed that preschool-aged children consider the world entirely from their own point of view and that this **egocentrism** is the cause of some of their difficulties in problem solving. A famous example of egocentrism is the "three-mountain problem"; when asked to select the view that would be seen by a doll placed at the opposite side of a diorama, preschoolers tend to instead choose a picture showing the scene from their own viewpoint. However, when Helen Borke modified the three-mountain task to represent a more familiar scene, even 3-year-olds demonstrated that they could imagine perspectives different from their own. The two versions of the task are logically identical; however, Borke concluded, although young children may have the *competence* to take the perspectives of others, their *performance* is affected by the demands of the task.
- Their tendency to focus attention on a single aspect of a stimulus may make it difficult for preschoolers to separate appearance from reality. Rheta De Vries showed children a cat wearing a dog mask. Most of the 3-year-olds believed that the cat had become a dog, whereas the 6-year-olds were confident that such a transformation was impossible. Interestingly, while 4- to 5-year-olds realized that a cat could not become a dog, they had difficulty in correctly answering questions such as "Can it bark?" John Flavell and his colleagues found appearance/reality confusion in children under 4 years of age in a variety of cultures. However, Carl Huelsksen and his colleagues showed that 3- and 4-year-olds could tell that a person dressed up in a costume was still the same person. And Catherine Rice and her colleagues found that young children showed understanding of the appearance/reality distinction when the knowledge was expressed as part of a task in which the children aided the experimenter in "fooling" another adult with a deceptive-

looking object. According to a study by Felicity Sapp and her colleagues, the difficulty for 3-year-olds is verbally expressing appearance/reality distinctions; when given the opportunity to respond nonverbally, children's responses were usually correct.

● When engaging in **precausal thinking,** preschoolers confuse cause and effect. According to Piaget, they think *transductively* (from particular to particular) rather than following the rules of inductive (from specific cases to general principles) or deductive (from general premises to particular cases) reasoning. For example, one child believed that, given their association with death, graveyards caused people to die and that, by avoiding graveyards, one could avoid dying. However, Merry Bullock and Rochel Gelman showed that even 3-year-olds grasped the working of an apparatus that caused a Snoopy doll to pop up when a marble was dropped into one of two slots, although 5-year-olds offered more adequate verbal explanations of the task. Still, later research has indicated that when a cause–effect problem is slightly complicated, 3-year-olds become confused and can neither solve nor explain it.

B. The Problem of Uneven Levels of Performance

The characteristics of preoperational thinking, shown in Table 8.2 of the textbook, show why Piaget considered young children to have difficulty in decentering their thinking. The box "Bearing Witness: Can Young Children Tell the Truth?" reveals how children's cognitive limitations may prove challenging when it is important to get from them an accurate account of events, as in a court case, and how improved interviewing methods can help. We have also seen how modifying tasks, especially by decreasing reliance on verbal interviews, has shown greater unevenness in development than was suggested by Piaget. Some researchers are pursuing alternatives to Piaget's concept of a preoperational stage in early childhood. Information-processing approaches account for cognitive change and unevenness in children's performance through general mechanisms such as an increase in short-term memory capacity and knowledge. Other competing approaches de-emphasize general mechanisms and focus on domain-specific psychological processes.

III. INFORMATION-PROCESSING APPROACHES TO COGNITIVE DEVELOPMENT

Information-processing models view people's thought processes as analogous to the workings of a computer, with the brain being analogous to the computer's hardware (*structural* components) and the activities and practices used by individuals for the purpose of remembering and using information being analogous to the computer's software (programs written to *process* information through the system). As shown in Figure 8.7 of the textbook, information is seen as first entering a *sensory register*, from which it is read into *short-term (working) memory*, where it is stored for several seconds and combined with information about past experiences from *long-term memory*. As shown in Figure 8.7, the flow of information is coordinated by *control processes*, such as attention, rehearsal, retrieval strategies, and decision making. According to this perspective, young children may experience difficulties at any point in the information-processing process. For example, when faced with a task, they may have trouble controlling their attention, or their ability to transfer information from short- to long-term memory may be slow, causing them to forget some of the information they need to use. Researchers who study children's memory have found that changes in "software"—that is, changes in the ways information is encoded, stored, and retrieved—are behind much of the improvement in children's memories during early childhood. One factor that is especially important is the increase in children's knowledge, which gives them a structure for incorporating new information. Another factor involves assistance from adults; children remember things better if adults talk with them about experiences as they unfold. In particular, children's memories improve when their mothers use an **elaborative style** in interacting with them, asking *wh-questions*, relating new information to the child's existing knowledge, following and discussing aspects of the events that the child finds interesting, and praising the child's verbal and nonverbal contributions to the interaction.

As preschool children grow older, the maturation of their brains and development of more efficient information-processing strategies contribute to improvements in cognitive performance and a reduction of the unevenness characteristic of this period.

IV. COGNITIVE DEVELOPMENT IN PRIVILEGED DOMAINS

Whereas Piaget's approach and that of information-processing theorists emphasize the importance of general intellectual processes in cognitive development, some developmentalists focus instead on changes within specific areas, known as **privileged domains,** that have evolutionary significance for humans. Research has focused mainly on the domains of physics, psychology, and biology.

A. The Domain of Physics

Naïve physics refers to children's early understanding of physical phenomena—for example, objects bumping into one another or water freezing into ice. As was seen in Chapter 5, infants have some understanding of physical laws—for example, that an object cannot pass through a physical barrier. As in infant studies, the violation-of-expectations method has been used in many investigations of young children's naïve physics. Kyong Kim and Elizabeth Spelke, studying children from infancy to 6 years of age, found that, while infants showed no understanding of the principles of gravity or inertia, 2-year-olds exhibited the beginning of understanding; 6-year-olds showed an appreciation of both concepts, although they had not fully mastered either one. Terry Au and her colleagues demonstrated that 3-year-old children understood physical substances still exist even after undergoing radical transformations such as being pulverized and then dissolved in water. Thus, by the time they are 5 or 6 years of age, children have developed ideas about the physical world that are the same as those of people everywhere.

B. The Domain of Psychology

Naïve psychology refers to children's early understanding of the relationship between people's mental states and their behavior. By the end of the first year, infants have some understanding that other people's actions are caused by their goals and intentions. Two-year-olds can make the distinction between their own and others' desires. Children's ability to understand others' mental states increases throughout early childhood; during this period, they develop a **theory of mind**—that is, they develop the ability to think about other people's mental states and form theories about how they think. Researchers study children's theory of mind using a **false-belief task,** in which the child, or a story character, is fooled into believing something that is not true. In a typical example, a child is shown a box on which a picture of candy appears. When asked what the box contains, the child says "candy" but finds, upon opening the box, that it holds pencils. Next, the child is asked what a friend who has not seen inside the box will believe it contains. Typically, 3-year-olds say that the friend will think the box contains "pencils" despite the picture of candy on it and despite their own experience of having been fooled. However, just as children show more advanced reasoning on Piagetian tasks when the problem is posed differently, they perform better on false-belief tasks when they are allowed to serve as co-conspirators with an adult accomplice to fool the experimenter. Kate Sullivan and Ellen Winner arranged such a task and found that 75 percent of 3-year-olds correctly predicted the experimenter's false belief compared to only 25 percent in the standard version of the task. In the scripted activity of "fooling someone else," the children were primed to think about another person's mental state. The ability to contemplate others' mental states seems to be in transition at 3 years of age and to become more solidified by 4 or 5 years of age.

C. The Domain of Biology

Young children's *naïve biology* has, as its starting point, making the distinction between living and nonliving things. Christine Massey and Rochel Gelman showed that 3- to 4-year-olds made correct generalizations about living creatures based on the ability for self-initiated movement. Young children also know that living things grow and change appearance and that, if neglected (for example, not given water), they may die. Developmentalists are not certain of how naïve biology originates; possibly, it is an outgrowth of naïve psychology that differentiates as children gain experience with living things.

D. Explaining Domain-Specific Cognitive Development

There are three major approaches to explaining knowledge acquisition in privileged domains: these emphasize either *modularity theory*, *theory theory*, or the culturally organized environment.

- Some theorists explain domain-specific intelligence in terms of **mental modules**—innate mental faculties that receive information from particular classes of objects in the environment and produce corresponding domain-specific information about the world. Modules are thought of as distinct from all others, with little interaction; it is believed that they are present at the start of development and need only to be triggered by environmental input. A line of evidence used to support modularity theory comes from studies of children with **autism**—a condition defined by the inability to relate normally to others. More information about autism appears in the box "In the Field: Supporting Brothers and Sisters of

Children with Autism." Interestingly, autistic children of any age may perform at the level of 3-year-olds on a false-belief task, despite much more advanced abilities in other areas; this suggests the possible existence of a "theory-of-mind" module. Simon Baron-Cohen and his colleagues conducted a study in which they asked 4-year-olds to arrange picture cards to make stories. The children were either autistic, mentally retarded, or developing typically. When the stories involved mechanical sequences, the autistic children outperformed the typically developing children; they were equally proficient on behavioral sequences involving obvious emotions. But when the stories involved mental events, the autistic children could not create meaningful sequences and performed worse than children in the other groups. In contrast, the mentally retarded children performed at much the same level on each type of sequence. Autistic children have also been found to perform well on naïve biology tasks and better than typically developing children on naïve physics tasks; in fact, they tended to apply physical reasoning to the psychological domain. Such findings have led some developmentalists to argue for the existence of isolated modules and to view autism as rooted in a defect in the theory-of-mind module.

- If autism can be explained by a defect in a theory-of-mind module, why do autistic children often improve when placed in intensive therapeutic programs? Modularity theory does not address the question of how experience influences domain-specific development. A theory that does tackle this question is **theory theory,** the theory that young children have primitive theories about how the world works, and that these theories influence how children think about and act within specific domains. Over time, children modify these theories in light of their experiences. Like scientific theory testing, children's thinking within privileged domains is accompanied by causal explanations and generates reasonable predictions. Parents, with the information they provide, as well as teachers, peers, and personal experience help children to construct their knowledge base.

- A third approach to explaining domain-specific development focuses on the importance of language and culture. For example, some cultures have many words for emotions; others have relatively few. It is unknown if lack of terminology for mental states has an effect on children's development of naïve psychology. No delay occurs with respect to performance on standard false-belief tasks. On other tasks, researchers have found delays or even the absence of the kind of theory of mind assumed by privileged-domain theorists to exist in all children. In countries where talk about mental processes is prevalent, children who hear a great deal of conversation about mental processes tend to demonstrate earlier on theory-of-mind tasks.

Cultural influences may be associated with beliefs that deviate from the knowledge thought to be part of privileged domains. For example, people may believe in magic or think that people can transform themselves into animals. It can also be argued that the very idea of domain-specific knowledge is at odds with the belief systems of many non-Western cultures.

V. COGNITIVE DEVELOPMENT AND CULTURE

As discussed in Chapter 1, Vygotsky's sociocultural theory has had a great impact on understanding how development is affected by the cultural contexts in which children participate. Cultural activities expand children's knowledge about the world; the resulting *cultural scripts* help explain both how this knowledge is gained and how culture may contribute to the unevenness of knowledge observed in young children.

A. Cultural Scripts

Children construct general event representations called **scripts** for routine events such as taking a bath, eating a meal, and going to a restaurant. Scripts specify who participates in an event, the social roles participants play, the objects that are used, and the sequence of actions that make up the event. Initially, scripts (taking a bath, for example) are more external to the child than internal; a bath is something done to, rather than done by, an infant. As children become more capable and more familiar with the scripted activity, they take on more active roles. Katherine Nelson points out that children rarely experience the world "raw"; instead, they experience it in a way that has been prepared according to the scripts prescribed by their culture.

Scripts include general knowledge (for example, what happens when you go to a restaurant) rather than specific information about a single experience (a particular restaurant visit). They are guides to action that tell children what to expect. Scripted knowledge frees them to attend to more than the superficial details of an activity; it also helps them coordinate their activities with others who share the same scripts. According to Nelson, knowing the script is a marker of maturity and adaptation.

B. Cultural Context and the Unevenness of Development

In familiar contexts, where they have scripted knowledge, young children may behave logically and in accordance with adult standards of thought. When contexts are unfamiliar, they may resort to illogical or magical thinking or may apply scripts inappropriate to the situation. Cultures influence the unevenness of children's development by (1) making specific activities available; (2) determining the frequency of basic activities; (3) relating different activities to each other; and (4) regulating the child's role in any activity.

VI. RECONCILING ALTERNATIVE APPROACHES

No single approach provides a complete explanation for the unevenness of young children's thinking. There is evidence for domain-specific and general changes; sometimes development appears stagelike and discontinuous, and other times it appears gradual. Kurt Fischer has emphasized the importance of the interaction between the specific cognitive processes being investigated and the context in which they occur. He proposes that, when the context provides support, change will appear more stagelike; however, when support is absent or the context provides distractions, change will appear more continuous.

Key Terms

Following are important terms introduced in Chapter 8. Match each term with the letter of the example that best illustrates the term.

1. _____ autism

2. _____ centration

3. _____ decentration

4. _____ egocentrism

5. _____ elaborative style

6. _____ false-belief task

7. _____ food insecure

8. _____ mental modules

9. _____ mental operations

10. _____ motor drive

11. _____ objectivity

12. _____ precausal thinking

13. _____ preoperational stage

14. _____ privileged domains

15. _____ scale errors

16. _____ scripts

17. _____ theory of mind

18. _____ theory theory

a. These refer to generalized event representations that specify the people, objects, and behaviors involved in, for example, birthday parties or a trip to the dentist.

b. Children with this disorder do not relate normally to others; however, they may demonstrate great ability in specific areas such as music or drawing.

c. A preschooler who points at a picture in a book and asks, "What's this?" not understanding that her mother can see only the outside of the book and not the picture she is indicating is showing this.

d. These involve mentally combining, separating, or transforming information within a logical system.

e. Examples are physics, psychology, and biology.

f. When John tells his preschool teacher, "When the trees outside move, it makes the wind," he is demonstrating this.

g. According to Piaget, this is a period during which children's thought is representational but not yet logical.

h. The ability to think about the mental states of others is called this.

i. According to some theorists, language is best explained as being one of these.

j. An example is when Lou tries to force a peg into a hole that is obviously too small.

k. This is used in research studies to determine what children know about what others are thinking.

l.   This important feature of scientific thinking is, according to Piaget, the main goal of cognitive development.

m. The tendency to be "captured" by one aspect of a stimulus or event and fail to take other aspects into account is called this.

n.   An example is when four-year-old Michelle runs and jumps just for the joy of movement.

o.   In this theory, developmental researchers hypothesize that young children have ideas about what others are thinking and that the children revise these ideas based on their experiences.

p.   That Derek's family does not always have enough food to ensure that everyone can stay healthy is an example.

q.   When Jaime's mother takes him to the zoo, she asks him questions about what the animals are doing and reminds him of what they have learned about them from their animal book at home is an example.

r.   Six-year-old Jessica is not fooled when the experimenter instructs her to show him "the big glass." She asks, "Which one, the big tall one or the big wide one?" Jessica is demonstrating this.

Multiple-Choice Practice Questions

Circle the letter of the word or phrase that correctly completes each statement.

1. By the time they are 5 years of age, children's brains have attained _____ of their adult weight.
    a. 25 percent
    b. 50 percent
    c. 65 percent
    d. 90 percent

2. According to studies carried out in several countries, the greatest risk of cardiovascular disease was found among adults who
    a. were overweight from the time of infancy.
    b. were thin until adulthood and later gained weight.
    c. were underweight for the first 2 or 3 years of life and then became overweight.
    d. were overweight during childhood and later became thin.

3. According to researchers, 2- to 5-year-olds sleep
    a. more than they did during infancy.
    b. more than is healthy.
    c. less than they should sleep.
    d. less than adults do.

4. In Piaget's framework, early childhood is associated with the _____ stage of development.
   a. sensorimotor
   b. preoperational
   c. concrete operational
   d. postsymbolic

5. Which of the following characterize(s) young children's thought, according to Piaget?
   a. inability to reason about others' points of view
   b. ability to think logically
   c. inability to use representation
   d. All these answers are correct.

6. When Rheta De Vries put a dog mask on a cat,
   a. 3-year-olds seemed to believe that the cat had become a dog.
   b. 4- and 5-year-olds could not give correct answers to questions such as "Can it bark?"
   c. 6-year-olds knew that the cat only looked like a dog.
   d. All these answers are correct.

7. Which of the following is "precausal" reasoning?
   a. reasoning from general premises to particular cases
   b. reasoning from specific cases to general conclusions
   c. reasoning from one particular case to another
   d. All these answers are correct.

8. On tasks that involve making appearance/reality distinctions or interpreting causality, young children perform better when
   a. they are asked to provide verbal explanations.
   b. they are encountering the situation for the first time.
   c. the task requires nonverbal responses.
   d. None of these answers are correct—they perform poorly on all such tasks.

9. Which occurs in short-term (working) memory?
   a. Information is stored for several seconds.
   b. Information is combined with information from long-term memory.
   c. Information is stored for several weeks; if not retrieved by then, it is forgotten.
   d. Both a and b are correct.

10. According to the information-processing view, children should have fewer difficulties remembering information when
    a. they have prior knowledge about the thing they are trying to remember.
    b. they have learned strategies for remembering—for example, repeating the information to themselves.
    c. their caregivers have helped them by elaborating upon the information.
    d. All these answers are correct.

11. Which is an example of a privileged domain?
    a. knowing that objects will reliably fall when dropped
    b. thinking about what other people might be thinking
    c. making distinctions between living and nonliving things
    d. All these answers are correct.

12. In what sense are privileged domains "privileged"?
    a. They have evolutionary importance for our species.
    b. Caregivers are especially likely to teach children about them.
    c. Children understand them fully by 3 years of age.
    d. They require no environmental input at all.

13. According to modularity theorists, mental modules
    a. are applicable to any domain of knowledge.
    b. are present in the human genome.
    c. interact closely with one another.
    d. require a great deal of environmental input to carry out their functions.

14. Children's mental representations of routine events such as going to the playground are called
    a. scripts.
    b. long-term memories.
    c. domains.
    d. modules.

15. According to Kurt Fischer, children's cognitive development should appear to be more _____ when the behaviors observed have _____ support from the culturally organized context.
    a. gradual; high
    b. gradual; low
    c. stagelike; high
    d. Both b and c are correct.

Short-Answer Practice Questions

Write a brief answer in the space below each question.

1. Discuss some ways that young children's developing gross and fine motor skills allow them to explore their environments in new ways.

2. What evidence is there that culturally organized activities can have an effect on the way young children's brains develop? Through what processes can this happen?

3. Sometimes, young children must be interviewed because they have been witnesses to, or victims of, a crime. What procedures can interviewers use to get the most accurate information from them? What should they avoid doing?

4. How does the special case of autism provide support for the idea of a mental module for theory of mind? What are the problems with this explanation?

5. Develop a script, from a preschooler's point of view, for "eating in a restaurant." Develop the same script for a college student. How do these scenarios differ? Pay special attention to how the supportive roles played by other people differ between the two.

Sources of More Information

Caplan, T., & Caplan, F. (1984) *The Early Childhood Years*. New York: Bantam Books.
This book gives an overview of development during the preschool years, covering motor and cognitive development, social development, early literacy experiences, sexuality, and family situations.

Hatano, G. (2002). *Young Children's Naïve Thinking about the Biological World*. New York: Taylor & Francis.
This book documents Hatano's work, carried out in North America, Australia, and Japan, on children's development of biological understanding.

Loftus, E. F. (1997). Memories for a past that never was. *Current Directions in Psychological Science, 6*, 60–65.
In this article, Elizabeth Loftus discusses how false memories of traumatic childhood events can be implanted even in older children and adults.

Newcombe, N. S., Drummey, A. B., Fox, N. A., Lie, E., & Ottinger-Alberts, W. (2000). Remembering early childhood: How much, how, and why (or why not). *Current Directions in Psychological Science, 9*, 55–58.
This article addresses the question of why people generally remember little of their lives before 5 or 6 years of age.

Paley, V. (1988). *Mollie is Three: Growing Up in School*. Chicago, IL: University of Chicago Press.
In these case studies of preschool children, the author vividly describes the unevenness of their thinking and the daily effort that small children make to understand the world.

Schreibman, L. (2005). *The Science and Fiction of Autism*. Cambridge, MA: Harvard University Press.
This book covers many important issues concerning autism and is aimed at students, parents, and beginning clinicians.

Selfe, L. (1983). *Normal and Anomalous Representational Drawing Ability in Children*. New York: Academic Press.
A psychologist provides a wealth of examples of extraordinary drawing ability by children, illustrating the kind of phenomena emphasized by modularity theories of development.

Answer Key

Answers to Key Terms: 1.b, 2.m, 3.r, 4.c, 5.q, 6.k, 7.p, 8.i, 9.d, 10.n, 11.l, 12.f, 13.g, 14.e, 15.j, 16.a, 17.h, 18.o.

Answers to Multiple-Choice Questions: 1.d, 2.c, 3.c, 4.b, 5.a, 6.d, 7.c, 8.c, 9.d, 10.d, 11.d, 12.a, 13.b, 14.a, 15.d.

9 Social and Emotional Development in Early Childhood

CHAPTER

Socialization begins at birth with infants' first interactions with their parents, and throughout infancy the values, standards, and knowledge of their society help to organize children's experiences. However, in early childhood, children develop a sense of personal identity and come to understand more about what is expected of them by their families and communities. At first, children follow the rules of their societies under adult constraint; eventually, though, they internalize these standards and follow them on their own. Developmentalists believe that a process called identification, in which children mold themselves after important people in their lives, is helpful in socialization, but they differ in their ideas of how identification comes about.

Preschool children face important developmental tasks in addition to making sense of the rules that govern their environment. They are expected to learn to regulate their own behavior, to control their impulses to hurt others, and to be helpful and cooperative when it is appropriate. They must come to terms with their identities as males or females and master the sex-role behaviors appropriate to their society.

The task of socialization is by no means completed at the end of early childhood, but by then children understand their society's rules and expectations enough to be ready for the increased responsibilities that middle childhood will bring.

Learning Objectives

Keep these questions in mind while studying Chapter 9.

1. How do children develop a sense of themselves as individuals, as boys or girls, and as members of a particular ethnic or cultural group?
2. How do children come to follow social rules, even when adults are not directly supervising their behavior?
3. In what ways do children's developing cognitive abilities help them to understand other people's feelings and to regulate the expression of their own emotions?

4. What contributions do the various theoretical perspectives make in explaining children's displays of aggression?

5. What factors contribute to children's development of prosocial behaviors such as helping, caregiving, and showing compassion to others?

Chapter Summary

During early childhood, children's social and emotional lives follow two paths: socialization, which leads children toward the standards, values, and knowledge of their society; and personality formation, which leads them to develop unique patterns of feeling, thinking, and behaving.

When children are newly born, parents already have expectations about how they will develop, and parents shape their infants' experiences according to these expectations. As discussed in Chapter 1, newborns display *temperament*—individual differences in activity level, responses to frustration, and reactions to novel situations. Children's personalities are formed as their temperamental styles are integrated with their cognitive understanding, emotional responses, and habits.

I. IDENTITY DEVELOPMENT

According to Erik Erikson, during early childhood, children face the challenge of **initiative versus guilt;** they must continue to declare their autonomy and their existence as individuals, but must do so in ways that begin to conform to the social roles and moral standards of society. This leads them to enjoy cooperating with others for the purpose of accomplishing specific tasks, for example, building sandcastles or baking cookies. A factor necessary for socialization is **identification,** a process in which children seek to be like significant people in their social environment. Identification can be studied with respect to many different categories, but sex-role identity and ethnic identity are two categories of particular interest.

A. Sex-Role Identity

Although male and female infants seem much alike, by the time children are 3 years of age their behavior is much more gender-typed. Boys and girls prefer different types of play, and they tend to prefer to play with others of their gender; this phenomenon is called **gender segregation.** Chapter 9 explores how sex-role identity develops according to the psychodynamic, social learning, cognitive-developmental, gender schema, and cultural views. These views are summarized in Table 9.1 of the textbook.

- *The Psychodynamic View.* According to Sigmund Freud, around the fourth year, children have moved beyond the oral and anal stages to the **phallic stage** of development, in which they begin to regard their genitals as a source of pleasure. During this period, Freud believed, boys have the desire to get rid of their fathers and replace them in their mothers' affections. These feelings cause fear, guilt, and conflict. Freud called this predicament the **Oedipus complex;** boys, he thought, typically resolved the conflict by *differentiating* (distancing themselves) from their mothers and becoming closer to their fathers, identifying with them and taking on many of their characteristics. In contrast, Freud believed girls' sex-role identity to be rooted in a different process, which his student, Carl Jung, labeled the **Electra complex.** Girls, Freud suggested, blamed their mothers for their lack of a penis. In response to their feelings of guilt over rejecting their mothers and competing for their fathers' affection, girls repressed their feelings for their fathers and identified with their mothers. Freud thought that this process of identity formation resulted in women being "underdeveloped" versions of men because they had never completely differentiated themselves from their mothers.

Critics have attacked various aspects of Freud's explanation, notably its characterization of women as "underdeveloped" men. They point out that, as discussed in Chapter 3, all human embryos initially follow a female path; thus, female development should not be thought of as secondary to male development. Also, research indicates that there is more to children's sex-role formation than identification with the same-sex parent at 4 or 5 years of age. Some aspects of identity formation may be observed well before that time.

- *The Social Learning View.* In contrast to Freudian theories that view identification as a way of resolving conflicts between children's fears and their desires, the social learning view assumes that identity is the product of two processes: **modeling,** in which children observe and imitate individuals of the same sex as themselves; and **differential reinforcement,** in which girls and boys are differently rewarded for engaging in gender-appropriate behavior. Children do not acquire gender-role identity only by imitating their same-sex parents; they also observe peers, siblings, and other adults, as well as gender stereotypes communicated through various media. The importance of siblings was supported by the research of John Rust and his colleagues. They found that children with older siblings of the same sex showed the most sex-typed behavior and children with opposite-sex older siblings showed the least sex-typed behavior; children without siblings were somewhere in between.

- *The Cognitive-Developmental View.* Lawrence Kohlberg proposed this approach to sex-role identity. It follows from Jean Piaget's view of children as actively structuring their own experience during cognitive development. Kohlberg believed that sex-role development goes through three stages: (1) sex-role *identity,* in which children label themselves as boys or girls; (2) sex-role *stability,* in which they understand that boys grow up to be men and girls grow up to be women; and (3) sex-role *constancy,* in which they understand that their sex remains the same despite alterations in appearance such as getting a haircut or dressing as a member of the opposite sex. There is evidence for this sequence of stages with respect to how children come to understand sex roles. However, contrary to Kohlberg's predictions, they display sex-typed behavior well before achieving the stage of sex-role constancy.

- *The Gender Schema View.* Gender schema theory, like the cognitive-developmental approach, regards the environment as affecting the child's understanding indirectly through a **gender schema**—a mental model containing information about males and females that is used to process gender-relevant information. This allows children to classify objects, people, and activities with respect to gender and to incorporate gender into their scripts about events such as barbecuing or shopping for groceries. In contrast to the cognitive-developmental approach, gender schema theorists believe that children's developing schematic knowledge exerts its influences even before the onset of Kohlberg's stages. They also employ an information-processing approach to describe the interaction of the cognitive and learning elements of the system, as illustrated in Figure 9.2 of the textbook.

- *The Cultural View.* Acquisition of gender roles illustrates how the tools of culture (in this case, gender categories) organize children's activities. For example, more gender stereotyping can be observed in preschools where teachers emphasize gender in classroom activities. Children's behavior is mediated by the content of behavior categories (which behaviors are considered "male" or "female") and by the rigidity with which the categories are defined. Thus, many Western cultures are more tolerant of girls engaging in typically masculine behavior and less tolerant of boys engaging in typically feminine behavior. Marion O'Brien and her colleagues found that, although preschool boys and girls were equally knowledgeable about male stereotypes, girls were much more knowledgeable than boys about female stereotypes. The view that cultural conceptions of gender mediate children's activities is consistent with the feminist approaches and other critical theories introduced in Chapter 1.

B. Ethnic Identity

Ethnic identity may be thought of as a sense of belonging to an ethnic group, and the feelings and attitudes that accompany the sense of group membership. The development of children's sense of racial or ethnic identity and their attitudes toward their own and other groups have important social, psychological, and economic implications. In the mid-twentieth century, Kenneth and Mamie Clark asked African American and European American children, 3 years of age and older, to indicate preferences for dolls representing the two ethnic groups. They found that African American children seemed to prefer the white dolls. This was interpreted as indicating that minority children define themselves in terms of the majority group. Although later research has supported such findings, it has not supported the interpretation that, if they prefer to play with a white doll, minority-group children have acquired a negative ethnic self-concept. Children's choices vary with the circumstances; for example, one study determined that Native American children who were tested in their own language preferred dolls representing their own group. And African American children's preference for white dolls has decreased over the years, according to more recent studies.

Developmentalists have become increasingly interested in **ethnic socialization,** the ethnic-based messages communicated to children. Among the types of messages communicated are *cultural socialization,* emphasizing ethnic heritage and pride; *preparation for bias,* stressing ethnic discrimination and prejudice; *promotion of racial mistrust,* encouraging mistrust of the majority ethnicity; and *egalitarianism,* emphasizing the equality of people of all ethnicities. Margaret Caughy and her colleagues, studying African American preschoolers, found that most parents incorporated a variety of ethnic socialization messages when interacting with their children. More parents (88 percent) communicated messages emphasizing cultural heritage and pride than messages promoting mistrust (65 percent). Similar results have been obtained in studies of Puerto Rican and Dominican parents in the United States. Caughy and her colleagues also found that African American children whose parents promoted ethnic pride and provided homes rich in African American culture tended to have stronger cognitive abilities and problem-solving skills and fewer behavioral problems compared with children whose parents provided other forms of ethnic socialization. This study indicates that the formation of ethnic identity is a process which begins early in life.

C. Personal Identity

Children's sense of self becomes increasingly complex during early childhood. **Personal identity**—a person's sense of him- or herself as it evolves over time—may be conceived of as consisting of two parts: the *I-self* who exists over time, and who acts and experiences the world in a particular way; and the *me-self,* which is the person's sense of his or her own objective characteristics such as appearance and abilities—the self that others see. The *I* and *me* shape one another over the course of development. When asked by developmentalists to describe themselves, young children typically provide a loosely connected list of behaviors ("I know my ABC's") that are not yet combined into generalized traits ("I am smart"). Their self-evaluations tend to be unrealistically positive, as they are not yet able to distinguish between their "real" and "ideal" selves. The process of developing a sense of self is influenced by children's increasing ability to use language and by their participation with caregivers in a variety of routine activities. Caregivers also help children create **autobiographical memory,** a personal narrative that helps them acquire an enduring sense of themselves. By the time most children are 4 years old, they have internalized the narrative structures appropriate to their culture and can recount their personal experiences by themselves.

II. A NEW MORAL WORLD

Developmentalists are interested in learning how children develop a personal sense of right and wrong. Three perspectives have dominated research on children's moral development: psychodynamic theory, cognitive-developmental theory, and social domain theory.

A. The Psychodynamic View

According to psychodynamic theory, children develop a personal sense of morality by *internalizing* the standards of their parents, especially their same-sex parent. Freud identified three mental structures that develop from early childhood. The **id** is present at birth and is the main source of psychological energy; it is unconscious, impulsive, and mainly concerned with the satisfaction of bodily drives. It operates on the *pleasure principle.* The **ego** develops from the id when an infant is forced by reality to cope with the social world; its primary task is self-preservation, accomplished through voluntary movement, perception, logical thought, and problem solving. It operates on the *reality principle.* By about 5 years of age, children's internalization of parental rules and standards results in the formation of the **superego,** which represents the authority of the social group and carries out the functions that parents have performed, especially passing judgment on the ego's efforts to keep the id under control.

B. The Cognitive-Developmental View

At first, children's ideas about moral issues are strongly influenced by the objective consequences (how much damage is done) and by adults' reactions to their behavior. Piaget called this **heteronomous morality.** As children enter middle childhood and have more experience interacting with peers in situations not directly controlled by adults, they develop *autonomous morality* in which moral judgments are freely and personally chosen. Both the psychodynamic and cognitive-developmental views emphasize how children move past relying on external authority to define right and wrong; they differ in their views of the processes that support this change.

C. The Social Domain View

According to **social domain theory,** the rules that dictate right and wrong fall into three domains, each at a different level of generality. Some rules are *moral rules,* based on principles of justice and the welfare of others; these are found in some form in all societies and are considered obligations not to be transgressed. At the next level of generality are *social conventions,* which are important in coordinating social behavior in a society; they include rules such as what clothing people should wear in public and appropriate behavior for men and women. Social conventions vary a great deal among societies and among subgroups within a society. Thus, children may have difficulty recognizing whether a rule they have broken is a moral rule or a social convention. Rules within the *personal sphere* are at the most specific level; they involve situations in which children can make decisions based on personal preferences, such as personal hygiene and some types of social relations. Children 3 or 4 years of age from a variety of cultures have been found capable of distinguishing among moral, social, and personal rules. Examples of each type of rule may be found in Table 9.2 of the textbook.

III. DEVELOPING SELF-REGULATION

While learning basic social roles, children also learn to act in accordance with their caregivers' expectations, even when they are not being directly monitored. **Self-regulation** involves the ability to control one's emotions, behaviors, and thoughts; it develops over a long time and involves all the developmental domains. Infants and young children need assistance with regulation, but the ability to self-regulate is important in order for a child to begin to function independently.

A. Regulating Thought and Action

Intentionally focusing one's attention, remembering to do something, and solving a problem each involve self-regulation. Sometimes, a task requires **effortful control**—the inhibition of an action already under way.

Various studies have explored children's ability to resist temptation and comply with adult norms. For example, Grazyna Kochanska and Nazan Aksan videotaped 2- to 5-year-old children as they interacted with their mothers. In one session, the children were given attractive toys to play with in their own homes. When the mothers asked their children to stop playing with those toys and to put them away, only some engaged in "committed compliance." Most engaged in "situational compliance" and had to be continually prompted by their mothers to do as they were told. In a second session, which took place in a laboratory, the mothers asked their children not to touch a particularly attractive set of toys; this directive was easier for the children to comply with than the instruction in the first session, which had involved effortful control.

Children's ability to control themselves is an example of internalization as described by Freud. Internalization is also important to the theory of Lev Vygotsky. Vygotsky viewed internalization as the process through which social regulations are transferred to a child's internal psychological system.

B. Self-Regulation and Play

According to Vygotsky, play also has an important role in self-regulation. When children can separate an object being played with from their thoughts about it (containing the *idea* or *meaning* of the object), they are regulating their thoughts and actions. An example would be a child talking into a block, using it to represent a telephone. Vygotsky believed that in this kind of imaginary play children both demonstrate and develop self-regulation.

Sociodramatic play, in which two or more participants enact a variety of social roles (for example, mother, father, and children), is an especially important type of imaginary play. A study by Cynthia Elias and Laura Berk assessed 3- and 4-year-old preschool children's sociodramatic play and their level of self-regulation. There was no relationship between the two at the time of the first assessment in the fall of the year; however, the children who engaged in a great deal of sociodramatic play also showed high levels of self-regulation when it was remeasured several months later. This was especially true for more impulsive children, who exhibited the greatest gains. Elias and Berk asserted that sociodramatic play may prove to be an important form of early intervention for impulsive children.

As discussed in the box "In the Field: Coping with Chronic Illness through Play," children with chronic illnesses that require painful medical treatments and have frightening symptoms often use play and games to help them get through these stressful situations. These activities create a zone of proximal development through which children gain a sense of control over situations that are uncontrollable.

C. Regulating Emotions

Young children, in order to become competent members of their social group, need to learn to interpret the emotional states of others, to control their own emotions, and to mask their true feelings when necessary. In early childhood, the *self-conscious emotions*—pride, shame, guilt, envy, and embarrassment—grow important as children participate in new and more complex social situations.

• As young children become better able to control their emotions, they deal more effectively with the disappointments, frustrations, and hurt feelings that are common at this stage. Evidence also exists that children who can moderate their own distress when another child is hurt or upset are better able to show sympathy to the playmate in distress. In order to sustain play, children must balance emotional expression and regulation.

- Babies are not born with the ability to regulate the expression of their feelings in socially acceptable ways. During early childhood, children learn to recognize when other people are masking their feelings. Girls are generally better than boys at recognizing and displaying masked emotions. There are cultural differences in the ages at which children learn to, or are expected to, mask their feelings.

  The ability to behave appropriately in social situations that evoke strong emotions is called **socioemotional competence;** it involves awareness of one's own and others' emotional states, the capacity for sympathy and empathy, and the ability to differentiate inner emotional states from outer expressions of emotion. Preschool children who display socioemotional competence are liked better by their teachers and peers.

- A culture's values and beliefs help to shape children's emotion regulation. For example, for children growing up the United States, greater emphasis is placed on personal achievement, whereas children living in China are encouraged to meet social obligations. As reported by Michael Mascolo and his colleagues, shame emerges for Chinese children at an earlier point in development than it does for American children. Figure 9.3 in the textbook shows how differences in the socialization of U.S. and Chinese children result in their different emotional responses to successes and failures.

IV. UNDERSTANDING AGGRESSION

Learning to control aggression is one of the most basic tasks of young children's social development.

A. The Development of Aggression

Two types of aggression can be identified during early childhood. In **instrumental aggression,** aggressive behavior is aimed at achieving a particular goal; **hostile aggression** is intended to injure the victim. As children's cognitive and linguistic skills increase, teasing becomes a more important part of aggressive exchanges. Instrumental aggression has been observed to increase when children are between 1 and 2 years of age. At this time, children begin to develop a distinctive sense of self and to worry about "ownership rights" to their toys. Up until approximately 18 months of age, physical aggression and teasing occur equally often; later, teasing becomes more prevalent. In general, boys are more aggressive than girls. As girls approach their second birthdays, they become less aggressive, whereas boys of the same age become more aggressive. Preschool and school-age girls, however, engage in more **relational aggression**—which involves harming other children's friendships or excluding them from a group—than boys do.

B. What Causes and Controls Aggression?

Developmentalists have noted that the earlier children develop problem behaviors relating to aggression, the more likely they are to behave in those ways later on. Thus, it is important to understand what causes aggressive behavior and how it can be controlled. Studies seeking to explain aggression have tended to focus on biological, social and cultural, or emotional and cognitive influences.

- Charles Darwin pointed out that members of a species are essentially in competition with one another to survive. According to this view, aggression is natural and necessary, and automatically accompanies biological maturation. Aggression is widespread among animal species but is kept in check by the formation of dominance hierarchies. F. F. Strayer and his colleagues observed that 3- and 4-year-olds in a nursery school also formed dominance hierarchies; once they were established, the total amount of aggression in the group decreased.

    Physiological factors have an important effect on aggression. For example, the difference in levels of aggression between boys and girls is associated with the differences in testosterone levels between them. Testosterone may act indirectly on aggression by increasing boys' activity levels. In fact, boys have been observed to have higher activity levels than girls.

- Another explanation of aggression stresses the importance of social and cultural influences. In this view, children learn to behave aggressively by imitating the aggressive behavior of others or being rewarded for aggressive behavior. For example, Gerald Patterson and his colleagues found that aggression by preschool children was generally followed by positive consequences for the aggressor. Patterson and Crosby observed that the parents of aggressive children often reinforce their aggressive behavior, signaling approval when the child is aggressive.

    Cultures vary in the amount of interpersonal aggression they consider normal. The box "The Spanking Controversy" discusses the use of physical punishment and its effect on aggression. There is cross-cultural evidence supporting the idea that children model the aggressive behavior of adults. When Douglas Fry compared the levels of violence in two Zapotec Indian towns in central Mexico, he found notable differences in the levels of aggression. When the children of each town were observed, it was determined that the children from the town characterized by greater violence performed twice as many violent acts as those from the town where violence was better controlled.

- Children's emotional reactions to events depend on how they interpret social contexts and how well they understand others' intentions and emotions. Aggressive children often misinterpret others' behavior in negative ways, which leads them to respond aggressively. Aggression may originate from the negative feelings that result when children are involved in frustrating situations (for example, when another child takes away something with which they are playing). Whether an aggressive response is made, however, depends on the children's temperaments and past social experiences. As shown in Figure 9.7 of the textbook, the unpleasant event can evoke a "fight or flight" response. Children's cognitive processes, including their thoughts about intentions and consequences, can modify these tendencies toward aggression or escape.

    Developmentalists have placed increasing emphasis on the influence of children's thought processes on aggression, especially their knowledge about emotions, goals, and behaviors and how they are linked. Children with a more advanced understanding should be less likely to behave aggressively. This view was supported by the results of a study by Susanne Denham and her colleagues in which puppets were used to assess the level of children's emotional knowledge. Jessica Giles and Gail Heyman examined another factor:

preschool children's beliefs about whether aggression is an enduring trait or a changeable behavior. They found that children who believed in aggression as an enduring trait were also more likely than other children to endorse aggressive solutions to conflicts.

Evidence exists that aggression can best be understood in light of children's thoughts and beliefs about their own and others' emotional lives. Reasoning with children has been found to be effective in controlling aggression, even with preschoolers.

Many people believe that offering children the opportunity to vent their aggressive tendencies in harmless ways will reduce the incidence of actual aggression. There is little convincing research evidence that such is the case; nevertheless, this idea is widely applied in psychotherapy with young, troubled children.

V. DEVELOPING PROSOCIAL BEHAVIORS

Prosocial behavior is voluntary action that benefits others—for example, sharing, helping, and showing compassion. The psychological states that correspond to prosocial behavior (in the same sense that anger corresponds to aggression) are *empathy* and *sympathy*.

A. Empathy

Empathy, sharing another person's emotions or feelings, is the foundation for prosocial behavior. Although empathy is possible at any age, children's ability to empathize broadens with age. Martin Hoffman has traced the development of empathy through four stages. During the first year, babies cry at the sound of another infant's cry (*global empathy*); this empathy is reflexlike, occurring even before infants have a real awareness of other people's feelings. During the second year, babies actively attempt to comfort another person who is in distress, although not always in ways appropriate to the other person (*egocentric empathy*). Preschoolers, with their more advanced language and cognitive skills, can empathize with a wider range of feelings and, through the media, with people they have never met or with characters in a story. A fourth stage emerges in middle childhood: at that time, children understand the relationship between others' emotions and their past histories. Hoffman's explanation is linked to Piaget's theory of cognitive development. It emphasizes children's ability to understand the feelings of others; children's actual emotions are not stressed in this explanation. Hoffman makes the assumption that the more children understand other people's feelings, the more intensely they will adopt them.

B. Sympathy

Other research places greater emphasis on the emotional component of empathy. As in Hoffman's theory, Nancy Eisenberg and her colleagues propose that empathy results in an emotional reaction similar to that experienced by another; however, they emphasize that empathy may turn into **sympathy** (feelings of sorrow or concern for another's distress), which is characterized by "other-oriented concern," and/or **personal distress** (a self-focused emotional reaction to another's distress). Sympathy and personal distress have differing effects on prosocial behavior. Children who exhibit sympathy in response to films showing characters in distress are more likely to exhibit prosocial behavior than those who respond with personal distress. Personal distress is associated with poor social skills; it is more likely to occur when another person's distress generates too much emotion in a child.

A study of 6- to 8-year-old children indicated that, for children who can regulate their emotions, higher levels of emotion are associated with greater sympathy. However, children who were rated low in regulation were also low in sympathy, regardless of their emotional intensity. A second study found a relationship between children's ability to focus their attention (another form of self-regulation) and sympathy for others. The researchers observed that children who were low in emotional intensity but high in attention focusing were higher in sympathy compared with those who were low in emotional intensity and also low in attention focusing.

VI. TAKING ONE'S PLACE IN THE SOCIAL GROUP

By the end of early childhood, children have accepted that conformity to social rules is inevitable. Their accomplishments during this period illustrate the two-sided nature of social development: socialization and personality development.

Key Terms I

Following are important terms introduced in Chapter 9. Match each term with the letter of the example that best illustrates the term.

1. _____ differential reinforcement

2. _____ effortful control

3. _____ ego

4. _____ ethnic identity

5. _____ heteronomous morality

6. _____ hostile aggression

7. _____ id

8. _____ initiative versus guilt

9. _____ instrumental aggression

10. _____ personal distress

11. _____ personality formation

12. _____ prosocial behavior

13. _____ relational aggression

14. _____ socialization

15. _____ sociodramatic play

16. _____ superego

a. The primary task of this part of a child's personality is self-preservation.
b. This is needed in order for children to, for example, stop playing with an attractive toy and put it away.

c. Janet hits another preschool child in order to gain possession of the doll she is playing with.

d. In Jared's opinion, a child who breaks three plates while helping his mother load the dishwasher has committed a worse act than one who breaks one plate while climbing the shelves to reach the forbidden cookie jar.

e. Altruism, cooperation, and sharing are examples of this.

f. The process by which children acquire their society's values, knowledge, and standards.

g. This part of the personality supplies a child's psychological energy.

h. Although she is growing up in the United States, Carla has a sense of herself as belonging to her community of immigrants from Oaxaca, Mexico.

i. Mike's parents reward him for doing masculine things and reward his sister Julia for doing feminine things.

j. John calls a fellow kindergartner "stupid" just to hurt his feelings.

k. This part of the personality serves as a child's conscience.

l. According to Erikson, children confront this challenge during early childhood.

m. Carrie and Maria decide that today they will not let Gina play with them at recess or at lunch.

n. A group of preschoolers play "mommy, daddy, baby, and big brother," with each taking on a different role.

o. Stephen has his own ways of thinking, feeling, and behaving that are different from those of anyone else in his family.

p. Brenda becomes extremely upset after Paul hurts himself at the playground, and runs away rather than helping him get up.

Key Terms II

Following are important terms introduced in Chapter 9. Match each term with the letter of the example that best illustrates the term.

1. _____ autobiographical memory

2. _____ Electra complex

3. _____ empathy

4. _____ ethnic socialization

5. _____ gender schema

6. _____ gender segregation

7. _____ identification

8. _____ modeling

9. _____ Oedipus complex

10. _____ personal identity

11. _____ phallic stage

12. _____ self-recognition

13. _____ social domain theory

14. _____ socioemotional competence

15. _____ sympathy

a. Boys prefer to play with other boys and girls with other girls.

b. A personal narrative that is initially created by children and adults together.

c. In acquiring sex-role identity, this occurs when children observe and imitate the behavior of individuals of the same sex.

d. Children engage in this when, for example, they are able to control their ability to tune out distractions.

e. This involves feeling sorrow or concern for another person.

f. Children's conceptions of sex roles that guide their behavior and influence the way they select and remember information.

g. This involves messages related to ethnicity that are communicated to children by their parents.

h. Jason tells his mother that he wants to marry her someday, "after Daddy dies."

i. Children's sense of themselves that contains the "I-self" and the "me-self."

j. The experience of sharing another person's emotions and feelings.

k. This perspective categorizes the rules of societies according to how broadly they apply and the consequences for violating them.

l. This is the Freudian stage during which children develop sexual jealousy toward the parent of the same sex.

m. Ability to discern other people's emotions is an important component of this.

n. A term for modeling oneself after another person.

o. According to Freud, this occurs when girls blame their mothers because they do not possess a penis; then, they transfer their affection to their fathers.

Multiple-Choice Practice Questions

Circle the letter of the word or phrase that correctly completes each statement.

1. _____ is the process by which children learn the standards, values, and knowledge of their society.
   a. Personality formation
   b. Prosocial behavior
   c. Affiliation
   d. Socialization

2. According to Freud, identification in males
   a. requires that they distance themselves from their mothers.
   b. requires that they distance themselves from their fathers.
   c. Both a and b are correct.
   d. occurs because they are rewarded for imitating masculine behavior.

3. According to Kohlberg's theory, which of the following needs to happen in order for children to develop a sex-role identity?
   a. Children need to be reinforced by adults for performing behaviors associated with their gender and punished for performing behavior associated with the opposite gender.
   b. Children need to resolve the Oedipus or Electra complex.

    c. Children need to come to understand that their sex is a permanent and unchanging characteristic.

    d. Children do not need to do anything; sex-role identities are genetically based and develop with maturation.

4. Research on the development of ethnic identity shows that

    a. the racial or ethnic preferences expressed by children in studies varies according to the circumstances of the interview.

    b. minority group children usually wish they belonged to the majority group.

    c. children usually prefer to play with dolls representing their own ethnic group.

    d. children are not aware of racial or ethnic groups until 6 or 7 years of age.

5. According to a study by Margaret Caughey and her colleagues, which was the most prevalent category of racial socialization messages used by parents?

    a. mistrust of the majority group

    b. preparation for bias

    c. cultural socialization

    d. all of these, equally

6. In Freud's theory, which part of the personality carries out the same functions as the child's parents?

    a. the id

    b. the superego

    c. the ego

    d. the unconscious

7. In thinking about moral issues, preschool children

    a. have no sense of right and wrong.

    b. believe in obeying the spirit of the law rather than the letter of the law.

    c. judge the rightness or wrongness of an action by adults' reactions.

    d. are inclined to question the judgment of people in authority.

8. _____ are the most general rules and the most likely to be found in similar forms in all societies.

    a. Social conventions

    b. Moral rules

    c. Rules related to sex roles

    d. Rules related to personal habits

9. When children are able to obey social rules even when no one is monitoring their behavior, they are exhibiting

    a. repression.

    b. empathy.

    c. prosocial behavior.

    d. self-regulation.

10. Which of the following is *most* difficult for young children to do?
    a. inhibit an ongoing action
    b. initiate a new action
    c. imitate a simple motor action
    d. accept a reward for performing an action

11. When children exclude another child from a group or harm the other child's friendship with someone else, they are engaging in
    a. self-regulation.
    b. hostile aggression.
    c. instrumental aggression.
    d. relational aggression.

12. Compared with girls, boys are more likely to
    a. engage in relational aggression.
    b. engage in direct aggression.
    c. mask their true feelings.
    d. All the answers are correct.

13. Aggression among children results from
    a. imitation of aggressive models.
    b. adults inadvertently rewarding aggressive behavior.
    c. inborn tendencies to compete with others.
    d. All the answers are correct.

14. Which leads to a reduction in aggression among children?
    a. the emergence of dominance hierarchies among children
    b. parents physically punishing children for aggressive behavior
    c. adults laughing when children behave aggressively
    d. All the answers are correct.

15. The ability to perceive the emotional states of others and ability to control the expression of one's own emotions are aspects of
    a. gender schema formation.
    b. socioemotional competence.
    c. resolving the Oedipus complex.
    d. the process of identification.

16. When newborns cry in response to another baby's crying, they are displaying the first signs of
    a. self-regulation.
    b. frustration.
    c. empathy.
    d. annoyance.

17. Which is necessary in order for children to be able to feel sympathy for others?
    a. ability to focus attention on other people
    b. ability to regulate one's emotions
    c. Both a and b are correct.
    d. the tendency to feel emotions very strongly

Short-Answer Practice Questions

Write a brief answer in the space below each question.

1. Briefly, what are the strengths and weaknesses of the main approaches used to account for the development of sex-role identity in children?

2. What do developmentalists know about how ethnic socialization occurs? What kinds of messages about ethnicity are associated with the best outcomes for children?

3. Describe several ways that interactions with adults and peers support children's development of self-regulation. How does their ability to self-regulate help to smooth their social interaction with others?

4. Describe some of the ways that culture affects children's regulation of their emotions.

5. What factors are thought to be responsible for human aggression? What might account for sex differences in aggressive behavior?

6. What is involved in *socioemotional competence*? How does it develop in young children? Give some examples of how to help children develop this ability.

Putting It All Together

In this section, material from Chapter 9 can be combined with information presented in earlier chapters.

I. One of the major accomplishments of early childhood is the growth of children's ability to regulate their own behavior. Show how developments in language ability and the growth of scripted knowledge help children to exhibit self-regulation and to interact socially with others.

II. Among preschoolers, the ability to reason about social categories such as sex is thought to influence the process of identification. Use examples to demonstrate the relationship between cognitive development (for example, categorization and perspective taking) and social development during early childhood.

Sources of More Information

Ames, L. B., & Haber, C. C. (1989). *He hit me first: When brothers and sisters fight.* New York: Warner Books.
This book discusses sibling rivalry from a biological-maturation perspective.

Dunn, J. (1993). *Young children's close relationships.* Newbury Park, CA: Sage Publications.
The author has studied children as they interact with their siblings in everyday family settings. The book is helpful in illustrating the relationship between cognitive and social development.

Eisenberg, N. (ed.). (1992). *The caring child.* Cambridge, MA: Harvard University Press.
A discussion of topics related to theory and research on the development of prosocial behavior.

Freud, A. (1979). *Psychoanalysis for teachers and parents.* New York: W.W. Norton.
This book contains four lectures in which Sigmund Freud's daughter, a noted children's analyst, discusses the early stages of psychosexual development.

Honig, A. S. (January 1985). Compliance, control, and discipline, Part I. *Young Children, 40,* 50–58.
Honig, A. S. (March 1985). Compliance, control, and discipline, Part II. *Young Children, 40,* 47–52.
These two articles discuss children's development of self-regulation and suggest techniques that can be used by adults to increase cooperation and compliance.

Lee, S. (ed.), & Editors of *Parents Magazine.* (2000). *Your three- and four-year-old: As they grow.* New York: St. Martin's Press.
Advice for parents of preschoolers on keeping them safe, fostering their development, and handling conflicts.

Paul, A. M. (January–February 1998). Do parents really matter? *Psychology Today,* 46–49. A brief discussion of the ways genetic predispositions interact with environmental factors in affecting children's behavior.

Answer Key

Answers to Key Terms I: 1.i, 2.b, 3.a, 4.h, 5.d, 6.j, 7.g, 8.l, 9.c, 10.p, 11.o, 12.e, 13.m, 14.f, 15.n, 16.k.

Answers to Key Terms II: 1.b, 2.o, 3.j, 4.g, 5.f, 6.a, 7.n, 8.c, 9.h, 10.i, 11.l, 12.d, 13.k, 14.m, 15.e.

Answers to Multiple-Choice Questions: 1.d, 2.a, 3.c, 4.a, 5.c, 6.b, 7.c, 8.b, 9.d, 10.a, 11.d, 12.b, 13.d, 14.a, 15.d, 16.c, 17.c.

10 Contexts of Childhood

Children's development is influenced by the many interacting contexts of their lives. Their families, for example, belong to communities that, in turn, are part of larger societies. Child rearing varies from society to society: a family of nomadic herders in North Africa and a family living in a New York City high-rise apartment will not teach their children the same survival and social skills. There are also differences in child-rearing strategies within societies and corresponding differences in children's behavior. Many factors influence a family's child rearing, including the personalities of parents and children, the parents' educational and occupational status, and the life stresses that affect the family at any particular time.

During early childhood, many children are cared for by relatives besides their parents or by child-care providers, in their own or other people's homes, or in child-care centers.

Even within the family, children are influenced by the world outside. Media such as television, newspapers, books, and electronic help to shape the behavior and beliefs of children and their family members.

Research shows that children whose environments combine a number of stress-producing factors are at risk for later problems. However, some are remarkably resilient in the face of difficult life circumstances. Supportive extended families, good schools, and even the child's own temperament may help to counteract life's stresses. Local communities, state and national governments, and international organizations such as the United Nations formulate public policies and contribute resources aimed at optimizing children's development.

Learning Objectives

Keep these questions in mind while studying Chapter 10.

✓ 1. In what kinds of family structures do people raise their children?
✓ 2. What goals do parents have for their children, and what parenting strategies do they adopt in order to fulfill these goals?

✓ 3. What kinds of child-care arrangements are adopted by parents in the United States? What effects does child care have on children's intellectual and social development?

✓4. How do stresses such as low income or single parenthood act to trigger developmental or behavioral problems in children?

✓ 5. How are children affected by exposure to media such as books, television, and the Internet?

✓6. What protective factors help children to overcome life stresses and develop into healthy adults?

Chapter Summary

Chapter 10 highlights the way the contexts in which young children develop influences the course of their development. These contexts—ranging from specific events within the family or preschool to global influences of mass media—may shape children's development directly or indirectly, through their effect on parents and other family members. It is useful to recall Urie Bronfenbrenner's ecological model, outlined in Chapter 1, which describes development as occurring within nested, interacting ecosystems: the *microsystem* at the most personal level, the *mesosystem* as connections between microsystem settings, and the *exosystem* at the most general level of influence.

I. THE FAMILY CONTEXT

When Beatrice and John Whiting organized observations of child rearing in six diverse locales around the world, they found differences in not only the circumstances of children's lives but also the overall patterns of their behavior. For example, the Gusii, an agricultural people in western Kenya, lived in polygynous families in which women did most of the farmwork, and infants and toddlers were cared for by older siblings and elderly family members. "Orchard Town," located in New England and representing the opposite experience, was populated by men who were wage earners and women who were mainly full-time homemakers. The Whitings determined that Gusii children were more likely both to offer help and responsible suggestions to others and to reprimand other children. The children of Orchard Town, on the other hand, were more likely to seek help and attention from others and to engage in horseplay with their peers. This difference in behavior highlights differences in how the children were socialized by the societies of which they were members. Whereas the children of Orchard Town spent their time in school, the Gusii children were expected to work and contribute economically to their families and to take care of younger children. Orchard Town children lived in small families in which there were close bonds between individuals; Gusii children lived in families that included members from several generations and formed attachments to the broader group.

A. The Biocultural Origins of Family

Developmentalists use the term **family structure** to refer to how a family unit is organized socially. For example, **nuclear families** consist of parents and their children; **extended fam-**

ilies include additional relatives. Nuclear families result in greater closeness among immediate family members, whereas extended families bind members to their ancestral line.

- According to historian Philippe Ariès, the nuclear family is unique to modern societies, resulting from the large migrations from rural areas to industrialized cities that occurred during the late eighteenth and early nineteenth centuries.

  However, the proportion of extended families has been increasing in the United States in recent decades, with approximately 8 percent of children currently living in a family that includes a grandparent. This is especially likely to occur when cultural traditions and values are consistent with extended family living, as is the case with Hispanic immigrants and African Americans. Grandparents and other family members are an important source of support, especially in cases of low income or social status, or when only one parent lives in the home.

- Researchers who study **allocaregiving** (child care and protection provided by group members other than the parents) recognize the importance of the many forms of support provided to children by extended kin. Siblings, uncles and aunts, grandparents, and nonkin members of the household may be allocaregivers. Studies of various cultures have found greater reproductive success among women whose children benefit from allocaregiving. This is also true among nonhuman species that engage in **cooperative breeding**—in which individuals form networks of support for the rearing of the young—as is the case for elephants, lions, wild dogs, and some bird species.

  These findings tie in with speculation about why human children take so long to reach maturity. The traditional explanation is that a long childhood allows the time necessary for the maturation of the large and complex human brain, and for the development of skills and cultural tools important to children's survival and success. However, an alternative view is that humans have large and complex brains precisely *because* they have a long childhood in which to mature, and that the support of families makes this long period of childhood possible.

B. Parenting Practices

All individuals who raise children have similar goals. How they reach them varies with the family's ecological context, cultural values, and beliefs about how children should behave.

- Anthropologist Robert Levine has proposed that families share three goals for their children: ensuring that their children survive, acquire economic skills, and acquire the basic cultural values of their group. These goals are hierarchical; thus, when threats to infant survival are high, parents typically respond quickly to their infants but show minimal concern about their emotional and behavioral development. When there is little threat to survival, parents show more concern about preparing their children for economic success.

  The **no-nonsense parenting**—characterized by high levels of control, including punishment, but also high levels of warmth—that is prevalent among African American single mothers can be best understood as a response to perceived threats in the environment.

• Research in the United States has revealed wide variations in *parenting styles;* however, they can be analyzed using measures of the amount of warmth parents display and the amount of control they exert. The parenting patterns to which these measures give rise are shown in Table 10.1 of the textbook.

Diana Baumrind and her colleagues measured the parenting styles of American families during the 1970s. They found that 77 percent of the families interviewed could be classified as falling into one of three patterns:

• In the **authoritarian parenting pattern,** parents try to shape their children's behavior according to a set traditional standard, stress obedience to authority, and discourage verbal give-and-take. They are relatively low in warmth and use punitive methods to correct their children's behavior.

• In the **authoritative parenting pattern,** parents set high standards and establish limits for their children's behavior, but recognize the children's needs and points of view. They are typically warm and responsive, and less likely to stress obedience to authority as a virtue in and of itself. They try to control their children's behavior by reasoning with them and encourage them to be independent and socially responsible.

• In the **permissive parenting pattern,** parents exercise less control over their children's behavior. In some cases, they believe that children need to learn how to behave through their own experiences (permissive parenting); in others, they do not take the trouble to discipline their children (neglectful parenting). The parents are typically warm toward their children, but do not demand the same level of achievement and mature behavior expected by authoritarian or authoritative parents.

Baumrind found that the children of authoritarian parents tended to lack social competence, spontaneity, and intellectual curiosity; the children of authoritative parents were more self-reliant and self-controlled; and the children of permissive parents were relatively immature and less responsible than those of the other groups. There are limits to the generality of these findings. For example, children's own characteristics probably influence the child-rearing strategies adopted by their parents.

C. The Role of Siblings

As shown in the box "Fathers," parents play a significant role in children's socialization. However, research studies indicate that siblings also influence one another's development. In agricultural societies such as that of the Gusii, many of the behaviors and beliefs of the social group are passed on through child caretakers who have responsibility for younger siblings. In industrialized societies, the increased participation of women in the workforce has led to more children being called on to help care for younger brothers and sisters; this is commonplace within African American families.

Sibling relationships can be loving and supportive and also hostile and competitive. A longitudinal study of 9- to 20-year-olds ascertained that the highest levels of intimacy were found in pairs of sisters. Same-sex sibling pairs maintained the same levels of intimacy over time; mixed-sex pairs declined in intimacy during middle childhood (possibly because of *gender segregation*) and then increased in mid-adolescence. Conflict between siblings declines throughout adolescence, but is affected by the emotional climate of the family.

The sibling relationship provides a context for teaching and learning. Margarita Azmitia and Joanne Hesser found that young children playing with building blocks spent more time consulting their older sibling than an older friend. Other studies have shown that older siblings are especially helpful when tasks become more difficult and when aiding much younger siblings.

D. Family Diversity

Because of changes in values, politics, economies, and transportation, families in many areas have become more diverse with respect to ethnicity, cultural heritage, and lifestyle.

- In the past few decades, the United States has experienced an influx of families from many parts of the world; more than 50 percent come from Latin America, 25 percent from Asia, 15 percent from Europe, and 8 percent from elsewhere. Immigrant children are the fastest-growing group of children in the United States.

  Baumrind's parenting patterns, formulated on the basis of research with middle-class parents, may not apply to other ethnic populations. For example, "authoritarian" does not have the same meaning for Chinese American and European American families; although Chinese parents typically exercise control over their children and demand obedience, it is within the context of a highly supportive, highly involved, and physically close mother–child relationship.

  Immigrant parents also differ in the values they seek to instill in their children, often placing great emphasis on education as the key to a better life. Unfortunately, many immigrant families experience hardships during their transition to American life, for example, a drop in economic and social status. Evidence exists that Latino and Asian immigrant children experience declines in health, school achievement, and aspirations as they remain longer in the United States.

- Approximately half of all children born in the United States spend some part of their childhood in a single-parent home; there has been a 280 percent increase in single-parent families among European Americans and a 543 percent increase among African Americans.

  Studies of children from single-parent families report a variety of social, behavioral, and academic problems. One difficulty in evaluating these findings is that the formation of a single-parent family may be associated with socioeconomic hardship and/or divorce.

  When Gunilla Weitoff and her colleagues conducted a study in Sweden comparing health outcomes for children in single-parent and two-parent families, they found that socioeconomic status was the most important factor in assessing differences between the groups. However, even when this was taken into account, the children from single-parent families remained at higher risk for a variety of problems.

  John Kesner and Patrick McKenry shed further light on the issue with a study of mainly African American families in the United States. In this sample, most of the single mothers had never been married and thus not experienced divorce. In addition, most had very supportive extended families. Under these circumstances, there were no differences between the children of single- and two-parent families in terms of social skills or con-flict-management styles.

- The number of gay and lesbian parents is also increasing. In some cases, gay and lesbian couples are co-parenting children they have from previous relationships. In other cases, gay and lesbian couples or individuals are raising children whom they have adopted or conceived by means of surrogacy or artificial insemination. Research suggests that children raised in gay and lesbian households are comparable in emotional, social, and intellectual development to those raised in heterosexual households. They may be more tolerant of same-sex experimentation and somewhat more likely to develop a homosexual identity than children raised by heterosexual parents.

E. Distressed Families

According to developmentalists who study *distressed families,* the most important factors that can impede development are poverty, adolescent parenthood, and abuse. The effects of divorce will be treated in Chapter 13.

- Poverty affects all aspects of family life, including access to adequate housing, health care, education, and safe surroundings. Statistics indicate that, as shown in Figure 10.4 of the textbook, 40 percent of children in the United States live in low-income households and 18 percent in poverty. Family income fluctuates over time and tends to increase as children grow older. However, poverty during early childhood has a greater effect on well-being—particularly academic achievement—than poverty later in childhood. Family socioeconomic status (SES) is the most accurate predictor of children's intellectual skills at the time they enter school.

    Children living in poverty are at risk for depression. Nonetheless, as shown in a study of Native American children conducted by Jane Costello and her colleagues, children's mental health improves if their family income rises above the poverty level. Poverty is also associated with health problems such as tuberculosis and asthma, and children living in deteriorating housing may be exposed to lead poisoning, from peeling paint and dust, and be at greater risk of developing associated learning disabilities.

    Parents experiencing economic hardship are more likely to be harsh and controlling in their child rearing, and to discourage independence and curiosity because the often dangerous circumstances of their daily lives make these characteristics too risky. Low-income parents are also at risk for depression, negative feelings of self-worth, and negative beliefs about the degree to which they can control their own life circumstances. Poverty also raises the risk of their becoming parents while still in adolescence.

- As shown in Figure 10.5 of the textbook, a drop in the proportion of adolescents giving birth in the United States occurred between 1990 and 2005. However, as shown in Table 10.2, the United States continues to have one of the highest teen birth rates among industrialized nations. For example, in 2005, 40.5 of every 1,000 American women aged 15–19 gave birth. Research indicates that the children of unmarried teenage mothers tend to be more aggressive, less self-controlled, and less intellectually advanced than those of older, married mothers. According to Frank Furstenberg and his colleagues, two factors contribute to this: (1) young mothers are less interested in bringing up children and vocalize less with their infants, thus giving them less intellectual stimulation; (2) young mothers, especially if unmarried, are often poorly educated, may be socially isolated, and have limited financial resources, with all the disadvantages that accompany low income.

Tom Luster and his colleagues found that "more successful" preschool-aged children of teenage mothers tended to be those who lived in more intellectually stimulating and less stressful environments and had mothers who had completed more education, were more likely to be employed, had fewer children, and lived with a male partner. A study of adolescent participation in welfare-reform programs found that highly involved mothers who took advantage of center-based child care, educational opportunities, and job training programs had children with more advanced intellectual abilities than the offspring of less involved mothers. The box "In the Field: Louisiana Swamp Nurse" describes one social program for teen mothers that aims to reduce risks and increase protective factors for their children.

- Child abuse is a problem in all areas of the world. However, because of cultural differences in the definitions of what constitutes "maltreatment," shown in Table 10.3 of the textbook, it is difficult for researchers to gather precise information on its prevalence.

  Parents who were physically abused by their parents are more likely to abuse their own children; however, only 30 percent do so. Factors such as poverty, recent job loss, marital discord, and social isolation contribute to abuse. It is also more likely to occur when the mother is very young, is poorly educated, abuses drugs or alcohol, or receives little financial support from the father.

  Some characteristics of children that are associated with abuse include age (under 3 years), gender (female), and ethnicity (Pacific Islander, Native American, or African American). A number of researchers view abuse as a social disease that accompanies the acceptance of violence in families, communities, and society. First, most abuse occurs when parents intend to physically discipline their children and then end up hurting them. Second, countries with low rates of physical punishment also have very low rates of physical abuse.

  Maltreated children are at risk for later depression, drug and alcohol abuse, sexual problems, and criminal behavior; however, approximately one-fourth do not experience long-term problems. Factors that serve as buffers are a warm relationship with at least one adult, a fairly stable family residence, positive experiences in school, and participation in extracurricular activities.

- Other factors can also put children's development at risk. For example, Suniya Luthar and Bronwyn Becker found that middle-school students from a wealthy community had high rates of depression and substance abuse. These children felt themselves under great pressure to achieve and tended to be isolated from adults and emotionally distant from their mothers.

II. NONPARENTAL CHILD CARE

By the time they are 3 years of age, more than 90 percent of children in the United States will regularly experience nonparental child care and more than 50 percent will spend over 30 hours per week in child care.

A. Varieties of Child Care

In **home child care,** children are cared for in their own homes, often by relatives; with this arrangement, they experience the least change from their normal routine. This is one of the most popular arrangements for caring for children under 5 years of age.

In **family child care,** children are cared for in the caregiver's home, along with children from outside their families. The routine is usually similar to that at home, but children are exposed to a more diverse social group and experiences than would exist at home.

Child-care centers have attracted the most public attention and study. Their programs vary in style and philosophy: some are schoollike, whereas others allow children to select their own activities. Many receive public funding and are therefore more accessible to researchers, who can study how their particular characteristics affect children's development. Child-care programs also vary in quality; Table 10.4 of the textbook suggests questions that parents should consider in selecting a program.

B. Developmental Effects of Child Care

Questions about the effects of child care concern intellectual development, social development, and emotional well-being.

- Children under 3 years of age who spend time in child-care arrangements with more than six other children become sick more often; however, there is no evidence that this affects their overall development. Infants and toddlers in child-care centers also experience more stress during the day, according to research by Sarah Watamura and her colleagues, who measured cortisol levels in children's saliva. The intellectual development of children in high-quality child-care centers is at least as good as that of their peers raised at home. Children of low socioeconomic status (SES) with less-educated parents may benefit intellectually from a high-quality center.

- Research results indicate both the positive and negative effects of child-care centers on children's social and emotional development. For example, children who attend child-care centers in the United States are more self-sufficient and independent, more comfortable in new situations, more knowledgeable about the social world, and more enthusiastic about sharing toys than children who do not attend child-care centers. However, they are also less polite, less agreeable, less compliant with adults, and more aggressive than children who do not attend child-care centers. The greater the number of years children spend in full-time non-parental care, the greater the likelihood that they will have behavioral problems in kindergarten. However, the negative effects of nonparental care tend to be mild compared with the effects of other factors such as the mother's sensitivity and the family's socioeconomic level. It may be argued that it is the quality, not the quantity, of out-of-home care that has the biggest impact on adjustment. John Love and his colleagues found that children from low-income families who received high-quality child care benefited in many ways and had fewer behavioral problems than children who did not. One study found that middle-class German mothers whose children were in child care compensated for their absence during the day with intense periods of interaction in the mornings and evenings. Lieselotte

Ahnert and Michael Lamb suggest that working mothers who are stressed may have little time and energy to engage in such high-quality interactions.

C. An Ecological Approach to Child Care

Deborah Johnson and her colleagues point out that ethnic-minority and immigrant children are often not included in research on child care; studies also fail to consider the fact that African American and Hispanic families may view parenting as a responsibility which involves a system of extended kin. Their ecological model of child care, illustrated in Figure 10.6 of the textbook, shows how interacting components of the macrosystem, exosystem, mesosystem, and microsystem affect the types of care available to and utilized by families subject to racism and segregation.

III. NEIGHBORHOODS AND COMMUNITIES

Neighborhoods and communities differ in the resources they provide to children and families. The term **social capital** is used to refer to these resources, which include schools, health services and the like, and also social structures, expectations for behavior, and the levels of trust and cooperation among community members.

A. Community and Culture

Communities play an important role in transmitting the values and beliefs of culture. Donna Marie San Antonio carried out a study that compared two communities in the rural northeastern United States. One community (Hillside) is a working-class community with low levels of education and median family income; the other (Lakeview) is a more affluent white-collar community. San Antonio found that the people of Hillside cherish tradition and family ties and consider social status to be determined more by social and civic connections than material wealth. The people of Lakeview value independence, family privacy, achievement, and upward mobility. San Antonio found these contrasting sets of values to be reflected in the language and social interaction of the children in each community. As pointed out in Chapter 2, culture affects children's development because it is rooted in their everyday activities.

B. Distressed Communities

Recently, there has been an increasing amount of research on the impact of distressed neighborhoods and communities on children's development.

- Research indicates that neighborhood economic disadvantage has a profound effect on children's development, over and above the effects of the income levels of their families. Low-SES children who live in substandard housing are at greater risk for emotional and academic problems, get sick more often, and miss more school than comparable children living in better housing. Children show improvements in school when their families move to better-quality housing.
- Distressed neighborhoods and communities are also subject to **neighborhood physical disorder,** which may include *physical deterioration* (garbage on the streets, abandoned

buildings, graffiti, etc.) and *chaotic activity* (crowding, heavy street traffic, and high noise levels). Another problem of such neighborhoods is **social disorganization,** which includes weak *social cohesion* (lack of trust and connection among community members), poor *neighborhood climate* (the level of fear related to crime and violence), and *perceived racism.* Children growing up under these conditions are at risk for poor quality of life and poor mental health.

The effects of physical and social disorganization on children's development can occur in any nation. One source of community disorganization that affects children in many parts of the world is war, as discussed in the box "Children and War."

IV. MEDIA CONTEXTS

The term **media** refers to such forms of mass communication as newspapers, books, magazines, comic books, radio, television, film, video games, and the Internet. Children in the United States are exposed to media for an average of 8.33 hours per day. It has been observed that children incorporate what they learn from media into their behavior in other contexts. Research on the effects of media on development focuses on the *physical form* of the medium and its *content.* Considerable controversy surrounds the effects of media on development.

A. Print Media

Children's average daily exposure to print media, as shown in Table 10.5 of the textbook, is less than their exposure to other forms and remains fairly stable throughout childhood. However, children read, or are read to, almost every day. Children's literature is a growing industry; adventures, mysteries, fantasies, and fairy tales are especially popular with children. Psychoanalyst Bruno Bettelheim conducted a famous analysis of the role of fairy tales in children's emotional development. He noted that many fairy tales include symbolic representations of universal childhood anxieties and concluded that children need fairy tales in order to deal with their inner conflicts and fears. Children's literature has also been used as a therapeutic device to help children cope with emotionally troubling events.

B. Television

On average, young children are exposed to television for over two hours each day, more than to any other medium. Research has focused on the potentially positive or destructive influence of television on children's development.

- *Television Form.* A special concern about television viewing is that children may have difficulty separating the actors from the characters they portray or understanding that the events depicted are not really happening. Even 4- and 5-year-olds, for example, may believe that Sesame Street is a real place. Children may also fail to comprehend what they watch, especially if this means linking together fast-paced scenes. And children may not, until 7 or 8 years of age, recognize the difference between television programs and advertisements.

- *Television Content.* Television exposes children to a wide range of content. How does this affect their development, positively and negatively?

    Nearly 70 percent of children's television shows contain acts of physical aggression; this averages to 14 violent acts per hour. Compared with children who watch less television violence, children who watch more violent programs show lower levels of moral reasoning and are more likely to believe that violence is acceptable under certain circumstances. This may be because violence generally goes unpunished in children's television and is often executed by attractive characters, such as "good guys" combating evil. Jamie Ostrov and his colleagues conducted a longitudinal study of preschoolers whose parents reported on their television viewing preferences. These children, from relatively high-SES families, preferred educational shows to violent ones; those who watched the most television also engaged in more prosocial behaviors than children who watched less. There were gender differences in the relationship between viewing and children's behavior. For boys, greater exposure to violent shows predicted higher levels of physical, verbal, and relational aggression. For girls, higher levels of exposure to violent shows predicted only verbal aggression. Interestingly, higher exposure to educational shows predicted relational aggression by girls.

    Researchers are also concerned about social stereotypes in children's television programming. Historically, European American male characters have dominated television programming; this is changing. However, gender stereotypes remain, even in children's programming. The misrepresentation of ethnic minorities and foreigners is a significant problem, too, although some improvements have occurred, notably in the depictions of African Americans. A study conducted with children between 10 and 17 years of age, from a variety of ethnic backgrounds, showed that children are keenly aware of the stereotyped depictions of people from minority groups. Stereotyping on television is of concern because it may create or maintain negative attitudes toward minority groups and influence minority children's attitudes about their own group and place in society.

C. Interactive Media

Interactive media rank close behind television in popularity with children.

- *The Form of Interactive Media.* Children find interactive video games to be exciting and challenging; they call upon cognitive skills such as divided attention, spatial imagery, and representation. They are also subject to young children's difficulty with appearance-reality distinctions. For example, many children have become visibly upset when their *Tamagotchis* (game toys that require constant attention in order to keep them alive) die.

    How do new media technologies affect children's relationships with peers? A United Nations report asserted that electronic networks have begun to replace face-to-face networks in many areas, leading to the erosion of social relationships. However, this concern has not been strongly supported by research findings; one study found that boys who play computer games spend more time with their friends than boys who rarely play computer games. Computer games also can bring families together for shared time. However, as children grow more knowledgeable than their parents about how interactive games work, this kind of interaction may become less frequent.

- *The Content of Interactive Media.* Much attention has been given to the amount of violence in interactive games, yet few studies have examined the effects of violent video games on children's behavior. Research generally has found that playing violent video games is associated with increases in aggressive, antisocial behavior. Video games also appear to affect children's perception of real-world crime. For example, third- to sixth-grade Flemish children who frequently played violent video games tended to overestimate the amount of violent crime in the real world. This may desensitize children to actual violence and reduce their empathy for other people's emotional distress. Furthermore, violent games actively reward children (with points or advancement to the next level of the game) for making repeated violent choices. For these reasons, adults often express concern about the content of the interactive media to which their children are exposed.

V. CONTEXTS, RISK, AND RESILIENCE

An area of research called **prevention science** examines the biological and social processes that lead to maladjustment as well as those that are associated with healthy development. Developmentalists are especially interested in identifying **risk factors,** personal characteristics or environmental circumstances that increase the probability of negative outcomes for children. Risk applies to groups, not individuals; thus, one can say that people with depressed parents are "at risk" for depression, but one cannot know for sure that any particular person is at risk. Serious problems are usually associated with a combination of biological, social, and environmental risk factors interacting over a considerable time. Many children who grow up under difficult circumstances are **resilient**—that is, they have the ability to recover quickly from the adverse effects of early experience or to persevere in the face of stress with no apparent negative psychological consequences. Developmentalists have searched for the source of children's resilience, which they refer to as **protective factors.** Some of the risk factors and protective factors that have been identified are listed in Table 10.6 of the textbook.

What needs must be met to ensure that children will develop into healthy, well-adjusted adults? In 1959 the United Nations General Assembly attempted to answer this question in a resolution called the Declaration of the Rights of the Child. You can see the information contained in this document in Table 10.7 of the textbook.

Individual governments also have worked to develop programs aimed at optimizing children's development. **Public policies** are laws and programs designed to promote the welfare of children and families. Examples in the United States are nutritional and education programs such as Women, Infants, and Children (WIC) and Head Start, as well as policies regarding children's television programming and advertising, and laws governing the age at which children can work, marry, vote, and join the military, or how long they must attend school.

Children's ecologies include a vast variety of interacting systems—far more than are discussed in this chapter. However, it is the individual child who interacts with, responds to, and finds meanings across this array of contexts according to his or her own characteristics and past experiences.

Key Terms

Following are important terms introduced in Chapter 10. Match each term with the letter of the example that best illustrates the term.

1. _____ allocaregiving

2. _____ authoritarian parenting pattern

3. _____ authoritative parenting pattern

4. _____ child-care centers

5. _____ cooperative breeding

6. _____ extended families

7. _____ family child care

8. _____ family structure

9. _____ home child care

10. _____ media

11. _____ neighborhood physical disorder

12. _____ no-nonsense parenting

13. _____ nuclear families

14. _____ permissive parenting pattern

15. _____ prevention science

16. _____ protective factors

17. _____ public policies

18. _____ resilient

19. _____ risk factors

20. _____ social capital

21. _____ social disorganization

a. Ben passes boarded up storefronts and trash-strewn lots on his way to school.
b. A child of refugees from a war-torn country becomes a well-adjusted adult.
c. Studies how biological and social processes lead to maladjustment or to healthy development.
d. This term refers to child care by anyone in a group other than the child's parents.
e. Books, films, and television are three examples.
f. This arrangement is considered the norm among North Americans, but has become somewhat less typical in recent decades.
g. In this child-care arrangement, care is given in the home of the provider, who may be a relative or a stranger.
h. This style of parenting is regarded as especially characteristic of African American single mothers.
i. Pablo lives in a town where people do not trust one another and are frightened of what may happen to them on the street.

j.   Examples are economic hardship or having poorly educated parents.

k.   In this arrangement, children are taken care of in their own homes, often by a relative.

l.   The WIC program and Head Start are examples.

m.   One example would be a family in which a child lives with his mother, father, and brother in the same home with his grandmother and two aunts.

n.   Julia's parents believe that she needs to find out on her own what will happen when she does not follow rules, so they do not keep track of whether she has completed her homework.

o.   A baby elephant is cared for and protected by many members of the herd; this practice improves the group's reproductive success.

p.   Some of these are schoollike in their philosophies.

q.   Jon's dad demands unquestioning obedience to family rules.

r.   Examples are having a supportive extended family or good experiences in school.

s.   Kyra's mother requires her to go to bed on time, but is willing to explain to her why she needs to do so.

t.   This includes such things as schools and health care, but also less tangible resources such as the community's expectations for people's behavior.

u.   A term that refers to family organization, for example, nuclear or extended.

Multiple-Choice Practice Questions

Circle the letter of the word or phrase that correctly completes each statement.

1.   Nuclear families
   a.   have always been the most common form of family structure in all human societies.
   b.   have only become common in the United States during the last 50 years or so.
   c.   are less common in the United States than they were 50 years ago.
   d.   are equally common among all ethnic groups in the United States.

2.   An advantage of cooperative breeding among humans and other species is that
   a.   it allows the young to have a longer period in which to mature.
   b.   it allows mothers to have more and healthier offspring.
   c.   Both a and b are correct.
   d.   it allows individual mothers to have fewer offspring.

3.   According to anthropologist Robert Levine, the most urgent goal for parents is
   a.   making sure that their children survive.
   b.   making sure that their children are prepared to become economically productive.
   c.   making sure that their children acquire the cultural values of their society.
   d.   making sure that they have as many children as possible.

4.   Diana Baumrind and her colleagues found that the parenting styles of middle-class Americans vary along dimensions of
   a.   aggression and love.   c.   guilt and initiative.
   b.   control and warmth.   d.   confidence and empathy.

5. Children of _____ parents tend to be self-controlled, self-reliant, and willing to explore.
   a. authoritative
   b. authoritarian
   c. permissive
   d. All of the answers are correct.

6. Children whose parents use a(n) _____ parenting style tend to be less mature than those whose parents use other strategies.
   a. permissive
   b. authoritative
   c. authoritarian
   d. None of the answers is correct.

7. Margarita Azmintia and Joanne Hesser found that, while trying to complete a block-building task, young children were most likely to consult
   a. a strange adult.
   b. an older friend.
   c. Either a or b is correct.
   d. an older sibling.

8. According to Tom Luster and his colleagues, teen mothers who are _____ are more likely to have "successful" children.
   a. more highly educated
   b. employed
   c. live with a partner
   d. All of the answers are correct.

9. Which is true about child maltreatment?
   a. The majority of children who are abused grow up to abuse their own children.
   b. Most abuse occurs when parents are attempting to discipline their children.
   c. Parents of all ethnicities and economic levels are equally likely to abuse their children.
   d. Boys are more likely than girls to be abused.

10. Children cared for in which arrangement experience the least change from their normal routines?
    a. home child care
    b. family child care
    c. a child-care center
    d. All of the answers are correct.

11. Children who attend child-care centers are _____ than those cared for at home.
    a. better behaved
    b. more self-sufficient
    c. more attached to their parents
    d. less intelligent

12. Children of all ages have greater exposure to _____ than to any other form of media.
    a. television
    b. books
    c. computer games
    d. audio

13. Bruno Bettelheim has argued that fairy tales
    a. are too frightening to be appropriate for children.
    b. stimulate violence and aggression.
    c. help provide solutions to children's inner conflicts.
    d. are useful as a means of teaching gender roles.

14. Which is a possible source of misunderstanding when preschoolers watch television?
    a. They may not be able to distinguish between advertising and programming.
    b. They may not understand that the events on the screen are not really happening.
    c. They may believe that the people they see on the screen can also see them.
    d. All of the answers are correct.

15. There is evidence that children who frequently play violent video games
    a. overestimate the amount of violent crime occurring in the real world.
    b. engage in more aggressive, antisocial behavior than children who do not play violent games.
    c. Both a and b are correct.
    d. are no different in their behavior than children who do not play violent games.

16. Which of the following is *not* a factor that puts a child at risk for developmental problems?
    a. living in an extended family
    b. having low self-esteem
    c. undergoing financial hardship
    d. living in a community with high levels of violence

17. Which of these is a protective factor that is associated with resilience in the face of threats to children's development?
    a. having an "easy" infant temperament
    b. adapting well to school
    c. living in a community with extensive, easily accessed services
    d. All of the answers are correct.

Short-Answer Practice Questions

Write a brief answer in the space below each question.

✓1. Discuss how different kinds of family circumstances might result in parents adopting authoritarian, authoritative, permissive, or no-nonsense parenting styles.

✓2. Research on children from single-parent families has found that they are more likely to suffer behavioral, academic, or social problems. What are some possible reasons for these findings?

3. Discuss some of the effects of living in poverty on children. How are children affected when their families' incomes improve?

4. In what ways do child-care experiences affect children's intellectual and social development? What positive effects have been noted? Negative effects?

5. How would you design an ideal child-care environment for a 3-year-old child? Explain how each element would be beneficial for him or her.

6. Imagine that you are a parent trying to monitor your children's exposure to media. Would you want to limit their exposure in any way? Why or why not?

Putting It All Together

In this section, material from Chapter 10 can be combined with information presented in earlier chapters.

It has been suggested that parents from distressed socioeconomic circumstances are more concerned with their children's survival, whereas middle-class parent are more focused on their children's preparation for economic success. Do you think this is true? Discuss the evidence discussed in this and earlier chapters.

Sources of More Information

Anderson, C., Gentile, D., & Buckley, K. (2007). *Violent video game effects on children and adolescents: Theory, research, and public policy.* New York: Oxford University Press.
This book discusses experimental and correlational research on the relationship between playing violent video games and aggression. It includes suggestions for parents and other caregivers.

Gee, J. (2008). *What video games teaches about learning and literacy.* New York: Palgrave Macmillan.
In this book, the author describes the cognitive and decision skills that children practice while playing a variety of video games.

Lemish, D. (2007). *Children and television: A global perspective.* Malden, MA: Blackwell Publishing.
This book presents research from many countries on children and television viewing.

NICHD Early Child Care Research Network (eds.). (2005). *Child care and child development: Results from the NICHD study of early child care and youth development.* New York: Guilford Press.
This volume contains information from the official NICHD study; it covers the age range up to first grade.

Pecora, N., Murray, J., & Wartella, E. (eds.). (2007). *Children and television: Fifty years of research.* Mahwah, NJ: Lawrence Erlbaum Associates.
This is a review of research on television viewing that includes an extensive bibliography.

Rosen, L. (2007). *Me, My Space, and I: Parenting the net generation.* New York: Palgrave Macmillan.
This book, written by a research psychologist who specializes in technology issues, discusses how parents can anticipate and help their children deal with issues that come up in the online world.

Wachs, T. (2000). *Necessary but not sufficient: The respective roles of single and multiple influences on individual development.* Washington, DC: American Psychological Association.
The author argues that the behavior of individuals is best understood as a result of influences from multiple domains, including genetics, neurology, nutrition, and culture.

Werner, E. (1995). Resilience in development. *Current Directions in Psychological Science, 4,* 81–85.
Emmy Werner describes the protective factors—individual, family, and community—that help children overcome great odds.

Answer Key

Answers to Key Terms: 1.d, 2.q, 3.s, 4.p, 5.o, 6.m, 7.g, 8.u, 9.k, 10.e, 11.a, 12.h, 13.f, 14.n, 15.c, 16.r, 17.l, 18.b, 19.j, 20.t, 21.i.

Answers to Multiple-Choice Questions: 1.c, 2.c, 3.a, 4.b, 5.a, 6.a, 7.d, 8.d, 9.b, 10.a, 11.b, 12.a, 13.c, 14.d, 15.c, 16.a, 17.d.

11 | Physical and Cognitive Development in Middle Childhood

CHAPTER

Between about 5 and 7 years of age, children change in a number of ways. Their bodies and facial features become more streamlined and their smiles show gaps and permanent teeth coming in. Less visible changes in their brains support more graceful movements and more efficient thinking. They are entering the developmental period called middle childhood.

During middle childhood, children's height, weight, and strength increase steadily. These changes are matched by new cognitive abilities and increasing competence in the many social contexts to which they have been exposed since the end of infancy. Already skilled speakers of their language, these older children can follow complex directions and perform assigned tasks without constant adult supervision. They are better at remembering things and their thinking is more consistently logical than during the preschool years.

A reflection of children's new abilities is that adults now send them to be educated in school. Because of the importance of schooling to later success, there has been great interest in tests that will predict school performance, and at present intelligence tests are routinely used for that purpose, at least in industrialized societies.

Children will still need the protection of their families for a good number of years beyond middle childhood. However, adults in societies throughout the world now begin to expect them to behave more maturely in the new situations that they will confront.

Learning Objectives

Keep these questions in mind while studying Chapter 11.

1. How do children's bodies change during the years of middle childhood? What factors affect their growth?
2. What characteristics of children's behavior during middle childhood lead adults to assign them greater responsibilities?

3. In what ways are changes in the structure and function of children's brains associated with their increased abilities?

4. How, according to Jean Piaget, is children's thinking different than it was during early childhood? Is this new way of thinking universal across cultures?

5. What roles do increases in cognitive abilities such as memory, the use of strategies, and knowledge about one's own thought processes play in helping children develop more powerful ways of thinking?

6. Why are intelligence tests used for measuring aptitude for schooling? What can be learned from these tests and what are their limitations?

Chapter Summary

In many cultures, adults develop new expectations of children once they reach 6 or 7 years of age. The children are expected to behave more maturely and take on additional responsibilities. They are able to work independently, formulate goals, and resist the temptation to abandon them.

I.   PHYSICAL AND MOTOR DEVELOPMENT

During middle childhood, children can do more than before, partly because they are bigger and stronger, and have more endurance. Changes are taking place in their brains as well as their bodies.

A. Patterns of Growth

Between 6 years of age and the beginning of adolescence (six or seven years later), children increase in height from about 45 inches to 60 inches and in weight from approximately 45 pounds to 90 pounds. Genetic and environmental factors interact to influence how much growth they experience.

- Both genetic and environmental factors contribute to height differences among children. Monozygotic twins resemble one another in height more than dizygotic twins, showing the influence of heredity. The effect of environment is illustrated by examples in which children move from one environment to another. For example, when the height of Mayan American children was compared with that of Mayan children living in Guatemala, Barry Bogin and his colleagues found that the Mayan American children were 4 1/2 inches taller, on average. In some countries (Guatemala and North Korea, for example), nutrition and health have important effects on growth. Children's growth slows during illnesses. When adequately nourished, they experience a period of "catch-up growth" after an illness; when their nutrition is inadequate, they do not catch up and their growth is stunted.

- Body weight is also influenced by both heredity and environment. A study of Danish adoptees found a strong correlation between their weight as adults and the weight of their biological parents, showing the effect of heredity. But environmental factors such as the quality and quantity of food available also have important impacts. The number of calories consumed per day can have long-term effects on children's growth. The box "In the Field: The Edible Schoolyard: Thinking Outside the Lunchbox" takes up the problem of childhood obesity and attempts to make children aware of the pleasures of growing, harvesting, cooking, and eating healthy foods. Today, approximately 15 percent of 6- to 11-year-olds in the United States are considered at risk for obesity.

B. Motor Development

Motor skills, strength, agility, and balance all increase during middle childhood. Advanced skills such as kicking and throwing require practice as well as physical maturation to develop. On average, boys are more advanced in activities that require power and force, such as batting, kicking, dribbling, and throwing balls; girls excel in fine motors skills, such as drawing and writing, and in gross motor skills that combine balance and foot movement, such as skipping, hopping, and the skills needed in gymnastics. Cultural expectations about the appropriateness of particular activities for boys and girls play a large part in shaping differences in behavior. Nonetheless, both boys and girls benefit from being active in sports; those who participate are more likely to have high self-esteem, a sense of belonging at school, and lower levels of depression.

C. Brain Development

During middle childhood—especially between 6 and 8 years of age—children's brains undergo growth and development that are believed to underlie changes in their cognitive skills: myelination continues, particularly in the frontal cortex; synaptic pruning continues, with more stable connections among remaining neurons; brain activity patterns, as measured by an electroencephalogram (EEG), reveal a shift from a predominance of theta activity (characteristic of sleep in adults) to mostly alpha activity (characteristic of engaged attention); and *EEG coherence*, the synchronization of electrical activity in different areas of the brain, increases significantly. Robert Thatcher has pointed out the importance of increases in coordination between the electrical activity of the brain's frontal lobes and that of other brain areas. There is some evidence that children's patterns of brain activity are related to their performance on problem-solving tasks. For example, it was found that children who succeeded on a standard Piagetian task had a different pattern of brain activity than those who failed at the task; older children who failed had brain activity similar to that observed in younger children. Another study examined the relationship between performance on standard intelligence tests and children's cortical thickness (measured using neuroimaging techniques). As shown in Figure 11.6 of the textbook, different levels of intelligence were correlated with particular developmental patterns of cortical thinning and thickening that took place between 7 and 19 years of age. So far, the evidence linking changes in the brain with changes in behavior is correlational: it is difficult to ascertain when changes in children's brains cause the changes in their behavior and when changes in children's experiences cause the changes in their brains.

II. CONCRETE OPERATIONAL DEVELOPMENT

During the transition to middle childhood, children begin to engage in *mental operations* that allow them to solve problems which involve combining, separating, or transforming information in a logical manner. Piaget called this stage of development **concrete operations**; its characteristics are shown in Table 11.1 of the textbook. Piaget invented problem-solving tasks to diagnose the presence of concrete-operational thinking.

A. Conservation

Conservation is Piaget's term for the understanding that some properties of an object or substance remain the same despite changes in appearance. For example, in the **conservation of number** task, two sets of objects are presented in one-to-one correspondence; then one set is modified—for example, by stretching out that row of objects—although the number of objects remains the same. Children who conserve number realize that on the basis of logic alone the number of objects in the two sets is still equal, despite the change in appearance. Children under 6 or 7 years of age rarely conserve number, unless the number of objects is very small.

The **conservation of volume** task examines children's understanding that the amount of liquid in a container remains the same, even when it is poured into a container of a different shape. Children of 3 or 4 years of age may believe that more liquid is present when it is poured into a taller, thinner container; they *centrate* or focus on the height of the container. Children undergo a transitional stage at 5 or 6 years of age: they recognize that both the height and circumference are important but have difficulty keeping both in mind simultaneously. By about 8 years of age, Piaget found, children understand that the increase in height of the new container is offset by the decrease in its circumference. Children are now able to respond to the conservation task by offering logical arguments: **identity** ("They were equal to start with and nothing was added, so they're the same"); **compensation** ("The liquid is higher, but the glass is thinner"); and **reversibility** ("If you pour it back, you'll see that it's the same").

B. Classification

Concrete operations also involve understanding the hierarchical nature of categories, including the *inclusion* relation between superordinate classes and their subclasses ("Are there more brown beads or more beads?"). So, for example, dogs and cats are subclasses of mammals. Children also become better able to classify objects according to multiple criteria. This is evident when they begin to collect and trade Pokemon and baseball cards, or to collect stamps, minerals, or comic books.

C. Planning

The ability to formulate a plan—that is, a cognitive representation of the actions needed to achieve a specific goal—is another aspect of thinking that improves during middle childhood. William Gardner and Barbara Rogoff, comparing 4- to 6-year-olds with 7- to 10-year-olds on a maze-solving task, found that when they instructed the children that both speed and accuracy were important, participants in both age groups planned a portion of their route through the maze ahead of time and then planned only when they encountered uncertain choice points. When instructed that accuracy alone was important, the older children planned all their moves ahead of time, realizing that this would result in fewer errors; however, the younger children proceeded just as they had in the other scenario. Research on the Tower of Hanoi game suggests that in reasoning tasks, as when solving mazes, older children show greater ability to plan their solutions ahead of time compared to younger children.

D. Metacognition

The development of **metacognition**, the ability to think about and regulate one's own thoughts, allows children to assess the difficulty of a problem and choose solution strategies in a flexible way. Researchers have found preschoolers and kindergartners to be more likely than older children to overestimate their knowledge and problem-solving skills. Candice Mills and Frank Keil asked kindergartners, second-graders, and fourth-graders to estimate their knowledge of how mechanical devices, including a toaster, work, both before and after giving the researchers an explanation and hearing an explanation delivered by a "toaster expert." Although the second- and fourth-graders revised their knowledge estimates downward after realizing that they knew less about toasters than they had recognized, the kindergartners actually rated themselves higher after hearing the expert's account.

E. Limitations of Concrete Operations

Concrete operations allow children to be objective, think logically, and apply knowledge flexibly to new situations. However, children's thinking is best in *concrete* situations that they have experienced directly. When children are asked to reason about abstract phenomena, difficulties may emerge. A study by Jason Low and Steve Hollis, in which children of different age groups and college students were asked to draw a picture of themselves with three eyes, found that 6-, 9-, and 12-year-olds all pictured the third eye near the other two, consistent with their experience of eyes in the real world. The college students, however, broke from the usual way of thinking about eye placement and their self-portraits were more imaginative and diverse.

III. INFORMATION-PROCESSING APPROACHES

Information-processing theorists explain the cognitive changes during middle childhood in terms of increased memory capacity and attention, more rapid and efficient mental operations, and the acquisition of new mental strategies.

A. The Role of Memory

Three factors are thought to bring about the memory changes that characterize middle childhood:

- *Increased Speed and Capacity of Working Memory.* A common behavioral method of measuring working memory is children's **memory span**—the number of randomly presented items of information that children can repeat immediately after the items are presented. The numbers' memory span of most 4- and 5-year-olds is approximately four digits; for 9- and 10-year-olds, it is six; and for adults, it is approximately seven digits. As shown in Figure 11.15 of the textbook, memory span increases along with the speed of naming items. Older children can name numbers more quickly, thus storing more of them in working memory and increasing the likelihood of retaining them in memory. Cross-cultural work supports this view. For example, Chuansheng Chen and Harold Stevenson found that Chinese children could recall more digits than their American age-mates; however, the Chinese words for numbers are shorter than the corresponding English words. When Stevenson and his colleagues measured memory capacity using lists of words that were of equal length in both Chinese and English, the researchers found no differences in memory capacity.

Brain development contributes to the change occurring in working memory during middle childhood. For example, when electrodes were placed over different areas of the brain to measure how quickly children's brains responded to complex stimuli, researchers found a gradual increase in speed throughout middle childhood.

- *Expanded Knowledge Base*. Older children usually have accumulated more experience with respect to any given topic than younger children; this provides them with a richer knowledge base with which to relate, and remember, new information. For example, Micheline Chi found that 10-year-old children who were experienced chess players were better able to remember the arrangements of pieces on a chess board that occurred during the course of a game than college students, although the college students' performance in remembering a random series of numbers was far superior. German researchers replicating the same study determined that the advantage of expert players was greatly reduced when the task was remembering random arrangements of chess pieces rather than their meaningful arrangements, thus removing the importance of knowledge.

- *Improved Memory Strategies*. Between early and middle childhood, children become better able to make use of **memory strategies**—deliberate actions that help them to remember.

  Rehearsal is the process of repeating the information to be remembered, as one might do when trying to remember a phone number. John Flavell and his colleagues found that in a 15-second interval between seeing a set of pictures and recalling them, most 10-year-olds engaged in rehearsal, whereas 5-year-olds rarely did. When children in each group who did not spontaneously rehearse were taught to do so, they did as well on the recall task as those who had rehearsed on their own.

  There is also a difference between younger children and those in middle childhood in the use of **organizational strategies**—strategies of mentally grouping the information to be remembered into meaningful clusters of closely associated items. For example, 7- to 8-year-olds often link words in a list to categories such as animals, foods, or geometric shapes, whereas younger children are more likely to use sound features such as rhymes or rely on situational associations. Over the course of middle childhood, children become increasingly better at using various strategies to help them remember.

  Elaboration is a process in which children identify or make connections between two or more items to be remembered. It is not until middle childhood that children begin to use this strategy spontaneously, and the use of elaboration strategies increases with age.

B. Thinking about Memory

Metamemory is a form of metacognition that involves the ability to think about one's memory processes. Five-year-olds understand that it is easier to remember a short list of words than a long one and that it is easier to remember something that happened recently than something that happened longer ago. But most 8-year-olds have a better understanding of the limitations of their own memories than 5-year-olds; they know, for example, that in order to remember a list of items, they need to study the list and test themselves on how well they remember it.

Children's metamemory seems to be related to their use of memory strategies. In one study, William Fabricius and John Hagen created a situation in which 6- and 7-year-old children used an organizational strategy on some trials and not on others; when they used the strategy, they almost always remembered better. The researchers found that children who recognized the usefulness of the strategy were more likely to use it in a future session (99 percent compared to only 32 percent of the children who did not attribute their improved remembering to using the strategy).

C. Increased Control of Attention

Children also become better able to control their attention during middle childhood. For example, Elaine Vurpillot, in a study of 3- to 10-year-olds, found that older children's visual search strategies were more systematic than those of younger children. Other research has shown that, during early and middle childhood, children also acquire the ability to ignore distractions and gain voluntary control over what to pay attention to.

D. Combining Memory Development and Logical Stages

In accounting for the increased mental abilities of children during middle childhood, how might the stagelike changes that occur in children's logical reasoning work together with the increases that occur in their memory and other information-processing capacities? Robbie Case and his colleagues have argued that when a child acquires a new cognitive scheme, working memory is stretched to capacity in applying the new scheme to new experiences. With practice over time, the scheme becomes automatic, freeing up space in working memory and permitting the child to attend to additional facets of experience.

To illustrate these ideas, Case and his colleagues conducted a number of studies that examined children's understanding of such areas as numbers, storytelling, and drawing. In the instance of numbers, they evaluated the performance of 6-, 8-, and 10-year-olds in solving math problems of four levels of complexity. They found that there was little difference between the performance of 6-year-olds and that of older children when the questions could be answered by thinking about a single number line; however, if two number lines needed to be coordinated, the 6-year-olds' performance deteriorated to a greater degree than that of 8- or 10-year-olds. As shown in Table 11.2 of the textbook, although the older children did better, they also experienced increasing difficulty as the problems became more complex (that is, made greater demands on working memory).

Andreas Demetriou and his colleagues found that speed of processing, working memory, and logical problem solving build on each other; increases in processing speed lead to increases in working memory, which in turn lead to increases in the effectiveness of problem solving.

IV. THE ROLE OF SOCIAL AND CULTURAL CONTEXTS

Cross-cultural research underscores the role of social and cultural contexts in the cognitive changes that occur between early and middle childhood.

A. Is the Acquisition of Conservation Universal?

Is the development of conservation a universal achievement of human beings? Piaget believed that conservation would occur in children of all cultures, although children in some cultures might, due to differences in experience, acquire it earlier than others. Research has found that children in nonindustrial societies who have not attended school achieve conservation a year or more later than reported by Piaget; however, in some cases, researchers have determined that adults in certain cultures never exhibit an understanding of conservation, as measured by traditional Piagetian tasks. It has become evident that unfamiliarity with testing procedures is partly responsible for these results. For example, Pierre Dasen and his colleagues found that rural Australian aboriginal children and Canadian Inuit children showed greater understanding of conservation after being familiarized with a similar task in a brief training session. Children participating in cross-cultural studies also perform better on conservation tasks when tested in their native languages. In one study, Raphael Nyiti found that Micmac Indian children in Nova Scotia performed less well than children of European descent when tested in English, but equally well when tested in Micmac. Similar results were obtained by Nyiti and others in studies carried out in Tanzania and Sierra Leone. Apparently, conservation and concrete operations in general are achievements of middle childhood for children in all cultures. However, cultural variations in children's familiarity with the specific tasks used to assess these skills may influence their performance.

B. Cultural Variations in the Use of Memory Strategies

Cross-cultural studies show that the development of memory skills during middle childhood is subject to cultural variations. For example, Michael Cole and his colleagues found that, unless they had attended school, children living in rural Liberia improved little after age 9 or 10 on a task that involved remembering a list of 20 items which belonged to familiar categories (for example, food, clothing, and tools). Liberian children attending school, like their counterparts in the United States, learned the stimulus list quickly and made use of the categories within it, clustering together items from the same category during recall. The nonschooled Liberian children, however, learned the list easily when the items were presented not randomly but as part of a story; items were clustered in recall according to their roles in the story. Similar results have been obtained with Guatemalan children from a Mayan village. The ability to remember is a universal intellectual requirement, but specific strategies for remembering—those most often studied by psychologists—are not universal, being associated with formal schooling.

C. Cultural Variations in Planning

A study of Navajo and European American children by Shari Ellis and Bonnie Schneiders revealed that Navajo children spent nearly ten times as long planning their way through a maze and made far fewer errors. This finding was of interest to the researchers because the two cultures differ in the value they place on doing things speedily; although Americans of European ancestry tend to consider speed of mental performance to be a sign of intelligence, the Navajo emphasize completing tasks thoughtfully rather than quickly.

V. INDIVIDUAL DIFFERENCES IN COGNITIVE DEVELOPMENT

While all languages have words that describe people's ability to solve problems, the exact meanings of the words differ across cultures. Some cultures define intelligence primarily in social terms (cooperation and obedience). Others, including many Asian and African cultures, define it as having both cognitive and social features. European and North American cultures give far more emphasis to the cognitive dimension of intelligence. In industrialized countries, children's scores on intelligence tests influence the kind of education they receive and the kind of work they will do as adults.

A. Measuring Intelligence

Once mass education became widespread, educators grew interested in finding out why some children had difficulty learning in school. In France a commission named by the minister of public instruction asked Alfred Binet and Théodore Simon to develop a test for identifying children who needed special educational treatment. They called their basic index of intelligence mental age (MA). According to it, a child who performed at the level of the average 7-year-old on his or her tasks had an MA of 7, regardless of chronological age. The concept of **Intelligence Quotient (IQ)**, introduced by psychologist William Stern in response to the Binet and Simon scale, is the unit of measurement we use today: MA/CA $\times$ 100, where MA is a child's mental age and CA is the child's chronological age. For example, a child performing at his or her chronological age has an IQ of 100; an 18-year-old with an MA of 16 has an IQ of 89. Although intelligence tests have undergone further refinement, they still use the logic of Binet and Simon: to define "average" performance for each age and compare individual children's scores against that average.

B. Persistent Questions about Intelligence

Three questions have dominated research on intelligence since the time of Binet and Simon.

1. The Nature of Intelligence: General or Specific?

Binet and Simon viewed intelligence as a basic characteristic of a person's mental life and, indeed, performance on different types of items within IQ tests is correlated, consistent with the idea of a "general intelligence." However, many scholars believe that a single dimension is inadequate to characterize intelligence and that it is composed of several distinct and separate abilities. For example, Howard Gardner has proposed a theory of "multiple intelligences," including, among others, linguistic, musical, logical-mathematical, and social intelligence. And Robert Sternberg has proposed a "triarchic" theory of intelligence that includes analytic, creative, and practical abilities. He argues that standard IQ tests measure only analytic intelligence.

2. What Explains Populations Differences?

Along with disagreements about whether intelligence is specific or general, developmentalists do not concur about the significance or source of differences across individuals and across groups in intelligence test scores. According to the *innatist hypothesis of intelligence*, some people are born more intelligent than others and these differences cannot be eliminated by training or other environmental manipulations. Beginning in the 1930s and 1940s, this view was countered by the *environmentalist hypothesis of intelligence*, which views intelligence both as including distinct and separate abilities and as being heavily dependent on experience. The **Flynn effect**, a steady increase in IQ performance over the past 100 years, lends support to the environmental hypothesis. Possible explanations for the rise in IQ scores range from improvements in nutrition and increasing years of education to experience with the greater complexity of modern life.

3. Are IQ Tests Culturally Biased?

As discussed in Chapter 2, it is difficult to specify the exact gene-environment interactions that contribute to human behavior, especially *polygenic* traits—those that are influenced by several or many genes acting in combination in a given environment. In addition, parents influence not only the genetic constitution of their children but also their environments. And, finally, children actively shape their own environments in response to both genetic and environmental influences.

Psychologists disagree about exactly what is measured by IQ tests. They do know that these tests are moderately accurate in predicting later school performance. But because all intelligence tests draw on a background of learning that is culture-specific and rooted in formal schooling, we cannot assume that an IQ test, like a yardstick, will yield equivalent measures in all cultural environments.

VI. RECONSIDERING THE COGNITIVE CHANGES IN MIDDLE CHILDHOOD

When we look at the physical and cognitive changes that occur between early and middle childhood as a whole, rather than as a collection of isolated achievements, we can understand why adults begin to give their children greater independence during this period. Chapters 12 and 13 will investigate these changes as they are displayed in a variety of contexts.

Key Terms

Following are important terms introduced in Chapter 10. Match each term with the letter of the example that best illustrates the term.

1. _____ compensation

2. _____ concrete operations

3. _____ conservation of number

4. _____ conservation of volume

5. _____ elaboration

6. _____ Flynn effect

7. _____ identity

8. _____ intelligence quotient (IQ)

9. _____ memory span

10. _____ memory strategies

11. _____ metacognition

12. _____ metamemory

13. _____ organizational strategies

14. _____ rehearsal

15. _____ reversibility

a. This is approximately seven items for adults, six for 9- and 10-year-olds, and four for 4- and 5-year-olds.

b. This supports the environmental hypothesis of intelligence.

c. A child realizes that the transformation performed in a conservation task can be undone—for example, by pouring the water back into the original container.

d. A number used to compare the intelligence of different people.

e. Writing a note and repeating information to oneself are two examples of this process.

f. Ryan knows that if he pours his glass of juice into a glass of a different shape, the amount of juice remains the same.

g. When a boy is asked if two lists of words are equally difficult to learn, he indicates that it will take him longer to learn the longer list.

h. Jill recognizes that two rows have the same number of pennies, even though one row is spread out so that it looks longer.

i. Kaylee remembers what she needs at the store by grouping the items into categories, such as breakfast foods, pet supplies, and snacks.

j. An example of this is being able to judge the difficulty of solving a particular problem.

k. In a memory task, children do this when they form connections between two or more of the things to be remembered.

l. Internalized actions (like combining or separating) that fit into a logical system.

m. A mental operation in which a child realizes that a change in outward appearance does not alter the actual substance involved.

n. Pat gets a phone number from directory assistance but has no pencil to write it down; he keeps the number in his memory by repeating it to himself over and over.

o. A child understands that when liquid is poured into a taller, thinner glass, the amount remains the same because the increase in the height of the container is offset by a decrease in its circumference.

Multiple-Choice Practice Questions

Circle the letter of the word or phrase that correctly completes each statement.

1. Which shows the effect of the environment on growth during middle childhood?
    a. Monozygotic twins resemble one another more than dizygotic twins.
    b. Children of Mayan descent who live in the United States are taller than those living in Guatemala.
    c. The weights of adopted children are correlated with the weights of their biological parents.
    d. All these answers are correct.

2. With respect to the development of motor skills during middle childhood, boys are generally more advanced than girls in
    a. fine motor skills.
    b. skills involving balance and foot movement.
    c. skills requiring power and force.
    d. All these answers are correct.

3. When children are between the ages of 6 and 8, their brains
    a. become more myelinated, especially in the frontal lobes.
    b. achieve greater EEG coherence.
    c. shift their electrical activity toward a greater preponderance of alpha waves.
    d. All these answers are correct.

4. A child who, in correctly answering a question about conservation of volume, says, "They're still the same because, even though the level now looks higher, the second container is skinnier" is justifying her answer in terms of
    a. negation.
    b. reversibility.
    c. identity.
    d. compensation.

5. One reason for preschoolers' problems on conservation tasks is that they focus their attention on
   a. only one aspect of the stimulus situation.
   b. two aspects of the stimulus at the same time.
   c. other stimuli besides those presented.
   d. their own actions with respect to the stimuli.

6. When children use concrete operations, their answers on the conservation of number task are based on
   a. the physical appearance of the stimulus display.
   b. what they wish to be correct.
   c. what must logically be true.
   d. what the experimenter tells them is correct.

7. Which way of organizing a stamp collection is especially characteristic of middle childhood?
   a. separating all the stamps into different piles according to country
   b. placing the stamps into one large, undivided pile
   c. placing U.S. stamps in one pile and all the other stamps in a second pile
   d. separating stamps according to country and, within countries, separating them according to subject (for instance, birds or people)

8. William Gardner and Barbara Rogoff found that age-related differences in performance on a maze-navigation task could be attributed to
   a. changes in knowledge base.
   b. differences in planning.
   c. strategies taught by teachers.
   d. differences between the performance of boys and girls.

9. When kindergartners, second graders, and fourth graders were asked about their knowledge of mechanical devices (such as toasters),
   a. younger children overestimated their knowledge more than older children did.
   b. older children overestimated their knowledge more than younger children did.
   c. children of all age groups overestimated their knowledge equally.
   d. children in all the age groups were more likely to underestimate their knowledge rather than overestimate it.

10. What is the relationship between children's memory and their knowledge base?
    a. The greater the knowledge base children have about a topic, the better their performance on a topic-related memory task.
    b. If children have a large knowledge base on one topic, their performance improves on unrelated topics as well.
    c. Knowledge base affects the memory performance of adults but does not affect the performance of children.
    d. Knowledge base has no effect on memory in adults or children.

11. Researchers have found that teaching 4- and 5-year-olds to rehearse material they are asked to remember
    a. has no effect on their memory performance.
    c. makes their memory performance similar to that of older children.
    d. improves the memory performance of children who use rehearsal spontaneously but not that of children who do not use it.

12. A child performing a free-recall memory task clusters like items together in recall (for instance, animals, toys, and clothing). This is an example of
    a. elaboration.
    b. increased memory span.
    c. an organizational strategy.
    d. rehearsal.

13. *Metamemory* refers to a person's
    a. memory capacity.
    b. use of strategies to aid in remembering.
    c. knowledge relating to the information to be recalled.
    d. knowledge about the process of remembering.

14. In a study comparing the performance of Navajo and European American children on a maze-solving task, Shari Ellis and Bonnie Schneiders found that
    a. European American children solved the maze more quickly and with fewer errors than Navajo children.
    b. Navajo children took much longer than European American children to plan their routes through the maze.
    c. European American children made more errors solving the maze than Navajo children.
    d. Both b and c are correct.

15. Schooled individuals have an advantage over unschooled people on which aspect of memory performance?
    a. memory capacity
    b. tasks using randomly presented items
    c. remembering stories
    d. None of these answers is correct.

16. Which of the following is true of intelligence?
    a. Only modern, industrialized countries describe people's abilities in ways that can be called intelligence.
    b. The meaning of intelligence is the same in all cultures.
    c. With modern testing methods, intelligence can be measured precisely.
    d. The concept of intelligence is used to explain differences in school performance.

17. A 9-year-old with a mental age of 10 has an IQ of
    a. 90.
    b. 100.
    c. 111.
    d. 119.

18. Which of these provides support for the environmental hypothesis of intelligence?
    a. the Flynn effect
    b. observations in the past that when people moved from rural areas to the city, their IQs rose
    c. observations that people tend to score similarly on the different types of test items found in IQ tests
    d. Both a and b are correct.

Short-Answer Practice Questions

Write a brief answer in the space below each question.

1. Discuss the biological and environmental factors that affect children's growth in height and weight.

2. What, according to Piaget, are the characteristics of concrete operational thought? Discuss the cultural factors that influence performance on the tasks Piaget used to evaluate concrete operational thinking.

3. What important changes take place in children's memory performance during middle childhood? How are these changes affected by cultural context?

4. What improvements take place during middle childhood in children's ability to plan ahead? How might they be related to changes in their brains during this period? How are they related to cultural factors?

5. Describe the basic elements of intelligence testing. What are the main sources of disagreements among researchers about the nature of intelligence?

6. Make up your own definition of intelligence. Describe how this type of intelligence might be affected by genetic, environmental, and/or cultural factors.

Putting It All Together

In this section, material from Chapter 11 can be combined with information presented in earlier chapters.

As children grow older, they learn more and more about the world. One thing they learn is that certain properties of objects and people remain the same despite changes in the way those objects and people look. *Using examples, show how this knowledge develops in various ways during infancy, the preschool period, and middle childhood.*

Sources of More Information

Cole, M., & Scribner, S. (1974). *Culture and thought.* New York: John Wiley & Sons.
This book describes studies of cognitive development carried out in Liberia.

Gardner, H. (1999). Intelligence reframed: Multiple intelligences for the 21st century. New York: Basic Books.
This book presents Gardner's theory that every person has a unique set of competencies which taken together make up his or her intelligence. Gardner describes how his theory has evolved and been revised since it was first introduced in 1983.

Inhelder, B., & Piaget, J. (1969). The early growth of logic in the child: Classification and seriation. New York: W.W. Norton.
The authors discuss their work on the development of children's skills in logical classification.

Rogoff, B. (2003). *The cultural nature of human development.* New York: Oxford University Press.
This book discusses the role of culture in responding to Piagetian tasks, and addresses topics relevant to schooling and learning through guided participation.

Siegler, R., & Ellis, S. (1996). Piaget on childhood. *Psychological Science,* 7(4), 211–215.
The authors describe what they consider to be the most significant features of Piaget's theory, highlighting the importance of variability in children's thinking as a motivator of cognitive change.

Tanner, J. (1990). *Fetus into man: Physical growth from conception to maturity,* rev. ed. Cambridge, MA: Harvard University Press.
A comprehensive review of normal physical growth and development.

Trotter, R. (August 1986). Three heads are better than one. *Psychology Today,* 20(8), 56–62.
This article presents Robert Sternberg's triarchic theory, which hypothesizes on the analytic, creative, and practical aspects of intelligence.

Answer Key

Answers to Key Terms: 1.o, 2.l, 3.h, 4.f, 5.k, 6.b, 7.m, 8.d, 9.a, 10.e, 11.j, 12.g, 13.i, 14.n, 15.c.

Answers to Multiple-Choice Questions: 1.b, 2.c, 3.d, 4.d, 5.a, 6.c, 7.d, 8.b, 9.a, 10.a, 11.c, 12.c, 13.d, 14.d, 15.b, 16.d, 17.c, 18.d.

12 School as a Context for Development

Throughout the world, middle childhood is a time when children are expected to learn the skills they will need in order to be productive adult members of their societies. In modern, industrialized countries, children of this age spend much of their time in school, learning literacy, mathematics, and other culturally valued knowledge.

When children begin school, they already know a great deal about language and may know the names of the letters of the alphabet, a system that represents each significant sound with a different symbol. They can usually count numbers and objects, perhaps using their fingers or other body parts to help keep track of quantity. In school, children will build on these skills, working within a specialized environment with its own rules and its own way of using language.

Many of the cognitive changes associated with middle childhood are not direct results of schooling; however, children who have attended school perform better on tasks that resemble school activities. Schooling has its greatest effect on opportunity: children who are not educated are less likely to experience later economic success and pass on opportunities to their own children.

In order to do well in school, children need not only aptitude but also an environment conducive to learning. For many students, a supportive atmosphere at home, in school, and within the culture at large can make the difference between success and failure.

Learning Objectives

Keep these questions in mind while studying Chapter 12.

1. In what ways does formal schooling differ from other methods of educating children, such as apprenticeships?
2. How do ideas about "top-down" and "bottom-up" processing affect strategies for teaching reading and mathematics?

3. How do families and preschools help in promoting children's school readiness?
4. What is the standard instructional format used in school and what are some alternatives to it?
5. What makes the "language of schooling" different from everyday language?
6. What cognitive skills are improved by participating in formal schooling? How do developmentalists study this question, given that nearly all children attend school?
7. What factors hinder children's ability to learn in school? How may these problems be remedied?
8. How do gender, socioeconomic status, and ethnicity impact access to education, and how is school success affected by the similarities between home culture and school culture?

Chapter Summary

Education is important in shaping children's lives and in improving the health of their communities. Educational quality is also important; even in the United States, where all children go to school, the quality of education available in economically impoverished neighborhoods may suffer. A study of African American families that moved from urban housing projects to new housing in a wealthier suburb found that children improved on a variety of academic measures, including a decrease in school drop-out rates and an increase in college attendance.

I. THE CONTEXTS OF LEARNING

Chapter 2 introduced the idea that children acquire the material and symbolic tools of their culture through *social enhancement*, *imitation*, and *explicit instruction*. **Education** is a social process in which adults engage in deliberate instruction of the young to ensure that they acquire specialized knowledge and skills. Explicit instruction is not an important activity in contemporary hunter-gatherer societies. Instead, skills are taught as a part of everyday activity, through social enhancement and imitation. Children learn by being included in adult activities. Once societies become more complex, **apprenticeship**, which combines instruction with productive work, provides a form of learning that is intermediate between the implicit socialization which occurs with family and community life and the explicit instruction of formal education. Apprentices learn through observation and practice; they often live with their adult master in a family setting and help with farm or household tasks to pay for their upkeep.

The earliest forms of formal schooling date back to about 4000 B.C., when young people were brought together to learn systems of writing and arithmetic. Schooling differs from apprenticeship training in several ways: (1) motivation (school knowledge typically cannot be put to use immediately and sometimes not for a long time); (2) social relations (schoolteachers are rarely relatives or family acquaintances); (3) social organization (in school, children learn in the company of other children of the same age, under the supervision of one adult, or work individually); and (4) medium of instruction (in school, a specialized type of oral and written instruction is used).

The problems children solve in school differ from those they encounter in other learning contexts. School problem solving supports the development and use of abstract reasoning, whereas everyday problem solving supports reasoning based on particular concrete experience. Table 12.1 of the textbook describes some of the typical differences between school problems and everyday problems.

II. SCHOOL READINESS

When children begin school, their academic success will rest partly on the **emergent literacy** (knowledge, skills, and attitudes that provide the building blocks for learning to read and write) and **emergent numeracy** (knowledge, skills, and attitudes that provide the building blocks for learning how to do math) that they have developed during infancy and early childhood.

A. Precursors to Reading and Writing

When children learn to read and write, their first step is recognizing the correspondence between *graphemes* (units of print) and *phonemes* (units of sound). This process of letter-sound translation is called **decoding**. The *phonological awareness* needed to detect and manipulate the phonemes in words does not occur, however, without deliberate instruction. And, according to Peter Bryant and his colleagues, children who find it difficult to break words into syllables and phonemes also have difficulty linking sounds and letters. Special instruction in oral language analysis (including, for example, rhyming or speaking "pig Latin") helps increase the literacy skills of poor readers.

B. Precursors to Learning Mathematics

In order to learn mathematics, children must learn to translate the words and symbols used for numbers in their culture into an understanding of specific quantities. Very young babies can distinguish between sets containing different numbers of objects. At 2 to 3 years of age, children begin to map quantities to symbols; the ability to envision numbers as discrete units on an abstract number line develops during middle childhood. Interestingly, the ability to identify and manipulate numeric units seems to emerge only within the context of school.

C. The Role of Family

In many cultures, parents provide children with toys and activities that promote literacy and numeracy. A study of 3-year-olds in the United States, Brazil, and Kenya, carried out by Jonathan Tudge and his colleagues, found differences in the types of school readiness activities practiced by families of different cultures and socioeconomic status. For example, in all three cultures, children from middle-class families were more likely to engage in academically oriented play and lessons. In Kenya alone, children from working-class families were more likely to be engaged with their parents in lessons about how things work, why things happen, and how to be safe; Kenyan working-class children also spent more time than children in any of the other cultural/socioeconomic groups engaged in work-related activities, such as shopping, cleaning, and repairing.

Numerous studies have shown that children's everyday activities have significant bearing on their intellectual development and academic success. For example, being read to at 14 months of age is related to language comprehension, vocabulary size, and cognitive functioning at 2 years. Thus, when young children are read to on a regular basis, their vocabularies increase; when their vocabularies increase, so do their daily reading activities in a kind of "snowball" effect.

D. Preschools

With greater recognition of the importance of school readiness for academic success, preschool enrollment throughout the world has tripled since 1970. However, as shown in Figure 12.5 of the textbook, there are vast differences in enrollment across geographic areas, and the children who are already at highest risk for malnourishment and preventable diseases are also those least likely to be enrolled in preschool programs.

In addition to cross-national differences in preschool attendance, differences exist within countries. Studies have shown that children of ethnic-minority immigrant families in the United States are less likely to be enrolled in preschool than their native-born, ethnic-majority peers. Possible reasons for this disparity include lack of financial resources and availability of family members to provide child care; cultural norms also affect participation. However, research has indicated that children from immigrant families profit greatly from preschool experiences. In particular, Hispanic children who have participated in preschool gain in language skills, English proficiency, reading and math, and are less likely to repeat grades.

III. IN THE CLASSROOM

Once in school, students experience different types of instruction according to the educational philosophies of the schools they attend. They also come to have different feelings about school, and some students put more energy than others into doing well.

A. Social Organization of the Classroom and Instructional Design

Opinion about the best way to design instruction in school oscillates between two extreme approaches. One approach, which emphasizes **bottom-up processing**, starts with teaching basic skills; once these skills are mastered, instruction moves on to more complex tasks. The other approach emphasizes **top-down processing** and focuses from the start on using skills to accomplish specific, meaningful tasks.

- *The Standard Classroom Format.* In schools, children usually sit in parallel rows, facing front, while the teacher sits or stands facing them. **Instructional discourse**, a distinctive way of talking that is typical in school but rarely encountered elsewhere, provides students with information specified by the curriculum and gives students and teachers feedback on children's efforts to learn the information. The **initiation–reply–feedback sequence** is the most common pattern for instructional discourse. In it, the teacher asks a question to which he or she already knows the answer, then provides feedback on the student's reply. Learning to respond to "known-answer" questions is an important aspect of schooling.

- *Alternative Forms of Classroom Instruction.* Alternatives to the standard instructional format seek to make children more active participants in the educational process, rather than passive recipients of information.

One alternative to the recitation script is **reciprocal teaching**, a method designed by Ann Brown and Annemarie Palincsar to integrate bottom-up and top-down processing through small-group discussion at the time of reading. It targets children who can decode simple texts but have difficulty making sense of what they read. In this approach, a discussion leader (teacher or child) initiates an exchange that includes a question about a segment of the text. That person then answers the question, summarizing the content in his or her own words. If there is disagreement about the summary, group members reread it to clarify its meaning. Finally, the leader asks them to predict what will happen next. These activities allow children to see and hear the teacher and other children model metacognitive skills that aid comprehension. Reciprocal teaching is an application of Vygotsky's "zone of proximal development" in that it allows children to participate in reading for meaning before they have acquired the full set of abilities that would allow them to do so independently. As shown in Figure 12.6 of the textbook, reciprocal teaching has been used not only to improve reading comprehension but also to aid mastery of course material in subjects such as science and social studies.

Another alternative approach, developed by Paul Cobb and his colleagues, is **realistic mathematics education**, which shifts the focus of mathematics instruction away from basic skills, procedures, and memorization toward a conceptual understanding and application of math to real-world problems. According to these researchers, realistic mathematics education should (1) use meaningful activities; (2) support basic mathematical skills; and (3) employ models in educational activity. Teachers introduce concepts in the context of a story and children use models to represent elements in the story. As children master the conceptual structures that the stories and models support, they learn to carry out the needed calculations without such aids. Children are expected to justify the reasoning behind their own answers and to understand the reasoning behind other children's solutions; they are also expected to share what they learn with other group members. A study by Jo Boaler examined differences between classrooms in England, one of which used a traditional recitation-script approach to learning mathematics and one of which used a small-group, problem-oriented approach. Students who learned under the traditional format scored higher on standardized tests measuring knowledge of mathematical procedures. However, students who learned under the problem-oriented approach did better on conceptual questions and questions that required them to apply their knowledge to a novel problem.

An approach to learning used in several European countries is **playworld practice**, which involves enacting, discussing, making art, and playing with themes based on works of children's literature; it is based on theories regarding the importance of play in children's intellectual development. A study carried out by Sonja Baumer and her colleagues found that, compared to standard instruction, the playworld practice format resulted in greater increases in children's language skills, especially their abilities to tell and understand stories. The box "In the Field: Learning after School in the Fifth Dimension" describes another example of the use of play in instruction. In the "Fifth Dimension" after-school program, children advance through a maze by playing games that foster progressive skill development. Participants have been found to score higher than nonparticipants in math and reading and to improve in their basic language skills.

B. Barriers to School Success

Many students have difficulty in school, regardless of instructional organization, because of learning disabilities or lack of motivation.

- *Specific Learning Disabilities.* The term **specific learning disabilities** is used to refer to the academic difficulties of children who have trouble learning in school despite normal IQ test performance. Specific learning abilities may not become apparent until children enter school; they may be manifested as problems with listening, thinking, talking, reading, writing, spelling, or arithmetic. The most widely used method to detect specific learning disabilities is to analyze children's performance on an IQ test and on an academic achievement test that covers parts of the curriculum. A child with a specific learning disability would have an IQ in the normal range but wide disparities between scores on different subtests. The child's academic performance should correspond to the pattern in the IQ test. For example, a child may show low verbal ability but high ability in math; he or she should have difficulty learning to read but not in learning arithmetic. This pattern of performance is called *dyslexia* and is the most common form of specific learning disability. Other specific learning disabilities are *dyscalculia*, which involves difficulty in learning math, and *dysgraphia*, which is a specific difficulty in learning to write.

  Why do children with dyslexia have trouble reading? One reason is that they may lack phonological awareness (the ability to detect and manipulate the phonemes in words), which is important for *phonological processing*—understanding and applying the rules relating phonemes and graphemes. Phonological processing can be tested using *pseudowords* such as "cigbet" that are meaningless but can be read by following the rules for converting graphemes into phonemes. Linda Siegel and her colleagues found that, by 9 years of age, normal readers were proficient in reading pseudowords; 14-year-old dyslexic readers, on the other hand, were no better at reading pseudowords than normal readers were at 7. Dyslexia is assumed to involve some kind of anomaly in brain development, but there is uncertainty about how specific difficulties in reading may be linked to abnormalities in specific areas of the brain. Paula Tallal and her colleagues have found that for some children with dyslexia who have phonological processing difficulties, a different part of the brain becomes active when they are, for example, asked to identify rhyming and nonrhyming letter names—that is, less activity occurs in both the visual cortex and Broca's area (the part of the auditory cortex specialized for language). Tallal devised computer games to help children make rapid sound discriminations. Practice with these games makes the brain activation patterns of dyslexic children comparable to those of normal readers.

- *Motivation to Learn.* A distinctive aspect of formal education is that children need to pay attention and try hard even when the material being taught is uninteresting to them or difficult to learn. They must also cope with the fact that their best efforts may not always be successful. Many children lose their **academic motivation**—the ability to try hard and persist at school tasks in the face of difficulties. Other children thrive in the face of challenges at school. Researchers have identified two ways in which children approach school tasks. Children with a **mastery orientation** are motivated to learn, to try hard, and to improve their performance; those with a **performance orientation** are motivated by their level of performance, ability, and the incentives for trying. Those with a mastery orientation are more likely to succeed in the long run and to use more advanced learning strategies. Those with a performance orientation may become discouraged when they fail at a task and may give up trying altogether. Interestingly, Carol Dweck and her colleagues found that these patterns are not related to children's IQ scores or academic achievement. Nevertheless, these different motivational patterns are related to children's conceptions of ability. Although even 2 1/2-year-olds can become discouraged and unmotivated after their problem-solving attempts fail, it is only when they begin formal schooling that children are directly compared with one another through grading practices. During elementary school, children begin increasingly to view ability as a fixed characteristic of people. By the time they reach middle school, they begin to articulate theories about what makes people intelligent. Some children have an **entity model of intelligence**, believing that everyone has a certain fixed amount of intelligence. Others have an **incremental model of intelligence**, believing that intelligence grows as one learns and has new experiences. Children who adopt an entity model see academic success as depending on fixed ability and not effort; they are likely to develop a performance orientation. Those who adopt an incremental model see academic success and ability as depending on effort; they are likely to develop a mastery orientation. In the challenging environment of middle school, there is an achievement gap between students who respond to failure by giving up and those who respond by trying harder. One approach to assisting children who have developed a helpless motivational pattern has been to train teachers to give feedback to their students in ways that foster mastery orientation. Another has been to retrain children themselves so that they attribute their failures to lack of effort rather than lack of ability.

IV. THE COGNITIVE CONSEQUENCES OF SCHOOLING

It is difficult to study the cognitive consequences of schooling because formal education is widely available throughout the world. Researchers have nonetheless used several strategies to do so: (1) *the school-cutoff strategy*; (2) *school-nonschool comparisons*; and (3) *second-generation studies*.

A. The School-Cutoff Strategy

In places where there is a minimum age for beginning school, it is possible to compare children whose birthdays fall just before the cutoff date with those who have just missed the cutoff; this is called the **school-cutoff strategy**. Frederick Morrison and his colleagues found that attending first grade increased children's recall ability and their use of active rehearsal. Other studies have shown that measures of conservation, coherence of storytelling, and the number of vocabulary words children understand improve as a consequence of age, rather than schooling.

B. Comparing Schooled and Nonschooled Children

Another method for assessing the cognitive consequences of a formal education is to study societies in which schooling is available to only a portion of the population.

- *Logical Thinking.* The evidence comparing schooled and unschooled children on Piagetian tasks measuring concrete operational thinking is split between studies that find more advanced performance among schooled children and those that do not. As discussed in Chapter 11, when schoolchildren do better on Piagetian tasks, it is largely because of their greater familiarity with the circumstances of test taking. When this is taken into account, the results suggest that the development of concrete operational thinking increases with age and is relatively unaffected by schooling.
- *Memory.* Schooling appears to be the factor underlying cultural differences on standard memory tests. Children from other cultures who go to school demonstrate memory performance more similar to that of their North American peers than to that of age-mates in their villages who have not attended school. The differences are most pronounced when the items to be remembered are not connected by an everyday script; the effects of schooling on memory performance disappear when the items are part of a meaningful setting. No evidence exists to support the notion that schooling increases actual memory capacity.
- *Metacognitive Skills.* Schooling seems to influence the degree to which children can reflect on and talk about their own cognitive processes and explain how they reach solutions to logical problems. Schooling also affects metalinguistic knowledge. For example, Sylvia Scribner and Michael Cole found that, although both educated and uneducated Vai people in Liberia could judge the grammatical correctness of sentences spoken in the Vai language, only the schooled subjects could explain what it was that made a sentence ungrammatical.

C. Assessing the Second-Generation Impact of Schooling

Evidence underscoring the general cognitive impact of schooling derives from studies of the child-rearing practices of mothers who have, and have not, attended school and the achievements of their children. Examining evidence collected in many countries and over several decades, Robert LeVine and his colleagues found that mothers who have attended elementary school have children with lower rates of infant mortality, better health during childhood, and greater academic achievement. This could be traced to habits and skills the mothers themselves had learned in school, for example, making use of information from health, education, and social welfare providers and interacting with their children in ways that prepare them for the school setting. In a study of Mayan mothers conducted by Pablo Chavajoy and Barbara

Rogoff, more educated mothers teaching their children to solve a puzzle gave them instructions, whereas less educated mothers simply participated with the child. Both methods are effective; however, the model adopted by the more educated mothers is more similar to the kind of instruction children will encounter in school.

There is little evidence that schooling changes the basic cognitive processes associated with middle childhood. Schooling improves children's performance by increasing their knowledge base, teaching them specific information-processing strategies that make them more effective in performing school-related tasks, and changing their attitudes and life situations, which they then pass on to their own children through child-rearing practices that promote achievement. One of the most important effects of schooling is that it serves as a gateway to health and nutrition, to greater economic power and social status.

V. CONTEMPORARY CHALLENGES IN A GLOBALIZING WORLD

Wide disparities exist both across and within countries in children's access to education; gender, socioeconomic status, and ethnicity can affect the amount and quality of the schooling they receive. There is also disparity across countries in children's school achievement. The box "Comparing Mathematics Achievement across Cultures" takes up this issue.

Throughout the world, large numbers of families are moving away from their native lands and making new homes in places with cultural practices that are new and different to them. For example, the fastest-growing group of children in the United States is children of immigrant families. In many areas, school districts are seeing an enormous rise in cultural and linguistic diversity. They face a major challenge in identifying and responding to the academic needs of students who vary so widely in native language and heritage culture and, in many cases, children and their families must also adjust to the unique culture and language of school.

A. The Culture of School

It has been suggested that each culture has a particular **cultural style**—a dominant way of thinking about and relating to the world that arises from a people's common historical experience. For example, some cultures place greater emphasis on promoting independence; this *independent* or *individualistic* cultural style emphasizes the individual and his or her personal choices. Other cultures consider interdependence to be a more important value; this *interdependent* or *collectivist* cultural style emphasizes the group and group harmony, and downplays individual achievement. The differences between the two styles are summarized in Table 12.5 of the textbook. Patricia Greenfield and her colleagues believe that children from cultures that value interdependence may be at a disadvantage in American schools. However, other researchers point out that children from cultures valuing interdependence are often quite successful in school, perhaps because of the positive role their parents play in their education. For example, Nathan Caplan and his colleagues, studying the children of refugees from Vietnam, Cambodia, and Laos, found that even though their parents did not know English well, the children benefited from being read to by their parents in their native language. Other studies have found that children from a variety of ethnic groups profit when their families make explicit efforts to pass on their native language and cultural heritage to them.

Other aspects of culture can prove disadvantageous in the standard American classroom. Wade Boykin conducted studies in which some African American children were given stories to remember and problems to solve under conditions that allowed them to run, jump, and dance; other children were presented with the same stories and problems under conditions that required them to behave in a more "schoollike" manner. The children who were allowed to express themselves physically outperformed those in the other group. According to Boykin, this reflects the importance of expressive movement as part of the everyday communicative behavior of African Americans, a cultural tradition that is suppressed in the typical classroom setting.

Clearly, cultural values and modes of behavior are important influences on children's success in school; however, there is no one "right way" to incorporate these factors into classroom practices.

B. The Language of School

Schools use language in distinctive ways, and children's experiences with oral and written language in the home will differ to some extent from language practices at school and those in other homes in the community. Over a period of years, Shirley Heath studied language use in three populations of children and their families from the same locale: European American schoolteachers; European American textile workers; and African Americans engaged in farming and textile jobs. Heath found that the teachers included a great deal of "instructional discourse" in conversations with their children, who tended to do well in school. The children of the European American textile workers did less well. Perhaps as a function of the language patterns used in their homes, they did well in the early grades, where there was more focus on the literal meaning of a text, and less well in the higher grades, where they needed to draw inferences from complex texts. The children from the African American homes were not exposed to the language patterns they would be expected to use in school—for example, their parents rarely asked them "known-answer" questions—and they tended not to perform well in school.

Because it is the goal of teachers to be successful with all children, designing educational interventions that will help everyone to learn effectively has become an important objective.

C. Culturally Responsive Classroom Strategies

Schools have grown more responsive to the home languages and cultures of their students and begun to make a place for them in academic curricula. For example, in an influential example of a culturally responsive approach to teaching, an expert teacher of the Odawa Indian tribe in Canada, while following the traditional recitation-script approach used in schools, modified the classroom setting, and employed language and feedback in ways that were consistent with Odawa cultural practices. In another example, Carol Lee drew on African American students' familiarity with the linguistic form called signifying to promote higher levels of literary understanding and interpretation.

It is possible to organize effective contexts for education by taking into account local variations in culture and social class. However, culturally specific strategies are likely to be applicable only when classrooms are culturally homogeneous.

VI. OUTSIDE THE SCHOOL

Although schooling is an important part of middle childhood, it does not represent all aspects of children's lives. Chapter 13 examines the characteristics of children's peer groups and the effects of peer-group experiences on development.

Key Terms

Following are important terms introduced in Chapter 12. Match each term with the letter of the example that best illustrates the term.

1. _____ academic motivation

2. _____ apprenticeship

3. _____ bottom-up processing

4. _____ cultural style

5. _____ decoding

6. _____ education

7. _____ emergent literacy

8. _____ emergent numeracy

9. _____ entity model of intelligence

10. _____ incremental model of intelligence

11. _____ initiation–reply–feedback sequence

12. _____ instructional discourse

13. _____ mastery orientation

14. _____ performance orientation

15. _____ playworld practice

16. _____ realistic mathematics education

17. _____ reciprocal teaching

18. _____ school-cutoff strategy

19. _____ specific learning disabilities

20. _____ top-down processing

a. A kind of verbal exchange that is frequent in schools, whereby a teacher asks a question, a student answers it, and the teacher then provides feedback.
b. This form of deliberate teaching is not characteristic of hunter-gatherer societies.
c. This keeps children persevering in school even when things may be going badly.
d. These are characterized by large differences among the subscales on IQ tests.
e. A kind of language used in schools that varies in important ways from everyday language.

f. In this kind of job training, the student often lives with the adult master's family.

g. Examples of this are "individualistic" and "collectivist."

h. This approach to learning is an application of Vygotsky's "zone of proximal development."

i. Learning this is the major task of beginning readers.

j. This approach to learning involves combining art, reading, and play and utilizes themes from children's literature.

k. This is one way to assess the effects of formal education on cognitive development.

l. An example of this is children's knowledge of what reading and writing are used for, even though they have not yet learned to read and write.

m. The belief that everyone is born with a fixed amount of intelligence.

n. This is emphasized in approaches to education that teach basic skills first and then move to more complex tasks after the basics are mastered.

o. This approach makes use of models and "real-world" math problems.

p. An example of this is a child pretending to be a grocery checker who adds up purchases, takes money, and makes change.

q. This approach to education emphasizes using skills to accomplish meaningful tasks.

r. The belief that intelligence grows with learning and experience.

s. Children with this orientation toward learning are motivated primarily by how well they do and by their perceived ability.

t. Children with this orientation toward learning are motivated to learn, try hard, and improve.

Multiple-Choice Practice Questions

Circle the letter of the word or phrase that correctly completes each statement.

1. In which way is apprenticeship training different from formal schooling?
   a. In apprenticeship training, relatively little explicit instruction is given.
   b. In apprenticeship training, knowledge is immediately put to practical use.
   c. The shop in which an apprentice works is likely to contain people of diverse ages and skill levels.
   d. All these answers are correct.

2. Decoding texts requires the translation of _____ into _____.
   a. phonemes; graphemes
   b. words; numbers
   c. graphemes; phonemes
   d. words; meaning

3. Learning to speak "pig Latin" is helpful to which aspect of learning to read?
   a. phonological awareness
   b. reading for meaning
   c. decoding
   d. All these answers are correct.

4. Which is an example of instructional discourse?
    a. On the first day of school the teacher asks a child, "What is your name?"
    b. After writing a word on the blackboard, the teacher asks, "What does this say?"
    c. The teacher asks the class, "Has anyone seen my red pencil?"
    d. All these answers are correct.

5. Which is most likely to be involved in realistic mathematics education?
    a. emphasis on mastering basic skills before moving on to more complex problems
    b. problems embedded in a make-believe situation
    c. emphasis on independent problem solving
    d. frequent exams to test children's developing skills

6. Which pattern of IQ test subscale scores might predict that a child has dyslexia?
    a. low scores on verbal subscales and high scores on quantitative ones
    b. low scores on all subscales
    c. high scores on all subscales but poor reading performance
    d. None of these answers is correct; there is no relationship between IQ subscale scores and dyslexia.

7. Researchers studying children's academic motivation have found that
    a. children who adopt a mastery orientation are more likely to succeed in the long run.
    b. children who adopt a performance orientation may become discouraged when they fail at a task.
    c. children who adopt a mastery orientation tend to be those who are less capable to begin with.
    d. Both a and b are correct.

8. The school-cutoff strategy allows researchers to investigate
    a. the effect of schooling on children's cognitive abilities.
    b. the effect of dropping out of school on children.
    c. the effect of teacher expectations on achievement.
    d. differences in achievement across cultures.

9. Schooling affects children's performance in which of the following areas?
    a. memory of items connected by an everyday script
    b. concrete operations in everyday contexts
    c. describing their mental activities
    d. All these answers are correct.

10. The clearest evidence for the general cognitive impact of schooling derives from studies of
    a. performance on free-recall tests.
    b. children who have had preschool experiences and those who have not.
    c. the child-rearing practices of mothers who have, or have not, attended school.
    d. None of the above have provided evidence for the effect of schooling.

11. Which is characteristic of an *independent* cultural style?
    a. It is considered okay to engage in confrontation with others.
    b. One's behavior is regulated by analyzing the costs and benefits to oneself.
    c. One's personal goals have priority over those of the group.
    d. All these answers are correct.

12. According to Wade Boykin, African American children are at a disadvantage in typical American classrooms because they are required
    a. to answer questions.
    b. to sit still.
    c. to interact with other children at recess.
    d. to use nonverbal communication.

13. Differences in mathematics achievement between American and Asian children most likely result from
    a. the fact that Asian students spend much more time in school studying mathematics than American students.
    b. the genetic superiority of Asian students in mathematics ability.
    c. the fact that American students use more objects that can be manipulated in learning mathematics.
    d. the fact that Asian classrooms are organized in a more decentralized way.

14. Shirley Heath found that the African American parents in her study
    a. asked their children questions related to the children's own experiences.
    b. rarely asked their children "known-answer" questions.
    c. rarely spoke to their children.
    d. Both a and b are correct.

15. Which is an example of a culturally responsive approach to education?
    a. heritage language classes for immigrant students
    b. Carol Lee's use of "signifying" to build African American students' literary analysis skills
    c. a Canadian teacher's use of Odawa cultural patterns in giving feedback to schoolchildren from that tribe
    d. All these answers are correct.

Short-Answer Practice Questions

Write a brief answer in the space below each question.

1. What are the main differences between "school problems" and "everyday problems"? Describe some examples from your own life.

2. Discuss some ways in which children's families can promote children's emergent literacy and numeracy skills.

3. Explain how the practices used in reciprocal teaching act as a zone of proximal development for children who need to improve their reading skills.

4. Think of two everyday problems and imagine how you might approach them if you had never been to school.

5. Some researchers believe that children from groups whose cultural style differs from that of the majority are at a disadvantage in typical American classrooms. Give one supporting example and one contradictory example.

6. What evidence exists that parents' use of "school language" in the home benefits children's school performance?

Sources of More Information

Bissex, G. (1980). *Gnys at work: A child learns to read and write.* Cambridge, MA: Harvard University Press.
This case study follows one child from age 5 to age 11 as he learns to read and write.

Eisenstein, E. (1985). On the printing press as an agent of change. In D. Olson, N. Torrance, & A. Hildyard (eds.) *Literacy, language and learning: The nature and consequences of reading and writing.* New York: Cambridge University Press.
This is a discussion of social change as it is related to the invention of literacy.

Garcia, E., & Miller, L. (2008). Findings and recommendations of the National Task Force on Early Childhood Education for Hispanics. *Child Development Perspectives*, 2, 53–58.
This article summarizes the findings of the task force, and their recommendations for enhancing the school readiness and academic achievement of children of Hispanic descent.

Graham, P. (2005). Schooling America: How the public schools meet the nation's changing needs. New York: Oxford University Press.
A look at the history of schooling in America, and its changing goals and strategies.

Kamii, C., & Housman, L. (2000). *Young children reinvent arithmetic: Implications of Piaget's theory*, 2nd ed. New York: Teacher's College Press, Columbia University.
This book describes a program for teaching mathematics that is based on Piaget's ideas. It includes activities for fostering numerical thinking in children of early elementary school age.

Schleppegrell, M. (2004). *The language of schooling: A functional linguistics perspective.* Mahwah, NJ: Lawrence Erlbaum Associates.
The volume discusses ways in which language is typically used in school settings and how school tasks differ for students of different social backgrounds.

Siegler, R. (1998). *Children's thinking*, 3rd ed. Upper Saddle River, NJ: Prentice Hall.
Addresses many topics relevant to children's cognitive development, including the development of academic skills.

Answer Key

Answers to Key Terms: 1.c, 2.f, 3.n, 4.g, 5.i, 6.b, 7.l, 8.p, 9.m, 10.r, 11.a, 12.e, 13.t, 14.s, 15.j, 16.o, 17.h, 18.k, 19.d, 20.q.

Answers to Multiple-Choice Questions: 1.d, 2.c, 3.a, 4.b, 5.b, 6.a, 7.d, 8.a, 9.c, 10.c, 11.d, 12.b, 13.a, 14.d, 15.d.

13

Social and Emotional Development in Middle Childhood

CHAPTER

As children enter middle childhood, many changes occur in their social and emotional domains as they move from the shelter of parental supervision to new contexts and challenges. More often 6- to 12-year-olds are left to the company of their peers than they were during the preschool period. They are expected to take responsibility for their actions, get along with other children, and follow the social rules of their societies, even when no one is watching. They are also expected to assume personal responsibilities, such as completing homework, practicing musical instruments, feeding pets, and regulating their own behavior in numerous other ways. Their play begins to include more complex and competitive games, and the role-playing of early childhood makes way for Scrabble and Monopoly.

During the middle childhood years, children's reasoning about moral issues and social conventions becomes more complex and abstract. Friendships take on an important role in children's lives as they learn to care for others who are not part of their immediate family circle. At this time, they also begin to evaluate their own behavior by comparing themselves with others and to imagine an ideal self toward which to strive.

Learning Objectives

Keep these questions in mind while studying Chapter 13.

1. In what ways do children's games help them to make the transition to more mature reasoning about moral issues?
2. What changes take place in children's thinking about moral rules and social conventions during middle childhood?
3. What causes children to be accepted or rejected by peers? Why do some children behave aggressively toward others?
4. What factors are important in children's forming and preserving friendships?

5. How do children's relationships with their parents change as the children grow older? How are they affected if their parents divorce?
6. How do the ways in which children describe themselves change over time? What influences them to develop a positive or negative image of themselves and their abilities?

Chapter Summary

During middle childhood, children spend more time than before with age-mates and less time with parents. At this time, peer influence emerges as an important form of social control with considerable power in shaping children's behavior. Children's relationships with their parents also undergo change and parents' socialization strategies make a corresponding shift. Instead of demanding blind obedience and simply removing children from dangerous situations, they use discussion and explanation to influence their children's behavior. When children spend more time with peers, their sense of self changes and they begin to form new identities appropriate to the new contexts they inhabit.

I. MORAL DEVELOPMENT

As discussed in Chapter 9, as children develop, their reasoning and behavior become less dependent on external rewards and punishments and more dependent on a personal sense of right and wrong. According to *psychoanalytic theory*, this internalization of society's rules and standards depends on the development of the superego. Jean Piaget and others holding a *cognitive-developmental* view of moral development also became interested in the shift from external to internal control; much of their work has focused on children's reasoning about right and wrong and on the relationship between children's moral reasoning and their moral behavior.

A. Piaget's Theory of Moral Development

In Piaget's view of moral development, introduced in Chapter 9, children shift from *heteronomous morality*, in which they judge right and wrong by the consequences of an act (for example, how much damage was done), to **autonomous morality**, in which they judge right and wrong on the basis of an individual's motives and intentions. What triggers the shift from heteronomous to autonomous moral reasoning? According to Piaget, it occurs in the context of peer activities—in particular, playing games.

After entering middle childhood, children continue the fantasy role-play of the preschool period; starting at 7 or 8 years of age, however, games based on rules become prominent. Now, whether the play is fantasy role-play or other rule-based games, the rules need to be agreed on beforehand and followed consistently. Changing the rules without the consent of the other players is cheating. Piaget studied children's ideas about rules by observing them play the game of marbles. Six- to 8-year-old children had "mystical respect" for the rules—that is, they would not agree to any alterations to them, believing that they had been handed down by authority figures and could not be changed (as in heteronomous morality). At 10 to 12 years of age, children began to treat the rules as social conventions that could be changed if the other players agreed (as in autonomous morality). Interestingly, children's conceptions of God also change during this period (from anthropomorphic to more abstract) as discussed in the box "Children's Ideas about God."

According to Piaget, games are models of society. He linked the ability to play within a system of rules to children's acquisition of respect for rules and to their new level of moral understanding. Through playing games, children come to understand that social rules make cooperation with others possible; this allows peer groups to be self-governing, and their members capable of autonomous moral thinking.

B. Kohlberg's Theory of Moral Development

Lawrence Kohlberg built on Piaget's ideas about moral reasoning. Based on subjects' responses to a series of stories about people faced with dilemmas, Kohlberg classified moral reasoning into six stages extending from childhood into adolescence and adulthood; the stages are grouped into three levels of moral reasoning: *preconventional*, *conventional*, and *postconventional*. Kohlberg found that children at stage 1, *heteronomous morality* (corresponding to the end of the preschool period and the beginning of middle childhood), adopt an egocentric point of view and base their judgments on objective outcome. Stage 2 reasoning, *instrumental morality*, is reached at 7 or 8 years of age. Children recognize that other people have interests that may conflict with their own; fairness is understood in the context of an exchange system, and morality is seen as serving one's immediate interests and letting others do the same. The transition to stage 2 is what allows children to get along without direct adult supervision. They no longer depend on an external source to define right and wrong, but regulate their behavior by reciprocal relations between group members. At the conventional level, moral reasoning is based on society's standards and rules, rather than external consequences. Stage 3, *good-child morality*, appears around 10 or 11 years of age; now, moral judgments are made from the social perspective of relationships with others and reasoning is similar to the golden rule (treat others as you wish to be treated). Kohlberg's stages are summarized in Table 13.1 of the textbook. The remaining three stages will be discussed in Chapter 14.

C. Prosocial Moral Reasoning

Prosocial moral reasoning, the thinking that is involved in deciding to share with, help, or take care of others when doing so may prove costly to oneself, also undergoes stagelike developmental changes, according to Nancy Eisenberg. Presenting children with story dilemmas which included a conflict between immediate self-interest and the interests of others, she found that whereas younger children focus on themselves and what they may personally gain, older children express more empathy for a person in trouble and a greater consideration of social norms.

Eisenberg and her colleagues, surveying a large number of studies on children's prosocial moral reasoning, found that higher levels of prosocial moral reasoning are positively related to high levels of prosocial behavior; however, being capable of prosocial behavior does not guarantee that a person will engage in it.

D. Social Domain Theory

Freud, Piaget, and Kohlberg viewed young children as deciding right and wrong based on external consequences and authority. However, some research within the social domain perspective has suggested that they demonstrate a strong sense of fairness, a concern for others' welfare, and an ability to question authority at earlier ages than once thought. When presented with stories that create a conflict between authority and fairness or others' welfare, children appear to give the morality of an act priority over the status of an authority figure. For example, they may question the legitimacy of an authority figure who, in a hypothetical situation, allows children to fight with one another. This suggests that they rely on concepts of harm and welfare, rather than authority, in judging moral behavior. Elliot Turiel and his colleagues concluded from this fact that children's reasoning about moral issues is different from their reasoning about authority and social conventions.

Many studies have shown that children distinguish between the moral domain and the social conventional domain when they judge how people should, or should not, behave; in each domain, there is development from more concrete to more abstract reasoning. In the moral domain, young children's judgments are based on concepts of harm or welfare, whereas older children's and adolescents' reasoning is based on more abstract concepts of justice and rights. Judgments about social conventions take rules, customs, and authority into account. Young children's reasoning emphasizes social rules, whereas older children consider more abstract concepts such as social roles and the social order. Over the course of middle childhood, children become increasingly concerned with social group roles and effective group functioning.

Cross-cultural studies have found Turiel's basic results in a variety of societies; however, according to some researchers, certain cultures may regard as moral issues matters that are seen as social conventions by North Americans. This issue will be discussed further in Chapter 14.

E. Moral Reasoning and Theories of Mind

Research indicates that how children judge someone's behavior may depend on their ability to understand the person's mental state (*theory of mind*). Bryan Sokol and Michael Chandler used a *Punch and Judy* puppet show to investigate this. Children rated the "badness" of Punch's behavior in one scenario in which he deliberately tried to knock Judy off the stage (but does not succeed) and in a second scenario in which Punch tried to rescue Judy but accidentally knocked her off the stage. The youngest children maintained what Sokol and Chandler described as an **objective view of responsibility**, rating Punch's responsibility according to the consequences of his behavior. Older children and adults demonstrated a **subjective view of responsibility**, evaluating Punch's behavior according to his intentions. Sokol and Chandler, in linking children's moral deliberations to their developing theories of mind, offer an alternative explanation for the shift in children's moral reasoning from reliance on external consequences to internal motives.

II. PEER RELATIONSHIPS

During middle childhood, children must learn to create a place for themselves within the social group. They must learn to compete for social status, come to terms with the possibility that others may not like them, and deal with any conflicts that arise.

A. Peer Relations and Social Status

Social structures—complex organizations of relationships between individuals—emerge in any group of children that exists over a period of time. Developmentalists who study social structures describe them in terms of *dominance* (who has, or does not have, power over others) and *popularity* (who is liked or disliked).

- *Dominance*. As is true for many other species, dominance hierarchies form in human social groups; they develop through a pattern of arguing or fighting and making up. Those who are skilled at managing the pattern of conflict and reconciliation establish dominance. **Dominant children** control resources such as toys, play spaces, and decisions about group activities. A crucial moment in development for children is the transition from elementary school to middle school, when new social groupings are being formed. For example, Andrew Pellegrini and Jeffrey Long found that bullying—which elementary and middle school children use as a means to influence dominance—peaks during sixth grade, the first year of middle school, and diminishes during seventh grade, once dominance patterns have been formed. The box "Bullies and Their Victims: The Darker Side of Children's Relationships" discusses the problem of bullying in more detail. The usual stereotype was that bullies and dominance hierarchies belong to the world of boys. Recent research has called this bias into question. Among girls, *relational aggression*—actions that threaten the relationships and social standing of their peers—takes the form of derogatory comments, spreading of rumors, and gossip intended to tarnish the reputation of others. According to research by Nicki Crick and her colleagues, this behavior, like other forms of bullying, peaks during the sixth and seventh grades, and may be used to raise one's status within the peer system. *Alpha girls*, at the top of the dominance hierarchy and well practiced in relational aggression, tend to be among the most popular.

- *Popularity*. The relative popularity of children in a group can be studied using the *nomination procedure* (asking children to name their friends or to name whom they would like to sit near or play with) or the *rating procedure* (asking them to rank every child in the group according to a specific criterion). With these data, researchers are able to construct *sociograms* showing how all the children in the group feel about one another. Figure 13.1 in the textbook shows a sociogram of relationships among a group of fifth grade students. Developmentalists have identified four main *popularity statuses*.

Popular children are those who receive the greatest numbers of positive nominations or highest rankings from peers; they tend to be rated as more physically attractive and seem more skilled at initiating and maintaining positive relationships. They are good at compromising and negotiating, and, overall, their behavior appears to be socially competent.

Rejected children receive few positive nominations or low rankings from peers; they are actively disliked. Some are rejected because they are shy and withdrawn. These children tend to be aware of their social failure, an awareness that makes them lonelier and more distressed about their social relationships. Aggressive behavior, however, is the most common reason for social rejection. Aggressive rejected children tend to underestimate how much their peers dislike them and to overestimate their social skills. According to Shelley Hymel and her colleagues, once children have been rejected, their reputations may persist even if they change their behavior; other children may even provoke the behavior that led a child to be rejected in the first place. Rejected children may experience difficulties beyond the school environment. They are more likely to be involved in delinquency and substance abuse, and to experience psychological difficulties, than children accepted by their peers.

Neglected children receive few nominations, positive or negative; they are ignored by peers rather than disliked. Neglected children are less sociable than others but are not aggressive or extremely shy, and are not especially distressed about their social situations. Compared with rejected children, they are more likely to improve their social status, perform better academically, are more compliant in school, and are better liked by their teachers.

Controversial children receive both positive and negative rankings. They may be aggressive, but have compensating social and cognitive skills; children who engage in high levels of relational aggression often generate this mixture of like and dislike. Controversial children are not distressed by their relative lack of social success and usually are liked by at least one other child.

B. Competition and Cooperation among Peers

The extent to which children are competitive or cooperative in their interactions with others depends on the contexts, and the cultures, in which the interactions occur.

- *The Role of Context.* Muzafer and Carolyn Sharif conducted a series of studies that addressed the role of context in fostering cooperation and competition in children's social groups. In one study, an experiment at summer camp, two cohesive groups of boys were put into competitive situations; this led to escalating hostility between the groups. The experimenters were able to reverse this by arranging for a series of problems that required the groups to engage in mutual cooperation.

  Many educational practices in Western cultures foster interpersonal comparisons and competition. Recently, there have been efforts to foster children's appreciation for their peers' success as well as their own through *cooperative learning programs*. According to Barry Schneider, when children care about each other's learning, they do better in school, engage in more prosocial behavior, and show improved relations with teachers and peers.

Cooperative learning is especially beneficial in classrooms of children with diverse cultural origins and ability levels.

Research such as that of the Sharifs shows the effects of context on the tendency to compete or cooperate, but culture also plays an important role.

- *The Role of Culture.* Researchers have studied cultural differences in competitiveness or cooperativeness through specially developed games that allow them to assess children's strategies. In general, they have found that children from North America tend to adopt competitive strategies, whereas those from Asia, Latin America, and other cultures that emphasize interdependence tend to adopt cooperative strategies.

Barry Schneider and his colleagues carried out a large cross-cultural study of seventh graders from Spain, Costa Rica, Cuba, and Canada. They reasoned that a culture's emphasis on independence or interdependence would be reflected in children's *basic social goals*, which would, in turn, influence the extent to which children would be competitive or cooperative in peer interactions. The researchers distinguished among *ego-oriented goals*, *task-oriented goals*, and *cooperation goals*. They also differentiated between two forms of competition: *hypercompetitiveness* and *nonhostile social comparison*. As shown in Figure 13.2 of the textbook, Schneider and his co-workers found more hypercompetitiveness in the friendships of Canadian and Spanish children than among the Costa Rican and Cuban children; there was no difference across groups in the amount of nonhostile social comparison. The researchers also found that the effect of hypercompetitiveness was different in different cultures. For example, whereas hypercompetition was related to the end of friendship among Canadian girls and all Latin American children, a moderate amount of hypercompetition among Canadian boys led to closer relationships between them.

Research suggests that competition between children is not invariably detrimental to peer relationships. Some forms are common across cultures and hypercompetitiveness affects relationships differently depending, in part, on the culture in which it takes place.

C. Relations between Boys and Girls

During middle childhood, children spend more time in sexually segregated groups. Studies in the United States have found that 68 percent of 6-year-old children have a "best friend" of the same sex; this number rises to 90 percent for 12-year-olds. According to Eleanor Maccoby, children aggregate in same-sex groups because of differences in activity preferences. *Male-style play* includes play fighting and high levels of physical activity, whereas *female-style play* includes more nurturing, prosocial play. When boys play with boys and girls with girls, they amplify each other's gender-typed behavior. Maccoby points out, however, that the extent of gender differentiation in a culture influences the degree to which children's play is gender-typed. The box "In the Field: Gender Politics on the Playground" describes a situation in which boys and girls exhibit vastly different views of how play should be conducted.

Sex segregation during middle childhood is not complete. Boys and girls still interact with one another, although they may sometimes do so in amusing ways, such as "cleansing rituals" afterward to get rid of "girl cooties" or "boy germs." Table 13.2 of the textbook describes some so-called rules for contact with the other sex, which Alan Sroufe and his coworkers abstracted from their observations of school-aged children.

D. Friendship: A Special Type of Relationship

Harry Stack Sullivan, an American psychiatrist, observed that close one-on-one relationships (*chumships*) between children begin when they are about 8 1/2 years of age. Sullivan believed the experience of friendship in childhood to be a necessary precursor of interpersonal intimacy later in development. Researchers have found that children with best friends score higher on measures of self-esteem and positive self-worth, whereas those with no friends are timid, overly sensitive, and at risk for later psychological problems. According to researchers, friendships provide children with (1) contexts in which to develop social skills, including communication, cooperation, and the ability to resolve conflicts; (2) information about themselves, others, and the world; (3) companionship and fun that relieve the stress of everyday life; and (4) models of intimate relationships characterized by helping, caring, and trust.

- *Making Friends*. Children tend to become friends with others who are similar in age, sex, socioeconomic status (SES), ethnicity, and general skill level in various activities. In a study by John Gottman, pairs of 3- to 9-year-olds who did not know one another were given several opportunities to play together. Those who became friends tended to have interactions characterized by common-ground activity; clear communication; exchange of information; resolution of conflicts; and reciprocity.

- *Keeping Friends*. Only about one-half of children's friendships are stable over the course of a school year. What causes some friendships to last, while others fall apart? Similarity of behavioral characteristics is important for friendship stability. Wendy Ellis and Lynne Zarbatany conducted a study of children in fifth through eighth grades, collecting information on their friendships and on behavioral characteristics such as relational aggression, overt aggression, and bullying by peers. They found that, in general, children's relationships were more stable when both friends scored high or scored low on a measure than when they were mismatched. The exception was children who engaged in overt aggression; they were no more likely to hold onto a friendship with another aggressive child than with a nonaggressive one.

- *A Cognitive-Developmental Approach*. During middle childhood, children develop a more sophisticated understanding of their friends' unique needs, motives, and goals. According to Robert Selman and his colleagues, increases in *social perspective taking* and decreases in *egocentrism*—associated with the transition to middle childhood—are important for successful relationships. Selman has proposed that there are three spheres of influence affected by the development of perspective taking: *friendship understanding* (a child's developing knowledge of the nature of friendship); *friendship skills* (specific action strategies that children use in developing their friendships); and *friendship valuing* (the child's personal commitment to and emotional investment in a relationship).

  In middle childhood, children acquire a variety of resources for managing their relationships; this is especially apparent when friends argue and fight. Brett Larsen and his colleagues, reviewing research on children's conflict resolution, found that during middle childhood children are more aware of the importance of **social repair mechanisms**— strategies that allow friends to remain friends even when serious differences temporarily drive them apart. Examples of these strategies are negotiation, disengagement from an escalating conflict, staying nearby after a fight to smooth things over, and minimizing a conflict's importance once it is over. When children interact in situations where no caregiver is present, they must be able to settle conflicts on their own.

III. THE INFLUENCE OF PARENTS

Middle childhood also sees changes in the relationships between children and their parents.

A. Changing Expectations

As children get older, their parents are less overtly affectionate and more critical of mistakes children make. They expect more responsible behavior from their children and adopt different strategies for correcting misbehavior when it occurs. There are cultural differences in the ages at which children are expected to display behavioral competence in various areas. For example, Jacqueline Goodnow and her colleagues found that Japanese mothers expected their children to display emotional maturity, compliance, and ritual forms of politeness at an earlier age than American, Australian, and Lebanese-born Australian mothers. American and Australian mothers expected their children to develop social skills and the ability to assert themselves verbally at a relatively early age. In contrast, Lebanese Australian mothers were more willing to let their children attain these competencies at their own pace. However, parents in all groups expected their children to master these social skills sometime during middle childhood.

During middle childhood, the issues that arise between parents and children in economically developed countries often center around schoolwork, academic problems, and school behavior issues. They also involve the extent to which parents should monitor their children's social lives and what chores children should be required to do. In less developed countries, parents may worry about their children's ability to take care of younger relatives or to help with economically important tasks such as caring for livestock. Parents attempt to influence their children's behavior by reasoning with them, appealing to their self-esteem or sense of humor, or arousing their sense of guilt; they are less likely to spank their children for breaking rules than to deprive them of privileges or ground them. Maccoby has ascribed the term **coregulation** to this sharing of responsibility between parents and children. It requires that parents work out ways of monitoring, guiding, and supporting their children when adults are not present, and children must also be willing to keep parents informed of their whereabouts, activities, and problems.

B. Parents and Peers

Parents have considerable influence in determining the contexts in which their children spend their time: the neighborhood in which they live and where they attend school. Parents also exert influence by monitoring their children's behavior. Children whose parents are not aware of where they are or what they are doing may be more likely to engage in antisocial activity and to face rejection by peers. Parents also influence their children's peer relations indirectly by providing the working models for how people should interact with each other. For example, they may encourage aggressive behavior in their children by engaging in coercive, power-assertive modes of socialization. Thomas Dishion found that boys who were exposed to more coercive family experiences at home were the students most likely to be rejected by peers at school. These boys tended to be overly aggressive and to behave badly in the classroom. Although boys from lower socioeconomic categories were more likely to fall into the rejected category, Dishion found that the effect of SES was indirect. Poverty increased family stress, making coercive discipline more likely, but when parents coped better with the pressures of poverty and did not engage in coercive discipline, their children were less likely to have low social status among their peers. Similar results were obtained in a study carried out in the People's Republic of China. Kerry Bolger and Charlotte Patterson also found that maltreated children are more likely to be rejected by peers. In this case, rejection seems to be related to the mediating effect of aggression, as shown in Figure 13.6 of the textbook.

Alan Sroufe and his colleagues have argued for a developmental "cascade effect" in which early family relationships provide support for engaging the world of peers, which, in turn, provides the foundation for deeper and more extensive peer relationships. This developmental cascade can be interrupted by disruptions in either the stability of the child's environment or patterns of parent–child interaction.

C. Divorce

Forty to 50 percent of all marriages in the United States end in divorce, affecting more than one million children per year; the rate of divorce is also rising rapidly in other places throughout the world.

Children whose parents have divorced are more likely to experience difficulties in school, to act out, to be depressed and unhappy, to have lower self-esteem, and to be less socially responsible and competent than children whose parents are still together. Following divorce, a family generally experiences a drop in income; as a result, about 30 percent of custodial parents find themselves living below the poverty level. Children often have to move away from friends and neighbors to poorer neighborhoods with fewer resources. Parents with sole custody may be overburdened with home, child-care, and work responsibilities. Children of divorce tend to receive less guidance and assistance and also lose out on important kinds of social and intellectual stimulation from their parents.

Developmentalists have used several different models to account for the consequences of divorce. In the *crisis model*, divorce was viewed as a specific disturbance to which parents and children needed to adjust over time. The *chronic strain model*, developed more recently, recognizes that ongoing hardships may affect children's lives for many years. Paul Amato's *divorce-stress-adjustment perspective* attempts to represent both the short-term trauma and long-term effects of divorce; it incorporates various stressors and protective factors that influence the short- and long-term adjustment of the family and its individual members. An alternative to the assumption that children's problems begin with the divorce itself is the *selection perspective*, which suggests that most of the negative effects of family disruption may be attributed to factors that predated the divorce and created an unhealthy environment for children, thereby contributing to their adjustment problems. Research has shown that the divorce rate is more similar in pairs of monozygotic twins than in pairs of dizygotic twins, which points to the possibility of a genetic component. Possibly, children from divorced families are more troubled because they have inherited tendencies that place them at greater risk for certain problems, including divorce.

There are individual differences among children in how they adjust to divorce. According to Amato, children's adjustment is aided by active coping skills, support from peers, and access to therapeutic interventions. Adjustment is impeded by avoidant coping mechanisms, a tendency toward self-blame, and feelings of lack of control. Divorce has different effects on different people, benefiting some while having a lasting negative effect on others.

IV. A NEW SENSE OF SELF

Changes in children's social lives during middle childhood are accompanied by changes in the ways they think about themselves.

A. Changing Conceptions of the Self

William Damon and Daniel Hart asked children between 4 to 15 years old to describe themselves. They found that children of all ages referred to their appearance, activities, relations to others, and psychological characteristics. However, although children between 4 and 7 tended to make categorical statements about themselves that placed them in socially recognized categories and seldom engaged in comparative judgments, children between 8 and 11 began to define their characteristics in relation to those of their peers—a process called **social comparison**. Table 13.3 of the textbook shows examples of the kinds of self-assessments children make at different ages. After spending a great deal of time with peers, children realize that questions such as "Am I good at sports?" have no absolute answers; success is measured in relation to the performance of others in the social group. At about 7 or 8 ears of age, children begin to describe themselves in terms of more general, stable characteristics (for example, "I am a good student" rather than "I can spell lots of words"). At the same time, they also start to assume that other people have stable traits which can be used to predict their behavior in different situations.

B. Self-Esteem

From Erik Erikson's point of view, during middle childhood children must resolve the crisis of **industry versus inferiority**. Now, they will either judge themselves (and be judged by others) as successful in meeting the new responsibilities and challenges they face at home and in school, or they will feel incapable and, therefore, inferior. Children's **self-esteem—**

their evaluation of their own worth—is affected by how well they demonstrate their capacity to themselves and to others.

- *Changes in Children's Self-Evaluations.* Susan Harter has studied the relationship between how children evaluate themselves and their self-esteem. High self-esteem in childhood is linked to satisfaction and happiness in later life, whereas low self-esteem is linked to depression, anxiety, and maladjustment in both school and social relations. Harter and her colleague Robin Pike studied the basis of children's evaluations of themselves; they showed pictures to 4- through 7-year-olds and asked them to indicate whether the images were a lot or a little like them. The pictures tapped the domains of cognitive competence, physical competence, peer acceptance, and maternal acceptance. The researchers found that the children combined physical and cognitive competence in a single dimension of competence and combined peer and maternal acceptance in a single dimension of acceptance. The self-evaluations of children who had been held back in school reflected low competence, whereas those of children who were newcomers to their school reflected low acceptance. In another study, Harter found that somewhat older children (8 to 12 years of age) made more differentiated self-evaluations, distinguishing cognitive, social, and physical competence. In addition, children of this age are able to integrate these components and form a general idea of their self-worth. During middle childhood, children also begin to form ideas about the person they would like to be—their "ideal self"—and to measure their actual self against it. This can be a source of motivation to improve or a source of distress and discouragement. At about 8 years of age, children's evaluations of their cognitive, social, and physical competence start to fit with the judgments of their peers and teachers.

- *Foundations of Self-Esteem.* Self-esteem has been linked to patterns of child-rearing. For example, Stanley Coopersmith found that 10- to 12-year-old boys with high self-esteem had parents whose style of child-rearing included acceptance of their children, setting of clearly defined limits, and respect for individuality—a pattern similar to that which characterizes *authoritative parenting*. A key to high self-esteem seems to be the feeling, transmitted in large part by the family, that one can control one's own future by controlling both oneself and one's environment. As shown by Coopersmith's results, children with high self-esteem know their boundaries. However, this does not detract from their feelings of effectiveness.

    Although promoting self-esteem has a prominent place in the child-rearing practices of American mothers of European descent, it may be a culture-specific concept. In a study of Taiwanese mothers, it was rarely mentioned. And a comparative study of European American and Mexican American families found a strong relationship between parenting practices and children's self-esteem among European Americans but a comparatively weak relationship among Mexican American families. While the authoritative parenting style has been associated with positive social and intellectual outcomes in European American families, families from other cultures can often not be classified according to Baumrind's categories. It is possible that parental warmth is the most important factor in children's well-being, not firmness or control.

V. RECONSIDERING MIDDLE CHILDHOOD

Freud described middle childhood as a period of *latency*, during which children experienced relative stability. However, as noticed by adults all over the world, many significant changes occur between the ages of 6 and 12. Adults in all cultures consider 6- and 7-year-olds to be in a new social category and assign them responsibilities accordingly. Peers also become more important during middle childhood, and children must learn to regulate their interactions with age-mates without constant adult supervision; through their interactions with peers, they develop new, more complex views of themselves. Children's growing cognitive capacities allow changes in the social domain, which, in turn, stimulate further cognitive development. And supporting all of this activity are biological factors: the proliferation of brain circuitry, changing relations between different kinds of brain-wave activity, and a significant increase in the influence of the frontal lobes. Finally, children's development takes place within the organizational construct of their culture, as transmitted through parenting practices and school curricula, as well as particular expectations for age-appropriate behavior, duties, and responsibilities.

Key Terms

Following are important terms introduced in Chapter 13. Match each term with the letter of the example that best illustrates the term.

1. _____ autonomous morality

2. _____ coregulation

3. _____ dominant children

4. _____ industry versus inferiority

5. _____ objective view of responsibility

6. _____ prosocial moral reasoning

7. _____ self-esteem

8. _____ social comparison

9. _____ social repair mechanisms

10. _____ social structures

11. _____ subjective view of responsibility

a. Judging the wrongness of an action on the basis of its outcome.
b. Without these, it is difficult to keep a friendship intact in the face of disagreements.
c. This kind of thinking may involve deciding to help someone even at a cost to oneself.
d. A child describing herself as "the best reader in the class" is an example of this.
e. Judging the wrongness of an action on the basis of the perpetrator's intention.
f. This is an indication of how children evaluate their own self-worth.
g. This term refers to Piaget's second and most advanced stage of moral development.
h. According to Erikson, this is the developmental challenge children face during middle childhood.

i. These tend to be organized according to dominance and popularity.

j. These children tend to control access to toys and play spaces and to make decisions about group activities.

k. This involves children and parents sharing responsibility for children's behavior.

Multiple-Choice Practice Questions

Circle the letter of the word or phrase that correctly completes each statement.

1. During middle childhood, _____ become(s) more important in children's play.
   a. rule-based games
   b. role-playing
   c. props such as blocks and dolls
   d. fantasy

2. Which is an example of *autonomous morality*?
   a. Right and wrong are defined according to the good or bad consequences of behavior.
   b. Right and wrong are defined by adults and other authority figures.
   c. Good and bad are defined according to people's internal motives and intentions.
   d. There is really no such thing as right and wrong.

3. Lawrence Kohlberg studied children's moral reasoning by
   a. observing their behavior in the playground.
   b. asking them to react to moral dilemmas presented in stories.
   c. asking them about the morality of their own behavior.
   d. exposing them to real moral dilemmas and observing their responses.

4. During middle childhood, the child who has the most influence over the activities of a group of children playing together is likely to be
   a. the most dominant child.
   b. the most controversial child.
   c. the most aggressive child.
   d. a bully.

5. Children who respond to the "Heinz dilemma" by saying, "He should steal the drug because someday he might be sick and need someone to steal it for him" are at which stage of morality, according to Lawrence Kohlberg?
   a. stage 1
   b. stage 2
   c. stage 3
   d. stage 4

6. Children who are rejected by their peers
   a. receive little attention, positive or negative, from peers.
   b. are sometimes very shy children.

c. are often aggressive children.

d. Both b and c are correct.

7. Which of the following is true of children's reasoning about social conventions?
   a. They do not distinguish social conventions from moral rules.
   b. Their reasoning does not change with age.
   c. Their reasoning advances with age, evolving from more concrete to more abstract.
   d. It is not possible to generalize about children's reasoning because it is specific to each situation.

8. According to research by Muzafer and Carolyn Sharif, which of the following methods would be the most effective in reducing conflict between groups of children?
   a. putting the groups in competition with each other
   b. requiring one group to share resources with the other
   c. having the groups engage in fun activities together
   d. requiring the groups to work together to solve a common problem

9. According to Eleanor Maccoby, gender segregation in play during middle childhood
   a. occurs much less frequently than in early childhood.
   b. only exists because it is imposed by culture.
   c. is mainly the result of differences in activity preferences.
   d. occurs only because boys do not want to play with girls.

10. Which of the following pairs of children is likely to maintain their friendship over a period of time?
    a. two boys who both rate high in overt aggression
    b. two girls who both rate high in relational aggression
    c. a girl who exhibits high relational aggression and a girl who exhibits low relational aggression
    d. Both a and b are correct.

11. According to Robert Selman and his colleagues, _____ during middle childhood leads to changes in children's conceptions of friendship.
    a. increases in egocentrism
    b. increases in perspective-taking
    c. increases in free-recall memory
    d. All these answers are correct.

12. Compared with the parents of younger children, parents of children in middle childhood are more likely to
    a. restrict the time children spend with peers.
    b. use physical force to control their children's behavior.
    c. rely on coregulation in controlling children's behavior.
    d. supervise their children closely.

13. Which are more likely to be issues between parents and children once the children reach middle childhood?
    a. schoolwork and household chores
    b. temper tantrums and fights
    c. establishing daily routines
    d. All these answers are correct.

14. According to which of the following views of divorce are most of the negative effects of divorce on children the result of longstanding dysfunctional family patterns that existed before the divorce?
    a. crisis model
    b. chronic strain model
    c. divorce-stress-adjustment perspective
    d. selection perspective

15. When asked to define themselves, 8- to 11-year-old children would be most likely to state which of the following?
    a. "I play baseball."
    b. "I am a good baseball player."
    c. "I play baseball, which makes me popular with the other kids."
    d. All these answers are equally likely.

16. Susan Harter has found that the self-evaluations of 8- to 12-year-old children
    a. are more differentiated (physical, cognitive, social) than those of younger children.
    b. reveal that children are forming ideas of their ideal selves.
    c. correlate relatively well with the judgments of peers and teachers.
    d. All these answers are correct.

Short-Answer Practice Questions

Write a brief answer in the space below each question.

1. Why did Piaget believe that rule-based games were an important part of middle childhood? What did he learn from studying children's games?

2. Give examples of the kinds of moral reasoning typical of children in Lawrence Kohlberg's stages 1, 2, and 3. What are some additional examples you have observed in everyday life?

3. Name some reasons why children bully others. If you were the teacher of one student who was a bully and another who was his or her victim, how would you approach the situation?

4. How do researchers measure children's popularity within a group? What factors have been found to influence children's popularity?

5. What factors result in some children becoming friends and others not doing so? What factors help children's friendships continue and what things drive them apart?

6. What challenges do children face when their parents divorce? What explanations have been developed to explain how divorce affects families?

Putting It All Together

In this section, material from Chapter 13 can be combined with information presented in earlier chapters.

I. Match each of the following examples of play to the developmental period of which it is most characteristic.

1. _____ Stirring a cup of sand "coffee" with a twig

2. _____ Playing "parents and children"

3. _____ Playing kickball

4. _____ Banging a wooden hammer on the table

5. _____ Jumping rope

6. _____ Cooking a meal on a play stove

7. _____ Dressing up as a princess (if a girl) or a superhero (if a boy)

a. early infancy (12 months or less)
b. late infancy (12–24 months)
c. the preschool period
d. middle childhood

II. Using examples from infancy, early childhood, and middle childhood, discuss how culture affects parents' expectations about their children's development and behavior, and helps to determine their parenting practices. How does culture affect the relationship between parenting style and measures of children's well-being?

Sources of More Information

Dunn, J. (2004). *Children's friendships: The beginnings of intimacy.* Malden, MA: Blackwell Publishing.
This is an account of children's early friendships at different developmental stages; it contains advice for parents and teachers on how to handle difficult situations.

Durojaiye, S. (1977). Children's traditional games and rhymes in three cultures. *Educational Research, 19,* 223–226.
This article compares games enjoyed by children in Great Britain, Nigeria, and Uganda.

Harter, S. (2006). The development of self-esteem. In *Self-esteem issues and answers: A sourcebook of current perspectives*, M. Kernis (Ed.), pp. 144–150. New York: Psychology Press.
This chapter gives a brief overview of the development of self-esteem in children, and refers to many important studies on the subject.

Killen, M., & Smetana, J. (Eds.) (2006). *Handbook of moral developmnt.* Mahwah, NJ: Lawrence Erlbaum Associates.
This handbook contains chapters by many different researchers working in the field of moral development.

Kowalski, R., Limber, S., & Agatston, P. (2008). *Cyberbullying: Bullying in the digital age.* Malden, MA: Blackwell Publishing.
The authors review the latest research on this problem and make suggestions for educators, parents, therapists, and policy makers.

Orpinas, P. (2006). Bullying prevention: Creating a positive school climate and developing social competence. Washington, DC: American Psychological Association.
The APA offers professional advice for dealing with an important social issue.

Piaget, J. (1997). *The moral judgment of the child.* New York: Free Press.
Piaget's report on his original work concerning the development of moral reasoning.

Power, C., Higgens, A., & Kohlberg, L. (1991). *Lawrence Kohlberg's approach to moral education.* New York: Columbia University Press.
This book describes how schools act as communities and proposes that school culture should become the focus of moral education.

Soyinka, W. (1981). *Ake, the years of childhood.* New York: Vintage Books.
An autobiographical account of growing up in an African village by a Nobel prize-winning playwright, poet, and novelist.

Wallerstein, J., Lewis, J., & Blakeslee, S. (2000). *The unexpected legacy of divorce: A 25 year landmark study*. New York: Hyperion.
This book summarizes, through the use of examples, the findings of a long-term study of adults and children affected by divorce.

Answer Key

Answers to Key Terms: 1.g, 2.k, 3.j, 4.h, 5.a, 6.c, 7.f, 8.d, 9.b, 10.i, 11.e.

Answers to Multiple-Choice Questions: 1.a, 2.c, 3.b, 4.a, 5.b, 6.d, 7.c, 8.d, 9.c, 10.b, 11.b, 12.c, 13.a, 14.d, 15.b, 16.d.

Answers to Putting It All Together I: 1.b, 2.c, 3.d, 4.a, 5.d, 6.c, 7.c.

14

Physical and Cognitive Development in Adolescence

CHAPTER

The end of middle childhood is marked by radical biological changes. During puberty, young people's bodies become adult, both in size and in their capacity for biological reproduction. In industrialized nations, the age at which puberty occurs has gradually fallen over the last 200 years; at the same time, technological developments have increased the amount of education young people need in order to become independent members of society. The result has been a shortening of middle childhood and a lengthening of adolescence—the transitional stage between biological maturity and the full independence of adulthood. According to some theorists, adolescence is a time of emotional upheaval and also a time of creativity and intellectual promise.

Developmentalists from various theoretical orientations agree that adolescents' thought processes are more sophisticated than those of younger children. Piaget believed that adolescence was characterized by the emergence of formal operations, a kind of systematic, logical thinking. Educational and cross-cultural differences complicate the picture, but thinking skills that resemble formal operations appear in people of all cultures, applied in specific contexts in which they are appropriate. Adolescents are also increasingly able to apply their more advanced thinking skills to reason about moral issues and to make important decisions about their lives.

Learning Objectives

Keep these questions in mind while studying Chapter 14.

1. Why have theorists historically viewed adolescence as a time of conflict and instability?
2. What biological changes occur during puberty? What impact do these changes and their timing have on adolescents' adjustment?
3. What health challenges confront adolescents and how well do they meet them?

4. How do cultures and nations differ in how they educate adolescents about sexual behavior?
5. How do the thinking capabilities of adolescents differ from those of younger children?
6. What new levels of moral reasoning become available starting in adolescence?
7. How do parents, peers, and situational factors influence the level of adolescents' moral reasoning and behavior?

Chapter Summary

The biological changes of puberty cause transformations in young people's bodies and in their feelings; they also affect the way in which others interact with them. At this time, young people encounter conflicting expectations about how they should behave and how they should relate to others. They are capable of more complex problem solving and abstract thinking, but may exercise poor judgment and take unreasonable risks.

Researchers and practitioners seeking to understand adolescent development are influenced by current views on the nature of adolescence, many of which are rooted in conceptions that have endured for thousands of years.

I. ADOLESCENTS AND SOCIETY

Adolescents inhabit a transitional area between childhood and maturity. In some ways they are expected to be knowledgeable, responsible, and independent; in others, they are encouraged to remain childlike and immature. Societies guide children through adolescence in accordance with their cultural beliefs and values and their economic structures. All recognize it is an important transition that requires special attention.

A. Historical Views

Accounts of adolescence from the time of Plato and Aristotle, and continuing through the Middle Ages and beyond, portray adolescents as impulsive, sensual, and passionate. Aristotle also called attention to the new powers of thought that come into being beginning at puberty. The idea of adolescence as a period of emotional conflict and instability, and higher intellectual functioning, persists into modern times.

B. Adolescents in the Industrial Age

During the late eighteenth and early nineteenth centuries, interest in adolescence increased as a result of the migration of young people to cities in search of work and also the expansion of schooling in response to the need for a more educated workforce. Scientists turned their attention to the factors that shape adolescent development; two theorists, G. Stanley Hall and Sigmund Freud, were particularly influenced by the biological aspects of adolescence.

II. BIOLOGICAL THEORIES OF ADOLESCENT DEVELOPMENT

Darwin's theory of evolution heavily influenced theories of adolescent development.

A. G. Stanley Hall

A major figure in developmental psychology, G. Stanley Hall considered adolescence to be a time of "storm and stress" due to the hormonal changes of puberty. He also embraced the idea that the evolutionary history of the species is repeated in the developing child. In adolescence, he believed, young people move beyond the biologically predetermined past to a period of new flexibility and creativity. For this reason, he viewed adolescents as the future of the human species.

B. Sigmund Freud

According to Sigmund Freud, adolescence corresponds to the beginning of the *genital stage,* the final stage in his theory of psychosexual development. The reawakening of primitive instincts by the events of puberty upsets the psychological balance existing among the id, ego, and superego, producing conflict and erratic behavior; during adolescence, young people must therefore reintegrate their psychological forces in a mature way that is compatible with their new sexual capacities.

There is some disagreement about whether, as Hall and Freud theorized, adolescence is necessarily a time of stress and conflict. However, it is widely accepted that adolescents are more prone than younger children to argue with their parents, experience fluctuations in mood, and engage in risky behaviors, as well as to think and act in creative and imaginative ways.

C. Modern Theories of Biological Development

Modern approaches emphasize how development is influenced by the evolutionary history of our species. For example, it appears that humans are the only primate species to experience the **growth spurt**—the rapid change in height and weight that marks the onset of puberty. For girls, the *takeoff velocity,* when the growth spurt starts, occurs at about $7\frac{1}{2}$ years of age; for boys, it takes place at about $10\frac{1}{2}$ years. As can be seen in Figure 14.1 of the textbook, the growth rate in humans is much slower than in our nearest primate relative, the chimpanzee, until the growth spurt occurs. This slow rate of growth delays the onset of reproduction in humans compared to other primates. This delay in reaching maturity aids our reproductive success by allowing humans time to learn and practice adult economic, social, and sexual behavior before they begin reproducing.

III. PUBERTY

Puberty is a series of biological developments that transform individuals from physical immaturity to biological and reproductive maturity. The process takes approximately three to four years to complete. The hypothalamus begins the process by signaling the pituitary gland to produce more growth hormones; these will stimulate the development and functioning of the *gonads:* the testes of boys and the ovaries of girls.

A. The Growth Spurt

One of the first visible signs of puberty is a growth spurt during which boys and girls grow faster than at any time since infancy and reach 98 percent of their adult height. Different parts of the body develop at different rates. As a result, adolescents develop a gangly appearance. Boys increase in muscle development and decrease in body fat; girls continue to have a greater ratio of fat to muscle. Puberty also leads to differences in strength. Boys develop greater strength and greater capacity for exercise; girls, however, once they've matured into women will, on average, live longer and be healthier and better able to tolerate long-term stress than their male counterparts.

B. Sexual Development

The **primary sex characteristics,** the organs directly involved in reproduction, enlarge and become functionally mature during puberty. During this time, **secondary sex characteristics**—anatomical and physiological signs that outwardly distinguish males from females—also appear.

- *Development of Primary Sex Characteristics.* During puberty, the reproductive organs become mature due to the action of *estrogen* and *testosterone.* In boys, testosterone increases to 18 times its level in middle childhood; in girls, estrogen increases to 8 times its previous level. Both hormones are present in boys and girls, though in differing amounts.

   Girls experience **menarche,** the first menstrual period, about 18 months after the growth spurt reaches its peak velocity. Ovulation typically begins 12 to 18 months after menarche. During this time period, the uterus grows and the vaginal lining thickens. However, the pelvic inlet—the bony opening of the birth canal—does not reach its full size until about 18 years of age.

   As a result of stimulation by testosterone, boys' testes begin to produce sperm cells and the prostate begins to produce semen, the fluid that carries sperm cells. The first sign of puberty in boys is thickening and reddening of the scrotal skin; the penis begins to grow at the time the growth spurt gets underway. A milestone that occurs about a year later is **semenarche**—the first ejaculation—which often happens spontaneously during sleep. For the first year after semenarche, the sperm in semen are less numerous and fertile than they will be in adulthood.

- *Development of Secondary Sex Characteristics.* The anatomical and physiological changes that distinguish males and females are shown in Figure 14.2 of the textbook. These characteristics appear at the same time that the reproductive organs are maturing and communicate to the adolescent—and to others—that sexual maturation is occurring. According to ethologists, secondary sex characteristics are important because they signal that individuals are capable of reproducing and, therefore, trigger sexually relevant responses from others.

C. Brain Development

New technologies such as magnetic resonance imaging (MRI) show that development of the brain continues during adolescence. Although the brain grows little in size during this period, having reached 90 percent of its adult weight by 5 years of age, changes occur in its organization and functioning, especially in the frontal lobes. These continue to develop until late adolescence and are associated with memory, decision making, reasoning, impulse control, and multitasking.

Changes in the brain involve both white and gray matter. White matter, evidence of myelination, increases fairly steadily from childhood to early adulthood. Gray matter increases rapidly in early puberty, possibly an indication of a new period of synapse production; it then declines again, suggesting a new period of synapse reduction in late adolescence. The overproduction of synapses may be triggered by hormones present at puberty. The difference between boys and girls in the timing of peak growth is consistent with such a possibility. This pattern of brain development—*synaptogenesis* followed by a period of *synaptic pruning*—parallels that of brain development during infancy. Presumably, synaptic pruning reflects the consolidation of neural pathways as a result of specific experiences. Researchers speculate that the brains of adolescents are particularly susceptible or vulnerable to certain experiences or effects, particularly those involving the use of drugs and alcohol.

D. The Timing of Puberty

There is wide variation among children in the age at which puberty begins. Both genetic and environmental factors play a part in this. As shown in Figure 14.4 of the textbook, children reach puberty at different ages in different countries; within those nations, children living in cities tend to reach puberty earlier than those living in rural areas. The role of genetic factors is illustrated by research showing that identical twins reach puberty much closer in time than fraternal twins. Further evidence of the role of genetics is the observation that African American children tend to reach puberty at earlier ages compared to European American children. The role of the environment can be seen in the effects of caloric intake and exercise on age of menarche. Dancers and other girls who participate in a high level of physical activity reach menarche later than average. Children who live in stressful family environments reach puberty earlier. In addition, a look at historical trends, as depicted in Figure 14.5 of the textbook, shows that in industrialized countries the age of menarche has been gradually on the decline. This **secular trend** is thought to result from improvements in nutrition and health care; it is more pronounced in African American girls than white girls. Developmentalists speculate that this ethnic difference, and the continuation of the secular trend, may both be accounted for by increasing levels of body fat. If so, the continued fall in the age of pubertal onset during recent years may be a sign of worsening health.

E. Puberty and Health

Adolescents experience fewer illnesses than younger children and older people. However, the increased rate of growth places new demands on adolescents' bodies.

- *Nutrition.* Nutritional needs are greater during adolescence than at any other time, particularly during the growth spurt. Optimal nutrition is important for achieving full growth and also for preventing disorders in later life such as heart disease, cancer, and osteoporosis. As shown in Table 14.1 of the textbook, the diets of American adolescents are low in essential vitamins and minerals and high in fats and sugars. Some of the vitamins and minerals that contribute to healthy development are *zinc,* which is vital for gene expression and plays a role in sexual maturation; *Vitamin A,* which contributes to reproduction, general growth, and the functioning of the immune system; and *folate,* which plays a significant role in biological processes affecting DNA. In many parts of the world, adolescents do not have access to healthy food. This is true not only in developing countries, but also in some communities within the United States. People in poor, urban neighborhoods have fewer grocery stores and fewer means of transportation to them. These same neighborhoods may have many fast-food outlets; this situation only encourages the excessive consumption of fats, salt, and empty calories. Figure 14.6 of the textbook shows how interacting psychological and socioeconomic factors contribute to nutrition-related diseases.

- *Sleep.* Adolescents often do not get enough sleep; they tend to stay up later at night than they did as children and—when possible—to sleep later in the morning. This pattern creates problems on school days, as students may be too sleepy to learn as well as they should. They may also use caffeine, nicotine, or other stimulants to cope with sleep deprivation. G. Stanley Hall called attention to adolescents' need for sleep, and contemporary developmentalists recommend that adolescents get at least 8 hours per night. However, the average bedtime of high school students in the United States is later than 11 p.m., and the average high school senior rises before 6:15 a.m., thus causing a large number of students to suffer from *chronic sleep deprivation.* The sleep-wake shift during adolescents results from an interaction of hormonal and environmental influences. Pubertal status may play a role; the sleep-wake shift occurs earlier in girls than boys. Environmental factors such as increased schoolwork and decreased parental control also are important. A study of Taiwanese fourth through eighth graders who were subject to intense academic pressure found that the increased demands of higher grade levels were more strongly associated than pubertal status with the sleep-wake shift.

- *Physical Activity.* Adolescents who engage in physical activity experience greater well-being than those who are less active; high levels of athletic activity are associated with less depression and drug use and with better relationships with parents and higher academic performance. However, many adolescents get too little physical activity, putting them at risk of obesity, and a British study of 11- and 12-year-olds found that sedentary behavior was associated with low levels of emotional well-being.

F. Puberty and Culture

The changes associated with puberty are noted in varying ways. In some cultures, special ceremonies mark the transition; in other cultures, institutional markers, such as getting a driver's license, serve as important milestones. Both kinds of markers are associated with changing expectations of how adolescents should behave.

- *Culture and Gender.* Boys and girls experience puberty differently in a psychological sense. It is more common for girls than boys to have mixed feelings about puberty. **Emotional tone**—the degree to which a person experiences a sense of well-being versus depression and anxiety—is different, on average, for boys and girls during adolescence. Whereas boys experience an increase in positive emotional tone during adolescence, positive emotional tone plateaus for girls only happen after early adolescence. This may be a product of the tendency for girls' bodies to be viewed as sexual objects to a greater extent than boys', making girls feel more self-conscious. Another physical change during adolescence is an increase in weight. For boys, this comes from increased muscle mass; for girls, it derives mainly from the accumulation of subcutaneous fat. Such changes are normal, but given cultural ideals emphasizing extreme thinness, adolescent girls may become dissatisfied with their new, mature bodies. In some cases, they develop eating disorders such as **anorexia nervosa** (which involves starving oneself, losing up to 25 percent of body weight) or **bulimia nervosa** (characterized by binge eating followed by self-induced vomiting).
- *Culture and the Timing of Puberty.* The age at which young people undergo puberty affects their reactions to the changes that occur with maturation. *Early maturation* is defined as the development of sex characteristics before 8 years for girls or 9 years for boys; *late maturation* is defined as the absence of sex characteristics at 13.4 years for girls and 14 years for boys. Early maturation, especially in girls, is a *risk factor,* contributing to such problems as depression, eating disorders, delinquency, suicide attempts, and early drug and alcohol use and sexual behavior. Two main explanations have been proposed for the link between early maturation and problem behavior. One suggests that early maturers who associate with older adolescents of similar physical maturity may themselves still be immature cognitively and socially; the other explanation is that early maturers are reacting to being out of synch with their peers and with their broader culture, which is not yet willing to give them the autonomy, freedom, and status that come with adulthood.

IV. THE EMERGENCE OF SEXUAL BEHAVIOR

The emergence of sexual behavior includes not only the physical act but also social influences and cultural meanings. Martha Nussbaum argues that Western culture associates feelings of shame with the body and its sexual behaviors and desires, and therefore does not address sexuality in an open manner; Freud's theory was inspired by the same idea. Perhaps partly for this reason, adolescent sexual development is most often addressed in the form of warnings about unwanted pregnancy or sexually transmitted infections (STIs).

A. Learning about Sex

Adolescents learn about sex from a variety of sources, in contexts that can range from casual and subtle to rigorous and formal. There is a great deal of family, ethnic, and cultural variability in what information is taught and how it is transmitted. For example, research found that adolescents whose mothers had interactive discussions about AIDS with them remembered more information than those whose mothers dominated the conversations. One study found that Hispanic American mothers were more likely than European American mothers to dominate the conversation, consistent with cultural expectations that children should be respectful and obedient toward parents. Differences also exist among societies in how adolescent sexual activity is viewed. In some European countries, there is easy access to contraceptives, confidential health care, and comprehensive sex education. Typically, these countries experience low rates of adolescent pregnancy, childbearing, and STIs. In the United States, in contrast, teenage sex is considered to be risky, and a source of unintended pregnancy and disease. In abstinence-only sex education programs, youths are encouraged to avoid premarital sex, and approximately 23 percent of adolescent females and 16 percent of males have taken "virginity pledges." However, research has found no difference between pledgers and nonpledgers in the ages at which they participate in various sexual acts.

B. The Sexual Debut

As shown in Figure 14.7 of the textbook, there is variation across countries in the average age at which adolescents first engage in sexual intercourse. Differences also exist in the timing of boys' and girls' sexual debuts. For example, in the United States and most Western European countries, boys tend to have intercourse at slightly younger ages than girls, whereas in Ethiopia and Peru, first intercourse occurs at younger ages for girls than boys. Cross-cultural variations are likely to result from a variety of biological and cultural factors.

Boys tend to report more positive feelings about their first experience of intercourse than girls. Many girls are less positive about their first experience because they have been coerced into sex; cultural attitudes may also play a role. Until recently, there has been little investigation of topics such as sexual desire, the social motives for engaging in sexual activity, and the sexual activities of lesbian, gay, and bisexual youth. More attention has been focused on identifying the risk and protective factors associated with having sex, and the consequences of adolescents becoming pregnant or contracting STIs. The box "Teenage Pregnancy" discusses the factors associated with teen pregnancy and shows pregnancy rates in various developed countries. The rate in the United States remains among the highest in the industrialized world.

C. Sexual Behavior and Reproductive Health

Approximately 25 percent of 14- to 19-year-old girls have at least one STI; among females, this rate of infection is higher than for any other age group. Rates are even higher among minority groups, with the exception of Asian-Pacific Islanders. Apart from their consequences on physical and psychological well-being, direct medical costs associated with the diagnosis and treatment of STIs are approximately $14.7 billion annually.

- *Clamydia.* Clamydia is among the most commonly reported infectious diseases in the United States. The rate of infection is highest among 15- to 19-year-olds; African American women are especially likely to become infected. Clamydia, if left untreated, can lead to pelvic inflammatory disease and infertility.
- *Human Papillomavirus.* There are two general categories of HPV: "low risk" (wart-causing) and "high risk" (cancer-causing). Most infections are low risk and eliminated by an

individual's immune system; although genital warts and cancer can be treated, no treatment exists for the virus itself. Recently, a vaccine has been developed that offers protection from the types of HPV that most often cause cancers and warts. It is recommended that girls be vaccinated when they reach 11 or 12 years of age.

- *HIV/AIDS.* The human immunodeficiency virus (HIV) is the virus that causes acquired immunodeficiency syndrome (AIDS), a deadly disease that attacks the immune system, preventing it from combating infections. HIV is contracted through anal, oral, or vaginal sex, through sharing syringes or needles with an infected person, or through prenatal exposure or breast milk. People under 25 years of age account for less than 15 percent of new HIV/AIDS cases; however, because the virus has a long incubation period, those infected during their teen years may not be diagnosed until their twenties or thirties. As many as 25 percent of infected people may be unaware that they have the virus.

  HIV/AIDS is especially prevalent among African Americans and Hispanics in the United States. In part, this may be because the disease is concentrated primarily in large metropolitan areas, where large populations of ethnic minority groups live; in addition, minority youth become sexually active at a younger age, which puts them at greater risk. Although no cure for AIDS exists, strides have been made in managing the disease. Consistent condom use is the most reliable means of prevention.

V. COGNITIVE DEVELOPMENT

The intellectual achievements of adolescence—reasoning, planning, deciding, and imagining—influence how adolescents interpret and react to the changes in their bodies, social lives, and relationships.

A. Piaget's Theory of Formal Operations

Piaget believed that changes in the way adolescents think about themselves, their personal relationships, and the nature of their society have their source in the emergence of **formal operations.** The characteristics of each stage of formal operations are shown in Table 14.2 of the textbook. In contrast to *concrete operations,* formal operations involve the ability to apply operations to operations—that is, to systematically relate relationships to each other. For this reason, they are called *second-order operations.* One example of a second-order operation is a proportion such as $^{10}\!/_5 = {}^4\!/_2$. Formal operations are necessary for systematic problem solving.

- *Reasoning by Manipulating Variables.* Inhelder and Piaget's studies of formal operational thinking typically involved problems that required subjects to hold one variable of a complex system constant while systematically searching through all the other variables. Possibly the most widely cited test of formal operational reasoning is the combination-of-liquids problem, essentially the combination lock problem with a twist. Concrete operational children are likely to go about the task unsystematically. However, formal operational adolescents solve the problem by trying all the combinations of liquids—systematically, beginning with the simplest possibility—until they discover the one that produces the color yellow.

- *Hypothetical-Deductive Reasoning.* A feature of formal scientific thinking is **hypothetical-deductive reasoning,** the ability to judge an argument on the basis of its logical form. If the conclusion follows from the premises, a statement is logical, whether or not the premises are true. Formaldeductive reasoning is rare before the sixth grade (11 to 12 years of age); it becomes progressively more likely between the fourth and twelfth grades (approximately between 10 and 18 years of age).

- *Promoting Formal Operational Thinking through Sociocognitive Conflict.* According to Piaget's theory, development occurs through the conflict of *assimilation* and *accommodation* leading to *equilibration* between previous levels of understanding and new experiences. Piaget considered social interaction to be an important source of cognitive conflict, as children are exposed to differing points of view; **sociocognitive conflict** is cognitive conflict rooted in social experience. Evidence for the importance of sociocognitive conflict came from a study by Rose Dimant and David Bearison. They asked college students to work through six sessions of problems similar to the combination-of-liquids task, either alone or in pairs. They found that the students benefited from sessions in which they worked collaboratively with another student on a set of increasingly difficult problems; sessions that included disagreements, contradictions, and alternative solutions were particularly effective. Students who worked alone or did not collaborate made smaller gains. The box "ICONS: Peacekeeping in a Virtual Classroom" describes an example of a program designed to induce sociocognitive conflict in the context of simulated negotiation about political issues.

- *Variability in Formal Operational Thinking.* Cross-cultural evidence that people rarely reach formal operations without extensive schooling led Piaget to conclude this stage depends on certain types of experience. Research shows that even well-educated American adults often are unable to solve formal operational problems. There is also variability within individuals: people may reason at a formal operational level in some task domains but not others. For this reason, modern researchers focus their investigations on the specific forms of reasoning associated with particular tasks and cultural practices.

B. Information-Processing Approaches

According to information-processing theorists, adolescents' expanded cognitive abilities derive from increases in working memory and in the ability to apply more powerful problem-solving strategies. Researchers have also explored adolescents' problem solving by examining how they make decisions about risk-taking behavior. Knowledge about adolescent thinking capability is relevant to legal issues such as whether adolescents who commit crimes should be tried as adults, whether adolescents should be allowed to undergo medical procedures without parental consent, or whether they can give *informed consent* to participate in research. In a study by Bonnie Halpern-Felsher and Elizabeth Cauffman, sixth to twelfth graders and young adults were presented with decision-making scenarios in which they were asked to help a peer solve a problem. The problems involved the domains of medical procedures, the family, and informed consent. The researchers found that the young adults demonstrated higher levels of decision-making competence compared with the adolescents, especially the sixth to eighth graders. Young adults were more likely to consider options, risks, long-term consequences, and applying a decision rule. However, many adolescents displayed high levels of competence, making it difficult to identify an absolute boundary between immature and mature decision making.

C. Sociocultural Approaches

Sociocultural approaches to adolescent thinking focus mainly on specific forms of thinking used in particular problem-solving situations. In addition, they emphasize the effects of social interactions on problem solving. Games provide an ideal setting for studying the development of complex reasoning skills in adolescence. Na'ilah Nasir used a Vygotskian approach to explore adolescents' reasoning in the context of dominoes, a game of strategy popular in many African American communities. In this study, in which individuals played in teams against one another, it was possible to observe transformations in domino play by children, adolescents, and adults. Adolescents were more adept than younger children at generating and evaluating the point value of possible moves, as would be expected from a Piagetian point of view. However, in keeping with the Vygotskian perspective, players also sought and received help from others in ways that scaffolded their knowledge of the game and mastery of game strategies. Intellectual development from childhood to adolescence emerges in the course of social participation.

VI. MORAL DEVELOPMENT

Issues of moral behavior take on special importance for young people during adolescence. The processes used to contemplate these questions undergo important changes between the ages of 12 and 19.

A. Kohlberg's Theory of Moral Reasoning

Kohlberg's system, as shown in Table 14.3 of the textbook, is based on the idea that moral reasoning progresses across three levels, each of which consists of two stages. As discussed in Chapter 13, at the start of middle childhood, moral reasoning occurs at the *preconventional level* (stages 1 and 2), in which children judge how right or wrong an action is on the basis of their own wants and fears; by the end of middle childhood, they attain the first stage of the *conventional level* (stage 3), in which they begin to take social conventions into consideration and to recognize shared standards of right and wrong. Kohlberg called stage 3 "good-child morality." He believed that for stage 3 individuals, being moral means living up to the expectations of significant people in their lives. Stage 3 remains the dominant mode of moral reasoning until people are in their mid-twenties. However, stage 4 reasoning, based on relations between the individual and a group, makes its appearance during adolescence. Stage 4 reasoning regards as moral behavior that which upholds the law, maintains the social order, and contributes to the group; for this reason, it is called "law and order morality." According to Kohlberg, stage 3 and stage 4 reasoning depends on partially attaining formal operational thought. Nevertheless, people who reason at stages 3 and 4 are still reasoning concretely in that they do not consider all possible relevant factors or form abstract hypotheses about what is moral. The transition to stage 5 reasoning marks a shift in the level of moral judgment; reasoning at the *postconventional level* requires going beyond existing social conventions to consider abstract principles of right and wrong. Stage 5 reasoning is called *social contract reasoning* because it is based on the idea of society being bound by a social contract agreed on by the group to serve the needs of its members. Rather than focusing on maintaining the existing social order, stage 5 thinkers seek possibilities for improving it. Stage 5 reasoning does not appear until early adulthood and is rarely observed even then. Stage 6 reasoning, the stage of *universal ethical principles,* is even rarer and involves reasoning on the basis of principles that transcend the rules of individual societies. Kohlberg did not see evidence of stage 6 in his investigations and came to consider it as perhaps only a philosophical ideal. However, behavior in line with stage 6 thinking is observed occasionally.

B. Feminist Approaches to Moral Reasoning

Is Kohlberg's conception of the nature of morality too narrow? Carol Gilligan, taking a feminist approach to moral reasoning, has asserted that Kohlberg's view reflects a **morality of justice,** emphasizing issues of rightness, fairness, and equality. Another important dimension that should be considered is a **morality of care,** stressing relationships, compassion, and social obligations. According to Gilligan, girls and women are more oriented toward morality of care, whereas boys and men are more oriented toward morality of justice. In fact, studies have shown few gender differences on tests of moral reasoning. However, Gilligan's conception of morality helps to orient researchers to broader contexts of moral judgment.

C. Parent and Peer Contributions to Moral Development

Who has more influence in promoting children's moral growth, parents or peers? According to Kohlberg, peers play a more important role because the sociocognitive conflict that stimulates higher levels of reasoning is more likely to occur in a relationship between equals than in a relationship in which one person has authority over the other. Research provides some support for the importance of peers: the quantity and quality of peer relationships are related to moral reasoning in adolescence. Furthermore, turbulent and conflict-ridden peer interactions are associated with the development of higher moral levels. Nonetheless, developmentalists have challenged the notion that parents have little impact in the moral realm. A longitudinal study by Lawrence Walker and his colleagues found that, in discussions of moral issues, parents provided a higher level of cognitive functioning than peers. When parents used a "gentle Socratic method," children's moral maturity was advanced. Also, authoritative, democratic, and responsive parenting is, in general, associated with higher levels of moral maturity. Thus, the evidence shows that peer and parent–child relationships each have an important influence on moral development, but in distinctive ways.

D. Cultural Variations in Moral Reasoning

Cross-cultural studies using Kohlberg's dilemmas reveal that people from small, technologically unsophisticated societies rarely reason beyond Kohlberg's stage 3 and often justify their decisions at the level of stage 1 or 2. Kohlberg suggested that this was the result of cultural differences in social stimulation; he did not believe that these results meant some societies are more moral than others. Other investigators, such as anthropologist Richard Shweder, have argued that Kohlberg's stage sequence itself contains value judgments specific to Western culture and democracy. In any case, using other approaches to measuring moral reasoning yields results different from Kohlberg's. According to these measures, the shift to postconventional reasoning in adulthood is quite widespread, and what cross-cultural differences do appear seem to be related to level of education. Using a *social domain theory*, Elliot Turiel and his colleagues provide evidence for agreement across cultures on moral reasoning, defined in terms of justice and rights; when cross-cultural differences occur, they tend to involve social conventions and personal choice, the importance of obedience to authority, and the nature of interpersonal relations. An example is provided by Cecilia Wainryb's work with 9- to 17-year-old Jewish and Druze children in Israel. When asked to make judgments on questions of justice, there was little difference between the responses of the groups. The only significant cultural difference was that Jewish children were more likely than their Druze counterparts to assert personal rights over obedience to authority. This fell in line with the hierarchical structure of Druze cultural norms, in which obedience to authority is a central value. Similarly, Joan Miller and her colleagues found that people both from India and from the United States made distinctions between moral infractions and personal conventions, even though they did not always agree on where to draw the line between them. For example, people from both groups judged a dress code violation to be a matter of social convention and theft to be a moral issue.

E. The Relation between Moral Reasoning and Moral Action

What relationship exists between adolescents' moral reasoning and their behavior? The link between reasoning and action is not especially close. Why do young people sometimes make moral choices that violate their principles and sometimes do not? Societal standards and expectations contribute to this variability. For example, adolescents may cheat in school, even though they know it is wrong, if they perceive that many of their peers are cheating and not being caught. In this case, perceiving of cheating as wrong no longer serves as a deterrent. A factor that helps adolescents act morally is the ability to understand the plight of others and to reason prosocially. Social domain theory provides another approach to examining the relationship between moral reasoning and behavior. For example, in a study of risky behavior, Tara Kuther and Ann Higgins-D'Alessandro found that adolescents who reported higher levels of drug and alcohol use were likely to see these behaviors as personal decisions rather than as moral or conventional decisions.

IV. IMPLICATIONS

Physical changes, new ways of thinking, and a new sense of morally appropriate behavior are all part of the transitions of adolescence. The social and emotional developments that are interwoven with these changes will be discussed in Chapter 15.

Key Terms

Following are important terms introduced in Chapter 15. Match each term with the letter of the example that best illustrates the term.

1. _____ anorexia nervosa

2. _____ bulimia nervosa

3. _____ emotional tone

4. _____ formal operations

5. _____ growth spurt

6. _____ hypothetical-deductive reasoning

7. _____ menarche

8. _____ morality of care

9. _____ morality of justice

10. _____ primary sex characteristics

11. _____ puberty

12. _____ secondary sex characteristics

13. _____ secular trend

14. _____ semenarche

15. _____ sociocognitive conflict

a. These involve the organs that are directly involved in reproduction.
b. In many countries, girls living in urban areas reach this developmental milestone at a younger age than those living in rural areas.
c. These outward signs of being male or female develop as a result of hormonal changes during adolescence.
d. This series of biological changes constitutes the most radical change in physical development since birth.
e. This is thought to help young people achieve higher levels of reasoning.
f. Reaching this milestone is a sign of sexual maturation in boys.
g. This is a kind of systematic logical thinking on which adolescent thought is structured, according to Piaget.
h. For boys, at least, this becomes more positive as adolescence progresses.
i. According to Carol Gilligan, Kohlberg's theory is based exclusively on this aspect of moral reasoning.
j. An example is "All cows are green. Bessie is a cow. Therefore, Bessie is green."
k. A symptom of this disorder is extreme self-starvation.
l. In industrialized nations, the average age at which girls reach menarche has declined over the past several decades and such a change is called this.
m. According to Carol Gilligan, this is more characteristic of girls and women.
n. This disorder is characterized by binge eating and self-induced vomiting.
o. This marks the onset of puberty.

Multiple-Choice Practice Questions

Circle the letter of the word or phrase that correctly completes each statement.

1. G. Stanley Hall believed that adolescents
   a. are not qualitatively different from younger children.
   b. have great potential to be creative.
   c. are subject to emotional ups and downs.
   d. Both b and c are correct.

2. In Freud's theory of development, the period of adolescence corresponds to the _____ stage.
   a. latency
   b. genital
   c. oedipal
   d. phallic

3. During adolescence, what events occur in the brain?
   a. synaptogenesis
   b. synaptic pruning
   c. No changes occur, because the brain has already reached full development.
   d. Both a and b are correct.

4. The _____ produce(s) the hormone that is responsible for the adolescent growth spurt.
   a. hypothalamus
   b. adrenal cortex
   c. pituitary gland
   d. ovaries and testes

5. Which are secondary sex characteristics?
   a. facial hair in boys and breasts in girls
   b. testosterone in boys and estrogen and progesterone in girls
   c. the testes in boys and the ovaries in girls
   d. All these answers are correct.

6. Which statement about the physiological differences between males and females in adolescence and adulthood is correct?
   a. Males are stronger, healthier, and better able to tolerate long-term stress.
   b. Males have a greater capacity for physical exercise, but females are healthier and live longer.
   c. Females have larger hearts and lower resting heart rates and can exercise for longer periods.
   d. There are no appreciable differences between male and female capacities for exercise and athletic performance.

7. Adolescents reach _____ of their adult height by the end of the growth spurt of puberty.
   a. 78 percent
   b. 85 percent
   c. 98 percent
   d. 100 percent

8. The timing of the events of puberty
   a. is earlier in many societies than it was 100 years ago.
   b. occurs later in children from families undergoing stress than in children from more harmonious families.
   c. is the same, on average, in all cultures.
   d. is equally similar for identical and fraternal twins.

9. There is concern that many adolescents do not get sufficient
   a. sleep.
   b. vitamins and minerals.
   c. exercise.
   d. All these answers are correct.

10. Studies have found early physical maturation to be _____ for girls.
    a. a risk factor
    b. an academic advantage
    c. a protective factor
    d. neither advantageous nor disadvantageous

11. Cross-cultural studies of sexual behavior indicate that
    a. adolescents in many cultures do not yet have sexual feelings.
    b. different cultures may have very different conventions for informing adolescents about sexual matters.
    c. the standards for adolescent sexual behavior are the same in all cultures.
    d. traditional societies are generally less restrictive about premarital intercourse than industrialized societies.

12. About 60 percent of girls under 15 years of age who have had sexual intercourse report that during their first sexual experience they were
    a. coerced.
    b. motivated by curiosity.
    c. satisfied with the experience.
    d. protected by contraception.

13. The combination-of-liquids problem requires the use of formal operational reasoning because
    a. it does not involve the use of real chemicals.
    b. it requires the participant to be systematic in testing the combinations.
    c. it is a test of conservation of liquid quantity.
    d. it requires the use of principles of class inclusion.

14. Formal operational reasoning
    a. is attained by all normal adults in all cultures.
    b. is attained by all educated adults in industrialized societies.
    c. is attained by most American adolescents and adults and is used fairly consistently.
    d. is attained by a minority of American adolescents and adults and is used in some situations but not others.

15. Research in which adolescents and young adults were asked to give advice to a person making a "real-life" decision found that
    a. both the young adults and adolescents demonstrated consistently low levels of reasoning.
    b. none of the younger adolescents reasoned at a high level, whereas most of the older adolescents did.
    c. the young adults were significantly more advanced in their reasoning than the adolescents.
    d. both the adolescents and young adults demonstrated consistently high levels of reasoning.

16. The most common level of moral reasoning on Kohlberg's dilemmas during adolescence is
    a. stage 2.
    b. stage 3.
    c. stage 4.
    d. stage 5.

17. Parents can help advance their children's moral development by
    a. using an authoritative parenting style.
    b. using a permissive parenting style.
    c. strictly limiting adolescents' interactions with peers.
    d. behaving more like peers and less like parents.

18. Adolescents in a variety of cultures are likely to agree about issues of right and wrong when they involve
    a. questions about justice and rights.
    b. questions about social conventions and personal choice.
    c. questions about obedience to authority.
    d. all of the above equally.

Short-Answer Practice Questions

Write a brief answer in the space below each question.

1. Discuss the factors, evolutionary and environmental, that influence the timing of puberty in humans.

2. Explain why early maturation can lead to problems for adolescents.

3. Discuss some of the health problems that are especially likely to occur during adolescence. Choose one problem and discuss—from the point of view of a parent, teacher, or health professional—how you would work to lessen its occurrence.

4. Why does the United States have such a high rate of teen pregnancy compared with other industrialized nations? What actions would you suggest to reduce the number of pregnancies among adolescents?

5. Describe an instance of "everyday" problem solving in which you, or others, make use of formal operational reasoning.

6. Discuss a situation you have observed or heard of in which adolescents or adults have failed to live up to their moral principles. What factors do you believe influenced them to behave this way?

Putting It All Together

In this section, material from Chapter 14 can be combined with information presented in earlier chapters.

It is theorized that *sociocognitive conflict* acts as a stimulant to developing higher levels of reasoning. Discuss examples from early childhood, middle childhood, and adolescence in which sociocognitive conflict helps to promote cognitive development and prosocial or moral development.

Sources of More Information

Epstein, R. (2007). *The case against adolescence: Rediscovering the adult in every teen.* Sanger, CA: Quill Driver Books/Word Dancer Press.
The author argues the case that adolescents are far more capable than adults give them credit for and should be treated accordingly.

Kohlberg, L. (1984). *The psychology of moral development: The nature and validity of moral stages.* New York: Harper and Row.
This volume brings together many of Kohlberg's most influential papers on moral development.

Lerner, R., & Lerner, J. (Eds.) (1999). *Theoretical foundations and biological bases of development in adolescence.* New York: Garland Publishing.
This collection of previously published articles contains a great deal of information on the biological changes of adolescence and how theorists have historically regarded this stage of development.

Levine, M., & Smolak, L. (2005). *Prevention of eating problems and eating disorders: Theory, research, and practice.* Mahwah, NJ: Lawrence Erlbaum.
This is a comprehensive view of the field of eating disorders and includes information on risk and protective factors, as well as what is known about prevention.

Linn, M., Clement, C., & Pulos, S. (1983). Is it formal if it's not physics? (The influence of content on formal reasoning). *Journal of Research in Science Teaching, 20,* 755--770.
This article examines how content and subjects' expectations affect performance on tests of formal operational reasoning.

Lopez, R. (2002). *The teen health book.* New York: W.W. Norton.
This book gives an overview of adolescence from a physician's point of view. It covers such topics as physical and emotional development, sleep, nutrition, substance abuse, and common ailments.

Malinowski, B. (1972). The social and sexual life of Trobriand children. In *Historical readings in developmental psychology,* Wayne Dennis (Ed.). New York: Appleton-Century-Crofts.
This observation, first published in 1929, describes the coming of age of children in a society very different from our own.

Piaget, J., & Inhelder, B. (1975). *The origin of the idea of chance in children.* New York: W.W. Norton.
Reasoning about chance and probability are examples of logical thought. Piaget and Inhelder report on their studies of the development of these concepts in children with reasoning levels from preoperational through formal operational.

Ruble, D., & Brooks-Gunn, J. (1982). The experience of menarche. *Child Development, 53,* 1557–1566.
This article reports on the attitudes and emotional reactions of adolescents and preadolescents to menarche.

Answer Key

Answers to Key Terms: 1.k, 2.n, 3.h, 4.g, 5.o, 6.j, 7.b, 8.m, 9.i, 10.a, 11.d, 12.c, 13.l, 14.f, 15.e.

Answers to Multiple-Choice Questions: 1.d, 2.b, 3.d, 4.c, 5.a, 6.b, 7.c, 8.a, 9.d, 10.a, 11.b, 12.a, 13.b, 14.d, 15.c, 16.b, 17.a, 18.a.

15 Social and Emotional Development in Adolescence

CHAPTER

Adolescence is regarded as a time of emotional upheaval, and it is true that, as adolescence progresses, young people report more negative feelings and less average happiness. However, adolescents' emotions eventually become less intense and their moods even out as they grow more adept at regulating their feelings.

Adolescents also face new challenges and risks, including the temptation to engage in dangerous or delinquent behaviors, or to risk their health with smoking or drug and alcohol use.

During adolescence, young people's attachments to their parents become less important and they look outside their families for friendship and romantic interest. Despite having access to a wider range of potential companions, they tend to choose friends who are similar to them in most ways. During this time, adolescents work to establish their identities, developing and committing themselves to their own points of view in many domains, including sexual and ethnic identity, educational and occupational choices, and political and religious affiliation.

The course of adolescent development varies across cultures, and young people growing up in traditional societies face a different set of choices than those in Western industrialized countries, who may pass through a further stage known as "emerging adulthood." However it is accomplished, the period of transition to adulthood is an important one in every human society.

Learning Objectives

Keep these questions in mind while studying Chapter 15.

1. How is emotional experience different in adolescence than in childhood?
2. How do biological processes and social processes shape adolescents' ability to regulate their emotions?
3. How do young people's social lives change during adolescence? What qualities are important in their friendships?

4. To what extent are adolescents at risk for engaging in risky or socially disapproved behavior? What factors contribute to such behavior?
5. What steps must adolescents go through in the process of forming an identity? How does this process differ according to sexual orientation, minority group membership, and culture?
6. In what ways do parents continue to influence the behavior of their adolescent children? Which parenting practices are most effective?
7. How does the experience of adolescence differ in traditional societies and in technologically advanced societies?
8. What is the stage of emerging adulthood, and how is it different from previous stages?

Chapter Summary

Adolescence is characterized by new ways of interacting with friends and with parents and by the search for identity. These social and identity developments converge in the period called "emerging adulthood."

I. EMOTIONAL DEVELOPMENT IN ADOLESCENCE

As discussed in Chapter 14, adolescence has long been considered a period of intense emotions and dramatic mood swings. Given adolescents' advances in cognitive development, is it true that they are also exceptionally impulsive?

A. The Experience of Emotions

It is difficult to document the emotional experiences of adolescence. One commonly used tool is the **experience sampling method (ESM),** in which participants carry electronic pagers that beep at random intervals, signaling them to fill out a brief report on their current feelings. Typically, the pager beeps every 1 to 2 hours, 15 hours per day, for a period of a week or more. This method has been praised for its *ecological validity.*

ESM studies have determined that emotional states change in type and intensity during the adolescent years. Reed Larsen and his colleagues conducted a longitudinal study spanning early to late adolescence, in which they found that more than 70 percent of the time, when paged, adolescents reported experiencing positive emotions. However, as shown in Figure 15.1 of the textbook, these same researchers also found that average happiness decreases between early adolescence and middle adolescence and remains relatively low throughout late adolescence. This decline in average happiness mostly results from an increase in negative emotions. Throughout adolescence, girls tend to have more positive average emotions than boys. There seems to be no one time during adolescence when young people are more sensitive or reactive to stressful life events; difficult circumstances are associated with equal amounts of negative emotion throughout adolescence. Over the course of adolescence, emotions become less intense and emotional ups and downs less frequent.

B. Regulating Emotions

A possible reason why emotions grow more stable over the course of adolescence is that young people become better able to control and regulate them, as well as the behaviors they may inspire. *Impulse control, inhibition,* and *persistence* are some of the main features of emotion regulation; they underlie the abilities to "down-regulate" negative emotions and "up-regulate" positive ones. Adolescents who have trouble regulating emotions are more likely to experience emotional, social, and behavioral problems. Regulating emotions involves the complex interplay of biological and sociocultural processes.

- *Biological Processes.* Adolescence is characterized by two important biological developments: (1) the influx of pubertal hormones during early adolescence and (2) the spurt in brain growth that begins in early adolescence but does not end until late adolescence. Some studies suggest that pubertal hormones may account for adolescents' **sensation-seeking**—the desire to participate in highly arousing activities. However, the infusion of hormones occurs at a time when the brain is still undergoing development—particularly in the frontal lobes, which are associated with processes such as decision making, judgment, and impulse control. Thus, according to Laurence Steinberg, there may be a gap between the emotions triggered by pubertal hormones and the brain's ability to regulate such emotions. Some support for the idea that adolescents are vulnerable to risky decision making comes from a study using a computerized driving game; the researchers found that adolescents made riskier driving decisions when playing with friends than when playing alone, whereas adults played similarly under both conditions.

- *Social Processes.* The ways adolescents regulate their emotions depend on the social contexts in which they develop. Families play an important role in how adolescents learn to manage their feelings. Warm supportive parenting is associated with the ability to regulate feelings, whereas emotional negativity within the family is associated with increased negative emotions and aggressive behaviors. Nancy Eisenberg and her colleagues conducted a longitudinal study to discover the relationships among parent–child interactions, adolescents' ability to regulate their emotions, and adolescents' behavioral problems. They found that parents' emotional warmth and expression of positive emotions when children were about 9 years old predicted higher levels of emotion regulation by children in early adolescence; this, in turn, predicted fewer behavioral problems in middle adolescence.

  Gender also affects adolescents' emotion regulation; males and females are socialized to manage emotional expressions in different ways. For example, boy and girl babies cry with equal frequency, but a gender gap in crying begins during early childhood and continues to widen through adolescence. This occurs because boys cry less and less often as they grow older, especially during adolescence. In contrast, girls' crying remains relatively stable throughout adolescence. Studies suggest that social expectations underlie this difference. A cross-cultural study of adolescents' emotions by Archana Singh-Manoux found that, among English subjects, girls reported feeling stronger emotions than boys and being preoccupied with them for a longer period. The difference between boys and girls was less significant among subjects in India; furthermore, it fell in the opposite direction, with boys reporting stronger emotions. This may be due to differences in cultural conceptions of adolescence.

II. RELATIONSHIPS WITH PEERS

As they enter adolescence, children's social activities and interactions with their peers change. Developmentalists distinguish between adolescents' *close relationships* with friends and romantic partners and their *peer networks,* which may include casual acquaintances as well as good friends.

A. Friendships

Friendship refers to a close relationship between two individuals. Friendships may have different bases that change over time. In contrast with the more superficial characteristics that bind together younger children, adolescents' friendships are distinguished by their reliance on *reciprocity* (the give-and-take of close relationships); *commitment* (loyalty and trust between friends); and *equality* (equal distribution of power).

- *Developmental Functions of Friendships.* Adolescents' friendships serve two important developmental functions: intimacy and autonomy. **Intimacy**—a connection between two individuals resulting from shared feelings, thoughts, and activities—is what comes to mind when we reflect on friendship. However, **autonomy**—the ability to govern the self and assert one's own needs—is necessary in order to avoid bowing to peer pressure to engage in risky behaviors. Healthy, well-balanced friendships contribute to adolescents' social and personality development, and adolescents with supportive friends report fewer school-related and psychological problems, less loneliness, and greater confidence in their acceptance by peers. Difficulty making friends may be part of a pattern of poor social adjustment that begins during early childhood.
- *Friendships and Gender.* Adolescent girls' friendships tend to be more intense and intimate than friendships among boys; one explanation is that boys are less trusting of their friends and less likely to share their emotions with them. For example, in response to an emotionally charged situation, boys may talk about more superficial aspects of the experience, whereas girls may share their feelings about it. Another possible explanation for boys' friendships being less intimate is that **homophobia**—a fear of homosexuality—may prevent them from demonstrating, or admitting to, strong feelings of intimacy toward their male friends.

  Boys' and girls' friendships also differ in their degree of competition. Among boys, friendly competition may increase the closeness of relationships. Girls' relationships tend to be less competitive. It has been suggested that boys and girls have different "goal orientations"—that girls focus on *communal goals* that emphasize relationship-enhancement and cooperation, whereas boys focus more on *agentic goals,* which emphasize dominance and self-interest.

B. Cliques and Crowds

New kinds of peer groups become prominent during adolescence. Family-sized **cliques** are small enough to serve as the primary peer group. Adolescents may be members of several cliques that meet in different settings; a clique can serve as an "alternative center of security" much like a family. Another type of peer group is the larger **crowd,** a mixed-gender group of friends and acquaintances that emerges when cliques interact. Crowds allow adolescents to meet new people, explore their identities, and develop romantic relationships. Crowds typically have public identities of their own, as is apparent from stereotyped labels such as "jocks," "brains," and "druggies." Being considered a member of a particular crowd reflects on an adolescent's social status. In some schools, "brains" occupy an intermediate status between elite and unpopular groups; in other schools—for example, in working-class African American communities—"brains" may be ostracized, leading young people to mask their abilities.

C. Romantic Relationships

In many cultures, a function of peer groups is to aid adolescents in transitioning to romantic relationships. Dexter Dunphy studied this transition during the late 1950s. He discovered that, as shown in Figure 15.3 of the textbook, during early adolescence, young people tended to gather in same-sex cliques. Cliques became part of a larger mixed-sex crowd. Eventually, the crowd dissolved into loosely associated groups of couples who were going steady or were engaged to get married. As proposed by Dunphy, mid-adolescence seems to be a turning point during which nearly 50 percent of adolescents report being involved in intense romantic relationships. Today, this pattern of dating still occurs in some parts of the world. However, in contemporary industrialized societies, marriage is often postponed until several years after the initiation of sexual activity. The box "Friends with Benefits" describes another exception to the pattern.

Despite the evidence of a stagelike process ending with individual romantic relationships, contemporary adolescents continue to "hang out with their friends" even as they begin dating. Thus, they must learn to maneuver between their relationships with friends and with their romantic partners. Ami Kuttler and Annette Greca studied how an ethnically diverse sample of adolescent girls managed romantic and friend relationships. They found that girls engaged in casual dating had closer relationships with their best friends; in contrast, those involved in "serious" romantic relationships spent less time with their best friends and reported less companionship with them.

There are subgroups within contemporary societies in which involvement in romantic relationships may be discouraged. And, given that most adolescent peer groups generally disapprove of homosexual relationships, peer influence is likely to be different in the formation of gay and lesbian relationships. In addition, cultures vary widely in the extent to which they support and provide opportunities for the development of romantic relationships.

D. Peer Pressure and Conformity

Although adolescents have more opportunities than younger children to meet people from different backgrounds, their friends tend to be even more similar to them than they were in elementary school. The degree to which friends are similar to each other is called **homophily.** High school friends tend to have similar views about school, academic achievement, dating, and other leisure-time activities, and also to feel the same way about drinking, drug use, and delinquency.

- *Selection and Socialization.* Denise Kandel and her colleagues found that adolescents seek out others who are similar to them in important traits and behaviors, especially those relevant to social reputation; this is called *selection*. Next, a process of *socialization* occurs; socially significant behaviors are modeled and reinforced in the course of ongoing interactions. Thus, friends become increasingly alike. In this way, adolescents friendly with delinquent peers are more likely to become delinquent themselves.
- *Conformity and Deviance.* Developmentalists have worried that it is unhealthy for adolescents to spend excessive time with their peers; left to themselves, they may engage in antisocial behavior. Frederic Thrasher studied a large number of Chicago gangs in the early years of the 1900s. He found that the gangs, which began as neighborhood play groups, only became a problem when they functioned without supervision and without opportunities to participate in socially acceptable activities. Uri Bronfenbrenner has also argued that children cannot learn culturally established patterns of cooperation and mutual concern if they have contact only with their age-mates.

It is not known how adolescents' behavior would develop if they were left to their own devices. However, plenty of evidence exists that deviancy can be socialized in the context of peer relationships. Thomas Berndt and Keunho Keefe found that seventh and eighth graders whose friends engaged in a high level of disruptive behavior in the fall reported an increase in their own such behavior when re-questioned later in the year; girls were more susceptible to this influence. Other studies show that when an adolescent's friends engage in smoking, using alcohol or illegal drugs, being sexually active, or breaking the law, he or she is likely to do these things as well.

It has been suggested that **deviancy training**—positive reactions to any discussion of rule breaking—contributes to antisocial behavior among adolescents. For example, Thomas Dishion and his colleagues found that positive reactions by 13- to 14-year-olds to talk about rule-breaking and other deviant forms of behavior predicted increased violent behavior, as well as the initiation of tobacco, alcohol, and marijuana use at age 15 or 16. Perhaps as a result of peer processes similar to deviancy training, Dishion and his colleagues also found that group counseling and therapy for delinquent adolescents may do more harm than good, actually increasing the participants' problem behaviors.

III. RELATIONSHIPS WITH PARENTS

Between fifth and ninth grades, the amount of time adolescents spend with their parents drops by about 50 percent, and they become more likely to turn to their peers for support and advice. Parents are also likely to be facing a variety of life stresses; as a result, conflicts may arise in their relationships with adolescent children.

A. Adolescent–Parent Conflicts

During adolescence, young people are caught between two worlds: one of childhood dependence and one of adult responsibility. This can lead to conflict between adolescents and their parents. Brett Laursen and his colleagues, reviewing a large number of studies carried out over several decades, found that patterns of conflict between parents and children change over the course of adolescence. The frequency and intensity of disagreements peak in early adolescence and then decrease. Interestingly, a recent study found that this pattern depended on family context. For instance, for a younger sibling close in age to a teenage brother or sister, his or her conflict with parents may peak in middle childhood—at the same time that the older sibling makes the transition to adolescence. What are the subjects of adolescent–parent conflicts? Often, they center around seemingly trivial matters of household responsibilities and privileges, dating and curfews, involvement in athletics, and financial independence; arguments over "big issues" such as religion or politics are less common. Parents and adolescents nevertheless may differ in their definition of big issues. For example, research from the perspective of social domain theory indicates that many adolescent–parent conflicts involve disagreements over where to draw the boundaries between the social conventional and personal domains. Thus, parents may view dressing appropriately for an event as a matter of social convention, whereas an adolescent may view it as a matter of personal choice. Middle-class African American families may have relatively restricted definitions of what constitutes adolescents' personal jurisdictions, compared with European American families. However, according to social domain theory, parents' expectations for obedience will vary across domains, so conflict in one area will not necessarily characterize the entire adolescent–parent relationship.

B. Parental Influences beyond the Family

During adolescence, parents continue to play an important role in addition to providing food, clothing, and shelter. According to a German study, adolescents whose parents demonstrate warmth, engage in discussions about academic and intellectual matters, and have high expectations for academic performance do better in school than those whose parents are less warm and involved. In one study with both African American and European American samples, positive identification with parents was strongly related to adolescents' valuing of academics. Parents also influence with whom their children interact, including what crowds their children are likely to become associated with. According to a study by Andrew Fuligni and Jacqueline Eccles, there is an interaction between the influences of peers and parents on adolescents' behavior. Children who perceived their parents as becoming stricter as they entered adolescence turned more to their peers for advice than children whose parents included them in decisions and encouraged them to express their ideas. Children whose parents set curfews and monitored their activities also turned less frequently to peers. Adolescents in the United States and China reported experiencing more positive emotions and better academic performance when they perceived their parents as supportive of their developing autonomy.

In studies of the family dynamics of normally developing and troubled adolescents, Hausser and his colleagues identified two main patterns of interaction: *constraining interactions* that limit and restrict communication through detachment, lack of curiosity, and other forms of discouragement; and *enabling interactions* that facilitate and enhance communication through explaining, empathizing, expressing curiosity, and encouraging mutual problem solving. The researchers argue that enabling interactions promote healthy psychological and identity development by making it safe for adolescents to "try out" new ideas and perspectives and to express new feelings. Studies of parenting style have found that children of authoritative parents are more competent in school and less likely to get into trouble than children of authoritarian or permissive parents; their friends also benefit from interactions with these authoritative parents. In general, the most common pattern of parent–child adjustment during adolescence is for children and parents to negotiate a new form of interdependence in which the adolescent is granted increasingly equal rights and more nearly equal responsibilities.

IV. IDENTITY DEVELOPMENT

It is widely believed that adolescence is the period during which an individual forms the basis of a coherent and stable identity. **Identity development** is the process through which individuals achieve a sense of who they are, what moral and political beliefs they embrace, the sort of occupation they wish to pursue, and their relationship to their communities and culture.

A. The I" and the "Me"

In order to understand what identity is and how it is formed, developmentalists distinguish between two components of the self: the **me-self** (*object-self*) includes all of the things that people know about themselves, such as social roles and relationships, material possessions, traits, and other features that can be objectively known; the **I-self** (*subject-self*) is the part of the system that guides and directs the object self. The I-self includes *self-awareness,* an appreciation of one's internal states, needs, thoughts, and emotions; *self-agency,* the sense of authorship over one's thoughts and actions; *self-continuity,* the sense that one remains the same person over time; and *self-coherence,* the sense that one is a single, integrated, and bounded entity.

According to identity theorists, social and historical contexts play an important role in how a person's self develops. A child growing up in a traditional society may have a limited number of social role possibilities and, therefore, a fairly clearly defined path of identity development. In technologically advanced societies, mass communications have accelerated and multiplied our relations to each other and to our communities. According to Kenneth Gergen, modern society has resulted in a **saturated self**—a self full to the brim of multiple "me's" that have emerged as a consequence of needing to conform to social roles and relationships that demand different, and sometimes contradictory, selves. The appearance of multiple selves in adolescents' self-descriptions means that they must deal with the fact that they are, in some ways, different people in different contexts. This makes the question of personal authenticity both compelling and anxiety-provoking.

B. Achieving a Mature Identity

A dominant theme of adolescence is the search for one's "true self." According to Erik Erikson, the search for identity is a lifelong task; however, its challenges come to a climax during adolescence. Adolescents must integrate a stable sense of self across various roles and responsibilities, creating a unified sense of identity; failure to do so results in "identity confusion." Thus, the crisis of adolescence is *identity versus role confusion.*

Erikson's ideas created a need for a way of assessing identity formation, and such a method was developed by James Marcia (the box "From Diaries to Blogs" describes yet another assessment method). Marcia focused on two factors identified by Erikson: **exploration,** the process through which adolescents actively examine their possible future roles and paths; and **commitment,** individuals' sense of allegiance to the goals, values, beliefs, and occupation they have chosen. Based on interviews with male college students about their choice of occupation, and beliefs about politics and religion, Marcia identified four patterns of coping with identity formation: *identity achievement,* in which young people had gone through a period of decision making and were pursuing their own goals; *foreclosure,* in which they had not gone through a period of exploration but had simply adopted their parents' identity patterns; *moratorium,* in which young people were actively engaged in a process of exploration at the time of the interview; and *identity diffusion,* in which they had neither explored nor committed to identity possibilities. Studies have indicated that identity achievement increases with age, whereas instances of identity diffusion and moratorium decrease, a trend that continues through the late college years.

C. Family and Identity

Adolescents' family relations influence the process of identity formation. Harold Grotevant and Catherine Cooper examined the relation between identity achievement scores and family interaction, using a "family interaction task" in which family members planned a hypothetical vacation together. In this and other studies, they found that adolescents who scored high on measures of identity exploration lived in families that supported their right to express their own points of view. Research has also found that secure attachment is positively correlated with identity achievement, whereas insecure attachment is related to identity diffusion.

D. Forming a Sexual Identity

Sexual identity refers to a person's understanding of him- or herself as heterosexual, homosexual, or bisexual. For **sexual minority youth**—those who develop identities as gays, lesbians, or bisexuals—developing identity can be complicated. A survey of a large sample of adolescents found that over 8 percent of boys and 6 percent of girls have had same-sex attractions or relationships. However, less than 2 percent of adolescents identify themselves as gay, lesbian, or bisexual.

Richard Troiden has proposed a stage model of forming a sexual minority identity. It includes the following stages: stage 1, sensitization, feeling different (during early adolescence, many sexual minority youths experience a feeling of being "different"); stage 2, self-recognition, identity confusion (at puberty, the individual realizes an attraction to the same sex and labels such feelings as homosexual); stage 3, identity assumption (the individual may move from private acknowledgment of homosexual preference to admitting it openly, at least to other homosexuals); and stage 4, commitment, identity integration (the stage reached by those who have come to terms with their homosexuality and are "out" in their communities). Commitment to a homosexual identity may vary in strength, depending on satisfaction with personal relationships, acceptance by family members, and functioning at work or in a career. Fear of rejection by parents or social stigma can make the public disclosure of sexual identity a major challenge. As shown in Table 15.2 of the textbook, the age of disclosure is similar in gay, lesbian, and bisexual youths. Sexual minority youths have the same concerns as other adolescents: they need their parents' love and respect, they must negotiate their on-going relationships, they are concerned with peer status, they desire love and sex, and they wonder about their futures.

E. Forming an Ethnic Identity

Identity formation is especially complicated for minority group children in the United States. Adolescents from minority groups face the task of reconciling two different identities: one based on the cultural heritage of their own group, and the other based on the cultural heritage of the majority group. Jean Phinney has described three stages in the formation of ethnic identity: stage 1, *unexamined ethnic identity* (children tend to accept and show a preference for the cultural values of the majority culture); stage 2, *ethnic identity search* (concern for the personal implications of their ethnicity), which, in some cases, involves a process of *oppositional identity formation* in rejection of the dominant group; and stage 3, *ethnic identity achievement* (secure self-confidence in their ethnicity and positive self-concept). A mature ethnic identity may be a protective factor against some risks; for example, a study of Native American students found that those with a greater sense of ethnic pride also had stronger anti-drug norms.

Jean Phinney and her colleagues, studying immigrant Armenian, Vietnamese, and Mexican families, found ethnic identity formation to be strongest when a native language is spoken in the home and adolescents spend time with peers who share their ethnic heritage. Positive ethnic identity formation is also fostered when parents uphold cultural conditions in the home and instruct their children in them. It is easier for the children of immigrants to develop a positive ethnic identity when they move into an existing community that shares their ethnic heritage; it can be more difficult when they move into areas that lack an established community and have little understanding of their culture. Adolescents may use art and music in the process of identity formation. An example of this appears in the "Hip-Hop Generation" box in the text.

F. Identity and Culture

Many researchers believe that identity formation can differ radically between cultures. For example, Hazel Markus and Shinobu Kitayama describe differences between cultures with an **independent sense of self**—in which individuals are oriented to being unique, expressing their own thoughts and opinions, and pursuing their own goals—and those with an **interdependent sense of self**—in which individuals seek to fit into groups and to promote the goals of others. Not all societies require the full range of decisions and choices related to work, marriage, and ideology that are faced by young people in Western cultures. Elliot Turiel has cautioned against categorizing societies into two broad groupings; he argues that cultures, and the people who live in them, are too diverse to be understood within such a system. However, as discussed in the box "Suicide among Native American Adolescents," cultural traditions and beliefs affect how adolescents understand themselves, and this, in turn, has implications for their mental health.

V. SOCIAL AND EMOTIONAL PROBLEMS OF ADOLESCENCE

An extensively studied topic related to adolescence is the increase of social and emotional problems during this period. Developmentalists distinguish between two categories of emotional problems: **internalizing problems,** which are more prevalent in girls and include disturbances in emotion or mood such as depression, worry, guilt, and anxiety; and **externalizing problems,** which are more common in boys and include social and behavioral problems such as aggression and delinquency.

A. Internalizing Problems

As shown in Figure 15.8 of the textbook, an increase in emotional distress occurs in both boys and girls between the ages of 11 and 15, and also a widening gender gap such that, by age 15, girls are approximately twice as likely as boys to experience serious depression. The increase in distress may be accounted for by a combination of the chemistry of puberty and a variety of possible social stresses. Girls also appear to be more concerned about how they are evaluated by others, including their peers, and more apprehensive about relationships.

B. Externalizing Problems

Externalizing problems also seem to peak during adolescence, rising sharply between early and mid-adolescence and declining thereafter. The gender differences are even greater than with internalizing problems; it is estimated that over 25 percent of all 16- to 17-year-old boys have been involved in at least one serious violent offense. During adolescence, the number of teens involved in antisocial behavior increases, as do such activities on the part of specific individuals. It is estimated that more than 50 percent of violent behaviors are perpetrated by only 6 percent of adolescents. Most of these youths are also involved in other externalizing behaviors such as theft or the frequent use of drugs or alcohol.

The more serious, chronic forms of externalizing behaviors account for the majority of referrals to adolescent mental health clinics and placements in special education classes. A team of researchers in New Zealand following 1000 individuals from birth to adulthood found that there were two distinctive developmental patterns with respect to externalizing behaviors. In one, *adolescent onset,* the problems emerged in adolescence, had a brief time course, and declined significantly in young adulthood; the boy/girl ratio for this pattern was 1.5 to 1. In the other, *childhood onset* or *life-course persistent,* high levels of aggression emerged in preschool and persisted throughout childhood and adolescence into adulthood; for this pattern, the boy/girl ratio was 10 to 1. Figure 15.9 in the textbook shows how temperament, child-rearing strategies, academic failure, and peer rejection combine to push children into a commitment to deviant peer groups and thus into delinquency. Why are girls less likely to develop externalizing problems? As discussed in Chapter 9, boys and girls have different biological predispositions toward aggression. In addition, norm-violating behaviors are less likely to be tolerated in girls, and their *communal orientation* may further diminish their involvement in externalizing behaviors.

VI. EMERGING ADULTHOOD

In technologically advanced societies, young people may continue to rely on their parents for support, engage in an extended period of identity exploration, and feel unprepared for the roles and responsibilities of adulthood. Some developmentalists argue for the existence of a unique stage, **emerging adulthood,** that reflects the new challenges faced by young people of 18 to 25 years of age. Decades ago, Kenneth Keniston proposed that individuals coming of age in societies undergoing fast-paced technological change experience a high degree of social, political, and cultural change as they adapt to new technologies. As a result, he argued, youth turn to each other, rather than to their elders, to sort out issues of identity and create a "youth culture" separate from that of the prior generation. More recently, developmentalists have investigated how 18- to 25-year-olds work toward achieving self-sufficiency, stable romantic relationships, and adult work roles. Several studies have found that emerging adults, in defining what it means to be mature, place considerable weight on accepting responsibility for oneself, making independent decisions, and becoming financially independent.

Some developmentalists have addressed intellectual changes during emerging adulthood; one of the most interesting areas of research is **epistemic development,** changes in individuals' reasoning about the nature of knowledge. For example, college students who were interviewed about their experiences in school revealed various views on the nature of knowledge: an **objectivist theory of knowledge,** in which knowledge is viewed as involving an accumulation of objective facts and definite answers; a **subjectivist theory of knowledge,** according to which there is no absolute truth, as truth can shift and change depending on one's perspective; and an **evaluativist theory of knowledge,** in which it is recognized that truth, although shifting and changing, is nevertheless subject to particular standards of evaluation. Studies have found a hierarchy in epistemic development: an objectivist theory emerges first, followed by a subjectivist theory, and finally, an evaluativist theory. However, cultural differences also exist, in that some cultures may emphasize one theory of knowledge over the others. Thus, traditional cultures that believe knowledge to be transmitted by authority figures may subscribe to an objectivist theory of knowledge, whereas a culture that believes knowledge should be evaluated according to scientific standards might subscribe to an evaluativist theory of knowledge.

Emerging adulthood is not viewed as a universal stage, but as depending on the cultural contexts in which children develop. The increasing levels of education required in technologically advancing societies delay an individual's entry into adult work and family roles, permitting a longer period in which to explore identity possibilities and different theories of knowledge.

VII. RECONSIDERING ADOLESCENCE

The transition to adolescence involves dramatic transformations in the physical, cognitive, and social domains. Evolutionary processes have played an important role. Humans are considerably delayed in reaching physical maturity compared to other primate species, and this delay allows the brain to develop areas associated with the advanced processes necessary for creating and using the sophisticated tools of human culture. Culture itself also plays a key role—for example, its effect on the age of puberty, which has been decreasing, initially with the greater availability of nutritious food and health care, and presently with the increase in obesity. Culture is also important in adolescent identity formation and in structuring the diverse ways by which the path to adulthood can be negotiated. For example, individuals growing up in traditional societies may have fewer questions about identity, career, and social role possibilities compared to those growing up in technologically advanced societies. In the latter, the array of possibilities for identity, relationships, education, and ways of understanding the nature of knowledge provides the context for a possible stage of emerging adulthood in which these issues may be explored.

Key Terms I

Following are important terms introduced in Chapter 15. Match the term with the letter of the example that best illustrates the term.

1. _____ autonomy

2. _____ clique

3. _____ crowd

4. _____ deviancy training

5. _____ epistemic development

6. _____ evaluativist theory of knowledge

7. _____ friendship

8. _____ homophily

9. _____ homophobia

10. _____ intimacy

11. _____ objectivist theory of knowledge

12. _____ sensation-seeking

13. _____ sexual minority youth

14. _____ subjectivist theory of knowledge

a. This term describes a close relationship between two people.
b. This is the idea that "truth" can shift according to one's perspective.
c. Examples of this are "jocks," "nerds," and "brains."
d. This is the ability to assert one's needs in a relationship.
e. This is more characteristic of friendships between girls.
f. This is thought to inhibit boys from sharing their emotions with one another.
g. This can undermine the effectiveness of group therapy sessions for adolescents.
h. According to this view, knowledge involves "definite answers."
i. This characteristic can result in risky behavior.
j. This group of friends is about the size of a family.
k. The tendency for adolescents to like others who have the same values, opinions, and preferences is called this.
l. According to this view, truth can shift and change, but is subject to standards of evaluation.
m. Examples are youths who develop identities as gay, lesbian, or bisexual.
n. Changes with age in reasoning about the nature of knowledge is known as this.

Key Terms II

Following are important terms introduced in Chapter 15. Match the term with the letter of the example that best illustrates the term.

1. _____ commitment

2. _____ emerging adulthood

3. _____ ethnic identity

4. _____ experiencing sampling method (ESM)

5. _____ exploration

6. _____ externalizing problems

7. _____ I-self

8. _____ identity development

9. _____ independent sense of self

10. _____ interdependent sense of self

11. _____ internalizing problems

12. _____ me-self

13. _____ saturated self

14. _____ sexual identity

a. If identity were a story, this would be the storyteller.
b. This is most characteristic of individuals living in traditional, collectivist societies.
c. These include delinquency and other antisocial behaviors.
d. This can be heterosexual, homosexual, or bisexual.
e. This emerges as a response to the need to conform to roles that demand different, sometimes contradictory, selves.
f. This term refers to an important aspect of identity formation that involves allegiance to the goals, values, and beliefs which individuals have adopted.
g. This is also known as the "object-self."
h. This is a stage of development that may occur in industrialized societies.
i. This term refers to a phase in which adolescents examine their future options.
j. This is used to help researchers study adolescents' emotions.
k. These are more likely to occur among girls than boys.
l. According to Erikson, this is the main developmental task during adolescence.
m. This can be an important aspect of identity among adolescents from immigrant families.
n. This characteristic of identity is typical of American or Western European culture.

Multiple-Choice Practice Questions

Circle the letter of the word or phrase that correctly completes each statement.

1. Over the course of adolescence, young people experience, on average,
   a. an increase in the level of happiness for both boys and girls.
   b. a decrease in the level of happiness for both boys and girls.
   c. an increase in happiness for boys and a decrease for girls.
   d. a decrease in happiness for boys and an increase for girls.

2. When Laurence Steinberg and his colleagues asked adults and adolescents in their study to play a driving simulation game, they found that
    a. both adolescents and adults made equally risky moves when playing alone and when observed by friends.
    b. both adolescents and adults made riskier moves when observed by friends than when playing alone.
    c. adolescents, but not adults, made riskier moves when observed by friends than when playing alone.
    d. adults, but not adolescents, made riskier moves when playing alone than when observed by friends.

3. Adolescents tend to choose friends
    a. who live close by.
    b. with similar values and attitudes.
    c. who are several years younger.
    d. from a different socioeconomic background.

4. Which describes an adolescent clique?
    a. a group of 15 to 30 boys and girls
    b. a loosely associated group of couples
    c. a small group of friends, usually of the same sex
    d. All these statements are correct.

5. During adolescence, children of _____ parents are less likely to get into trouble than those whose parents use other styles of interaction.
    a. authoritative
    b. authoritarian
    c. permissive
    d. None of these answers is correct—adolescents are equally likely to get into trouble regardless of parenting style.

6. According to Erik Erikson, establishing _____ is the fundamental task of adolescence.
    a. intimacy
    b. identity
    c. autonomy
    d. foreclosure

7. Research shows that the majority of young people have reached a state of identity achievement by the time they are
    a. 12 to 14 years old.
    b. 15 to 17 years old.
    c. 18 to 20 years old.
    d. 21 to 24 years old.

8. _____ may be the response of minority young people to the shocking experience of being rejected because of their ethnic background.
   a. Ethnic identity search
   b. Internalization of ethnic identity
   c. Developing an interdependent sense of self
   d. Indifference to ethnic identity

9. An *independent sense of self* is
   a. typical of cultures that emphasize individuality.
   b. based on the view that identity formation is a personal process.
   c. characteristic of middle-class American society.
   d. All these answers are correct.

10. Externalizing problems of adolescence
    a. is more common among boys than girls.
    b. involves behaviors such as aggression and delinquency.
    c. Both a and b are correct.
    d. involves primarily emotional problems such as depression and anxiety.

11. According to a large Scottish study, which group is *most* likely to experience serious depression?
    a. 15-year-old girls
    b. 15-year-old boys
    c. 13-year-old boys and girls equally
    d. 11-year-old boys and girls equally

12. Compared with those growing up in Western industrial societies, adolescents living in traditional cultures
    a. have a larger number of important decisions to make about their futures.
    b. are more likely to develop an independent sense of self.
    c. are more likely to develop a "saturated self."
    d. face fewer decisions about activities such as marriage and occupation.

13. The increase in violent behavior observed during adolescence may be attributed to
    a. greater numbers of adolescents participating in such behavior.
    b. a greater amount of such activity on the part of a few adolescents.
    c. Both a and b are correct.
    d. girls participating in such behavior to a greater extent than before.

14. "Emerging adulthood" is a stage of development that
    a. occurs in technologically advanced societies.
    b. reflects challenges faced by young people 18 to 25 years old.
    c. occurs among young people who feel unprepared for the challenges of adulthood.
    d. All these answers are correct.

15. Regarding the nature of knowledge as an accumulation of objective facts is characteristic of which theory of knowledge?
    a. evaluativist
    b. objectivist
    c. subjectivist
    d. All these answers are correct.

Short-Answer Practice Questions

Write a brief answer in the space below each question.

1. What factors contribute to the "crying gap" between male and female adolescents? What does this say about how males and females are socialized to express their emotions?

2. How do peer groups help adolescents make the transition from associating primarily in small, same-sex groups to maintaining romantic relationships?

3. What factors contribute to adolescents having friends who are similar to them? What implications do you think this has for their social development?

4. Discuss how the process of identity formation might differ for either sexual minority or for ethnic minority youth.

5. What are some reasons for the difference between male and female adolescents in the types of problems (internalizing or externalizing) they typically face?

6. Do you think that *emerging adulthood* is a distinct stage of human development? What evidence supports or contradicts this view?

Putting It All Together

Look back at material from Chapter 9 to help answer this question.

Imagine that you have friends or family members from another culture who have recently immigrated to the United States and are planning to start a family. How would you advise them on raising their children to develop a positive sense of ethnic identity?

Sources of More Information

Bem, D. (1996). Exotic becomes erotic: A developmental theory of sexual orientation. *Psychological Review, 103,* 320–335.
This article presents a theory on the development of sexual identity that attempts to explain same- and opposite-sex desire in both males and females.

Erikson, E. (1994). *Identity: Youth and crisis.* New York: W.W. Norton.
In this book, first published several decades ago, the author discusses adolescent identity formation and some of the difficulties involved in this process.

Hofer, M., Youniss, J., & Noack, P. (1998). *Verbal interaction and development in families with adolescents.* Stamford, CT: Ablex.
This book discusses issues relevant to the communication between adolescents and their parents; much of its research was done with German families.

Kroger, J. (1996). *Identity in adolescence: The balance between self and other.* New York: Routledge.
This book pays careful attention to each of the major theories of identity formation. The biographical accounts of the theorists place their work in a cultural-historical context.

Marcia, J. (1980). Identity in adolescence. In *Handbook of adolescent psychology,* J. Adelson (ed.). New York: John Wiley & Sons.
In this chapter, the author discusses his findings on adolescents' identity statuses.

Pipher, M. (1994). *Reviving Ophelia: Saving the selves of adolescent girls.* New York: G.P. Putnam's Sons.
The author, a psychologist with extensive experience working with adolescents, suggests ways to prevent problems caused by aspects of contemporary culture that are destructive to girls.

Savin-Williams, R. (1987). *Adolescence: An ethological perspective.* New York: Springer-Verlag.
This book describes a naturalistic study of adolescents at a summer camp. It provides a good illustration of the way psychological processes are manifested in social interactions.

Whiting, J. (1990). Adolescent rituals and identity conflicts. In *Cultural psychology: Essays on comparative human development,* J. Stigler, R. Shweder, & G. Herdt (eds.). New York: Cambridge University Press.
This work discusses identity formation and identity conflicts in a variety of cultures.

Answer Key

Answers to Key Terms I: 1.d, 2.j, 3.c, 4.g, 5.n, 6.l, 7.a, 8.k, 9.f, 10.e, 11.h, 12.i, 13.m, 14.b.

Answers to Key Terms II: 1.f, 2.h, 3.m, 4.j, 5.i, 6.c, 7.a, 8.l, 9.n, 10.b, 11.k, 12.g, 13.e, 14.d.

Answers to Multiple-Choice Questions: 1.b, 2.c, 3.b, 4.c, 5.a, 6.b, 7.d, 8.a, 9.d, 10.c, 11.a, 12.d, 13.c, 14.d, 15.b.